DiMaggio's Yankees

ALSO BY LEW FREEDMAN
AND FROM MCFARLAND

*The Day All the Stars Came Out: Major League
Baseball's First All-Star Game, 1933* (2010)

*Early Wynn, the Go-Go White Sox and
the 1959 World Series* (2009)

*Hard-Luck Harvey Haddix and
the Greatest Game Ever Lost* (2009)

DiMaggio's Yankees
A History of the 1936–1944 Dynasty

LEW FREEDMAN

McFarland & Company, Inc., Publishers
Jefferson, North Carolina, and London

All photographs are courtesy of the National Baseball
Hall of Fame Library, Cooperstown, New York

LIBRARY OF CONGRESS CATALOGUING-IN-PUBLICATION DATA

Freedman, Lew.
 DiMaggio's Yankees : a history of the 1936–1944 dynasty /
Lew Freedman.
  p.   cm.
 Includes bibliographical references and index.

 ISBN 978-0-7864-5906-3
 softcover : 50# alkaline paper ∞

 1. New York Yankees (Baseball team)—History.
 2. DiMaggio, Joe, 1914–1999. 3. Gehrig, Lou, 1903–1941.
 I. Title.
 GV875.N4F74 2011
 796.357'64097471— dc23   2011035292

BRITISH LIBRARY CATALOGUING DATA ARE AVAILABLE

© 2011 Lew Freedman. All rights reserved

*No part of this book may be reproduced or transmitted in any form
or by any means, electronic or mechanical, including photocopying
or recording, or by any information storage and retrieval system,
without permission in writing from the publisher.*

On the cover: (left to right) Tony Lazzeri, owner Jacob Ruppert,
Joe DiMaggio and Frank Crosetti (National Baseball Hall of Fame
Library, Cooperstown, New York)

Manufactured in the United States of America

*McFarland & Company, Inc., Publishers
 Box 611, Jefferson, North Carolina 28640
 www.mcfarlandpub.com*

Table of Contents

Introduction — 1

1. A Kid Named Joe — 7
2. Replacing Ruth — 19
3. Co-Starring Gehrig and DiMaggio — 26
4. Ruff Was Tough — 37
5. Monte, Pat, Bump and Grandma — 47
6. The Real Italian Stallion — 59
7. Dickey Linked Them All — 68
8. The Crow Makes a Mark — 78
9. The Yankee Way — 87
10. Joe D. Gets Hitched — 97
11. Shut Up and Play Like King Kong — 108
12. The Search for Fresh Arms — 116
13. New Guys on the Block — 125
14. Gehrig and the Other Babe — 134
15. Diagnosis and Death — 143
16. The Yankees Lose a Pennant — 152
17. The Streak — 162

18. A Brooklyn-Bronx Subway Series 175
19. War Changes Everything 185

Epilogue 196
Chapter Notes 199
Bibliography 209
Index 211

Introduction

The history of the New York Highlanders and all of their failures might as well have been on parchment paper by 1935, disappointments recorded for posterity and stored away in a dusty attic, but forgotten by fans whose good old days began in 1920.

The Highlanders had become the Yankees and Babe Ruth had made the Yankees into the best team in baseball, a royal outfit that presided from the top of the American League standings. Ruth had virtually invented the home run as a weapon, his bigger-than-life bombardments of opposing pitchers meshing neatly with his bigger-than-life lifestyle.

Ruth was a man of gargantuan appetites, a big, cuddly Teddy Bear for the kids, an admired sportsman for the fans, and a party animal for those in the know in an era when gossip did not travel quite so far or quite so quickly as it does in Internet days.

Famously, one of his assigned roommates, Ping Bodie, was asked what it was like to share quarters with the great slugger. "I don't know," Bodie replied. "I don't room with Babe Ruth. I room with his suitcase."[1]

Ruth was the Bambino and gave new meaning to "hitting them where they ain't," the old Wee Willie Keeler pronouncement about placing singles and doubles where fielders did not roam. Ruth just hit the ball over their heads, sending it into orbit beyond the boundaries of ballpark fences.

When the Yankees worked their way north each spring for the start of the major league baseball season, they played exhibition games and advertised their involvement with signs reading, "Babe Ruth, the Home Run King," as if the rest of the world champions were a back-up band.[2]

His feats of strength and drama eclipsed the lure of anything playing on Broadway, and the demand for tickets to watch Ruth pummel the ball and the Yankees win games, pennants and World Series was so great the team built a new structure in the Bronx. It was called Yankee Stadium officially, and "The House That Ruth Built" unofficially.

Where once the pre–Ruthian Yankees' offense sputtered and gasped, it was now a juggernaut. The pennants accrued, World Series titles were claimed, and the Yankees throughout the 1920s were the most triumphant and popular team in the sports world. The 1927 "Murderers Row" were anointed the greatest team of all time and 85 years later the argument can still be made.

The Yankees of the 1920s lived history and wrote it. Ruth set home run records that astonished baseball supporters, collecting 54, 59, and 60 in individual seasons with blows so spectacular he made station-to-station advancement around the bases a relic of the past. He was the leader of a revolution. Despite ebbs and flows in popularity, neither the stolen base, nor the hit-and-run, has ever regained their cache.

In his prime in 1930, Ruth was earning $80,000 a year from the Yankees, an annual salary of $5,000 more than President Herbert Hoover. The discrepancy was pointed out to Ruth, who said, "I know, but I had a better year than Hoover."[3]

For the first time the Yankees were the toast of their town, the kings of the National Pastime in the high-spirited communications capital of the world. They were fawned over, pinstriped symbols of success in The Roaring Twenties era of excess.

Those Yankees set a standard of performance — and expectation — that has continued throughout the rest of the twentieth century and more than a decade into the twenty-first century. No one could know then what baseball fans know now. It would have been impossible to imagine that the Yankees would become a sort of permanent gold standard of the sport, that for many fans they would become the team others loved to hate because they won too much for their tastes.

In the 1920s and into the early 1930s, the Yankees were a team to admire because of their achievements. Ruth was Herculean. Nobody had ever seen anyone like him. He was certainly the symbol of a team and an era. But Ruth alone did not build the Yankees. He had plenty of help, most notably from Lou Gehrig, who latched onto first base and never let go.

Earle Combs, Bob Meusel, and Tony Lazzeri provided even more firepower, and they were all members of the 1927 club with Ruth and

Gehrig, too. Waite Hoyt, Herb Pennock and Urban Shocker were the moundsmen who dominated. Miller Huggins was the manager, small in physical stature, but fierce in demeanor.

Between 1921 and 1928, the Yankees won the American League pennant six times and the World Series three times. They won again in 1932 after the Philadelphia Athletics threw in a mini-dynasty of their own, capturing three straight pennants under Connie Mack.

One of the greatest challenges in sports is to repeat a championship season. From one year to the next players age, players get injured, new talent comes along, and squabbles over salaries and playing time materialize. Things change and not always for the better. So each season is an individual ride, and teams that can hold their rosters and outlooks together to reproduce success are rare.

The Yankees owed some of the stability to the management team of owners Colonel Jacob Ruppert and Captain Tillinghast L'Hommedieu Huston and business manager / general manager Ed Barrow. The savvy group understood how to construct a winning team.

What the late 1920s and early 1930s presented was the challenge of how to keep a good thing going. Ruth was aging. During the waning days of the 1929 season, Huggins died from sepsis. He was only 50.

Huggins was replaced by Art Fletcher for the last 11 games of the 1929 campaign and Bob Shawkey for one year. Ruth was friendly enough to hunt and golf with Shawkey, but he wanted the position. Yankees management informed him it did not want a player-manager. A year later, though, when Shawkey was ousted, Ruth was again given no consideration and Ruppert issued one of the most famous put-downs in baseball history. "How can you manage a team when you can't manage yourself?" Ruppert said point-blank.[4]

The Yankees may not have wanted a player-manager, but mainly, they didn't want Ruth. The exchange engendered bitterness in Ruth for years and contributed to his difficult relations in 1931 with Joe McCarthy, one of the greatest managers of all time. McCarthy was resented by Ruth because he did not play in the majors and Ruth felt he, not a "busher," should have been offered the job.

Other Yankees were coming to the end of their careers in the post–Huggins era and were no longer capable of starting for a pennant contender. With the rise and new apparent domination of the A's, it was a legitimate question to wonder if the Yankees had slipped back to the pack, if they were backsliding to the old Highlanders days.

Winning three straight pennants, as the A's did between 1929 and 1931, has only rarely been accomplished in baseball history. The A's, anchored by pitcher Lefty Grove and sluggers Jimmie Foxx, Al Simmons and Mickey Cochrane, might well have become established as the greatest team of all if owner-manager Mack could have kept adding key pieces and kept winning.

Instead, hammered economically by the Depression, Mack reluctantly sold off valuable players to keep the franchise afloat. Mack gutted his phenomenal team and the proceeds went into the general team coffers for expenditures merely to keep the team in business. Grove and Foxx ended up with the Boston Red Sox, Cochrane with the Detroit Tigers and Simmons with the White Sox. All ended up in the Hall of Fame.

Although the Depression resulted in tough times for baseball, as well as the nation at large, with diminished attendance, the better-endowed Yankees weathered financial problems much more smoothly than the A's. While Philadelphia was self-destructing and most of the rest of the American League was enduring, the Yankees were able to make a turnaround.

The transition from a Babe Ruth-led deep and talented squad to a new generation of leaders was not seamless. And Ruth did not want to go quietly into that good night—at least not without a guarantee from the bosses (never delivered) that he would be the next manager of the Yankees.

In 1935, the unthinkable occurred. Ruth had broken into the majors in 1914 with the Red Sox. In 1920, he was sold to the Yankees in perhaps the worst deal in the history of professional sports. But in 1935, unwanted by the team he had transformed into the most glamorous in sport, Ruth wore the uniform of the Boston Braves. There was no sentimentality in the Yankees' front office outside of an offer for Ruth to manage AAA Newark, and ever since then New York has retained that image.

Ruth appeared in 28 games for Boston. He hit six homers, three of them in a stunning finale against the Pittsburgh Pirates. That day Ruth blasted three homers and a single after his old teammate Hoyt, now in the Pirates locker room, had warned pitchers to just intentionally walk his old pal, even if he did seem finished. No one listened and Ruth had a grand last laugh to his career.

Introduction

He retired with a record 714 home runs and then vanished from any active baseball roster and any direct involvement with the Yankees.

Ruth was gone, but the Yankees were still around. The time period is sometimes overlooked, sandwiched as it is between the Yankees' Ruth Dynasty and World War II, and then the rise of the Yankees all over again under Casey Stengel and Mickey Mantle. But the Second Yankees Dynasty proved to be an astonishing stretch of high-caliber baseball.

There had to be baseball people who believed the post–Ruth Yankees' era was going to be a flop. Some had to believe that Ruth was irreplaceable and that five new players couldn't make up for his departure. They were all wrong. The Yankees of 1936 to 1944 were every bit as good as their predecessors, and while the new star on the scene was a very different sort of man from Ruth, the new leader's on-field flair and force of personality in a completely different manner was just as compelling.

The Yankees moved directly from counting on Babe Ruth for his big swings to relying on a new fella named Joe DiMaggio to carry them in the clutch.

1

A Kid Named Joe

The story has been told many times and when they hear it for the first time, or the fifth, fans of the New York Yankees chuckle. The future of the franchise rode across the country from San Francisco to spring training in Florida in an average sedan as reliable as the roads connected coast to coast long before the interstate system was built.

Tony Lazzeri, ultimately elected to the National Baseball Hall of Fame, and Frank Crosetti, who as a player and a coach appeared in a record 23 World Series for the Yankees, invited their fellow San Francisco–area rookie of Italian heritage to ride the 3,000 miles with them to spring training in St. Petersburg, Florida, in 1936.

The three would share the driving and arrive by the reporting deadline of March 1 with ease. Lazzeri, who owned the vehicle, drove the first leg of the journey. When he tired he turned the wheel over to Crosetti. When Crosetti became road-weary it was DiMaggio's turn. They were stopped for gas when Lazzeri said, "OK, champ, it's your turn to drive."[1]

It was then, not before the trip, or at any time during casual conversation during the first couple of thousand miles, that DiMaggio said, "I don't drive."[2]

Lazzeri suggested they let DiMaggio walk the rest of the way, but naturally that did not occur. The story is usually told in a manner that suggests DiMaggio was still a naïve 21-year-old and reflective of his upbringing in an insular world where his father and brothers fished for a living rather than mingled much with outsiders. In retrospect, decades later, after DiMaggio evolved into a somewhat mythic hero, a prince of sorts, one might say that even then he was being chauffeured through life by protective friends.

In an era when hype was confined to word-of-mouth and the occasional newspaper story, the glare of the spotlight was not too bright on young ballplayers. DiMaggio was somewhat of an exception because the New York newspapermen knew who he was. DiMaggio made as many waves in the Pacific Coast League playing for the San Francisco Seals as the real Pacific did on the nearby beaches. But without 24-hour sports talk radio, television, sophisticated scouting services, or any other way for the casual baseball fan to learn his face and background, DiMaggio seemed just a step up from an average guy signed for the 1936 Yankees, not someone thought of as the next Babe Ruth. Ruth's brilliance still shone too brightly for anyone to escape his shadow. Yet not even Ruth could play at his prime level forever. He was, contrary to public opinion, only human.

The fading of Babe Ruth's youth and skills on the baseball diamond concurrently paralleled the fortunes of the United States as the care-free Roaring Twenties devolved into the Great Depression. There were tough times for all. As the Yankees were eclipsed by the Philadelphia A's between 1929 and 1931 and measurements of wealth plummeted for so many, the National Pastime endured a decline in attendance as paying customers cinched their belts and focused more on feeding their families than entertaining them.

Although the Yankees were built on the broad shoulders of Ruth, the assembled management team had come to believe that being a member of the Yankees organization meant something besides how you played on the field. Gradually, steadily, the men who ran the team shaped the image into one where fans would associate the ball club with success and class, much as Cadillac came to be a symbol of those very things.

Time has a way of eroding history for each new generation, and probably the most underestimated and overlooked great Yankee of the past was the innocuously titled business manager Ed Barrow, who purchased Ruth from the Red Sox, pieced together the first pennant-winners in the 1920s, and kept right on building, as if he were a developer of skyscrapers seeking to dominate a big-city skyline, which in a sense he was.

Ed Barrow was born in Springfield, Illinois, on May 10, 1868, and by 1900 he owned the Toronto team in the Eastern League. In 1903, he became manager of the Detroit Tigers. Some years passed before Barrow arrived on his true path to greatness. Of all things, given the way events played out and how most of American League baseball history was affected by developments Barrow had a hand in during the twentieth century, he was the manager of the Boston Red Sox in 1918 when they won their last World Series crown until 2004.

Barrow, a short, stern man who seemed to smile primarily when he was winning, left the Red Sox to become business manager of the Yankees in 1920 when the notorious Sox owner Harry Frazee began shedding payroll to fund Broadway shows. It was Barrow who, as manager, first used Ruth in the outfield on days when he was not pitching and who, when he linked up with a new employer, engineered the sale of Ruth to New York.

Ed Barrow was always seen in a suit and tie during his 25 years in the Yankees' front office as business manager and then president. Brisk and efficient, he invested enough to keep his bosses winning pennants and World Series, but never spent a penny more on salaries than he had to despite negotiating with stars like Babe Ruth, Lou Gehrig and Joe DiMaggio.

The history-making swap of Ruth for $125,000 led to instant Yankee's triumphs and the crumbling of the Sox empire that had been so successful during the first two decades of the American League's existence. Following the departure of Ruth, the Red Sox did not win another World Series for 86 years and during the later stages of the drought were dogged by the annoying phrase "The Curse of the Bambino." This was a tidy way of saying the years of futility were all Frazee's fault for disposing of Ruth.

Barrow, who had also been president of the International League, had wide-ranging responsibilities with the Yankees as a personnel manager and custodian of the purse strings. Although he worked for wealthy men, Barrow guarded their expenditures as if every request for an increase in player salaries was raiding the piggy bank he had filled with cash for his retirement.

While the average fan of baseball history recalls the steal that gave the Yankees Babe Ruth, others think that at least one acquisition in team history was more important. Sportswriter Joe Williams once wrote that hiring Barrow "was the best deal the Yankees ever made."[3]

When Barrow arrived, the Yankees were owned by Colonel Jacob Ruppert and Tillinghast L'Hommedieu Huston. Although he intended to attend Columbia University and passed the exams for entrance, Ruppert was a beer baron, a man of inherited wealth. His family scotched the notion of college and Ruppert worked his way through the ranks at the family brewery from the time he was a teenager, until he ran the entire operation. His family was of German heritage, but Ruppert was born in the United States. Sometimes, he slipped into a German accent, as if it was something else inherited from his family that he could not avoid.

Once ensconced at the head of the brewery, it appeared from all accounts that Ruppert did whatever he wanted. That included expanding the business and adding to the family coffers, but it also meant high society womanizing (he never married), collecting Chinese jade, porcelain and oil paintings, and raising St. Bernard dogs and collecting monkeys. Ruppert gained his colonel's rank in the National Guard. Elected to Congress, he served four terms.

Huston was a character of a different sort. A civil engineer, as a captain Huston led a company of volunteers in the Spanish-American War in Cuba in 1899, and then became a colonel in World War I. Huston made his fortune in Cuba between those wars on construction projects and his company improved the quality of several harbors, notably Havana's.

At different times and through different contacts, Ruppert and Huston were fascinated by the New York Giants, either as baseball fans or potential future owners. Huston developed a friendship with the Giants' legendary manager John McGraw, and Ruppert knew Giants owner Andrew Freedman and supposedly had a handshake agreement that if Freedman ever wanted to sell the team he would offer it to Ruppert first. That did not happen.

Both were tied to New York, but totally unimpressed with the Highlanders/Yankees. Ruppert and Huston were brought together by American League President Ban Johnson, who respected their bank accounts and convinced other American League owners they would be worthy additions to their club. In 1915, Ruppert and Huston became partners and bought the Yankees for $460,000.

The entrepreneurs had been skittish about buying the Yankees because the team's track record was so poor and the Giants, under "Little Napoleon" McGraw, were so clearly the dominant team in the market. To sweeten the deal the other teams in the league said that if Ruppert and Huston purchased the Yankees, they would throw in some players to help improve the roster. It's hard to picture the Yankees as a charity case, but after the duo signed the paperwork only the Tigers followed through, anyway.

Ruppert and Huston, strong-willed men who had signed on to a 50–50 power-sharing arrangement with the Yankees, were ticked off by the other teams reneging. Ruppert and Huston started out trying to make their own personnel decisions, but when big money spent for little results emerged as a pattern rather quickly they hired a McGraw pal named Harry Sparrow and gave him the title of business manager.

It is uncertain how a longer Sparrow tenure might have changed the course of history, if the Yankees would ever have obtained Ruth, or been able to build such a strong team. However, Sparrow died in 1920, opening the position for Barrow. While Huston went off to war, Ruppert argued against the hiring of Wilbert Robinson, another crony of McGraw's from their old Baltimore Orioles days together, as manager. Once again, Ban Johnson stepped in. He recommended the Yankees hire Miller Huggins based on his background with the St. Louis Cardinals.

Ruppert did so, without consulting Huston, who was a Robinson man. The action created a serious breach between the owners that colored their dealings for years, even though Huggins turned out to be a brilliant selection for the job.

The owners had their own worries. Huston was embroiled in World War I. The passage of the nation's Prohibition laws in 1920 put a crimp in Ruppert's beer business. He had to manufacture non-alcoholic beer to survive. After World War I ended and the Barrow tenure in the front office began with the acquisition of Ruth, the good times rolled in the 1920s. Stubborn men with Alpha personalities, one thing that pleased Ruppert and Huston was winning.

Still, the strong-willed men were not destined to remain business partners long-term. In 1923, Ruppert bought out Huston for $1.5 million — a nice profit — and made the Yankees his own.

From the dregs of the league, the Yankees had risen to the top and stayed there, enhancing the public profiles and egos of the team's owners. But as the 1920s ended, the Great Depression dug in with a tighter grip, and simultaneously some of the best Yankee players grew older, the team faced new challenges. Between 1929 and 1935, the Yankees won just one pennant.

Although New York finished second five times as opposed to dropping into the second division in an eight-team league, for Ruppert that was no satisfaction. Placing anywhere but in first place was like the proverbial tie with the reward of kissing your sister. He got no charge out of that. Then, as would be exemplified by the long Yankees ownership of George Steinbrenner, it was win or else, or in the modification of Vince Lombardi's football proclamation, "Winning is the only thing."

Following the in-house controversy over his hiring, Huggins had been a winner for the Yankees. His death before the end of the 1929 season shocked the team. It took two tries to get it right, but when Joe McCarthy came aboard in 1931, the Yankees had their next great manager in place.

With Louisville in the minors, McCarthy had won so often the Chicago Cubs hired him in 1926. McCarthy brought a pennant to the North Side in 1929, but owner William Wrigley Jr. was impatient and in a colossal blunder fired McCarthy because he hadn't captured the World Series. The Cubs still have not won the Series since 1908.

When Ruppert greeted McCarthy with his marching orders in 1931, he offered an olive branch of surprising patience, but left no ambiguity that he expected the new manager to lead the Yankees to the promised land soon enough.

"McCarthy, I finished third last year," Ruppert said. "I realize that you are confronted with problems that will take you a little time to solve, so I will be satisfied if you finish second this year. But I warn you, McCarthy, I don't like to finish second."

McCarthy had the right answer for his new boss: "Neither do I, Colonel," he said.[4]

The problems holding the Yankees back in the standings were pitching and fielding. When McCarthy, who loved his new spring-training digs in St. Petersburg even more than he did the Cubs' spectacular layout on Catalina Island off the California coast, was asked what kind of operation he planned to run, he said, "All work and no play."[5] If it sounded as though he was going to be working out the Yankees in a military boot camp, he didn't mind the interpretation.

McCarthy sought to put his own stamp on the club. The weather might be sunny and warm, but his disposition was more that of a drill sergeant. There was no goofing off under McCarthy. He was a 110 percent guy, squeezing every bit of effort out of every single player.

He was neither gregarious nor unfriendly, but kept to himself, didn't share jokes with the press as Casey Stengel would famously do some years later, but believed in running things with a firm hand. He had no plans to coddle Ruth, but did not want to insult him or his legacy, either, despite his awareness that Ruth coveted his job.

What McCarthy tried to do was treat Ruth like everyone else and play him as Ruth deserved. In McCarthy's first year Ruth was still the Sultan of Swat, clubbing 46 home runs, driving in 163 runs, and batting .373. It was an astounding season for a 36-year-old veteran who had not exactly taken care of his body like Jack LaLanne. It took another couple of seasons for Ruth to fade, but in between, in 1932, the Yankees won 107 games, the pennant and the World Series. Ruth cracked his "called-shot" home run off of the Cubs' Charlie Root in that Series.

Whether McCarthy's job was ever in question or not, in his first four seasons he produced three second-place finishes and one World Series title for Ruppert. Ruppert must have appre-

The man who wrote out the lineups, juggled the players, chose the starting pitchers and replaced them with relievers during the Second Yankee Dynasty was manager Joe McCarthy, who won seven pennants with New York. Stern-faced, McCarthy was known for seeing everything on the field and having the recall to pull out helpful tidbits when needed.

ciated McCarthy's diplomacy and his willingness to stand up to Ruth because despite the owner's disdain for finishing second, McCarthy was still in command in 1936. He was about to receive, via that long, drawn-out car ride, a new player of spectacular ability.

Giuseppe DiMaggio, Joe's father, left Italy for the United States in 1898 and sent for his wife Rosalie in 1902. He emigrated to improve the financial health of his family in the Land of Opportunity and settled in the North Beach section of San Francisco in an Italian enclave where many heads of household performed the same tasks they did in the old country—fishing.

While Giuseppe was in a new world, he raised his family in an old way. He expected his five sons to follow him into the crab fishing business. Joe DiMaggio tried fishing, but he hated it more than if he had been forced to high-kick with a chorus line in a Broadway show. He got seasick and even despised the smell of the catch. Meanwhile, his father had no appreciation for the American sport of baseball. To him it was a time-wasting game with no anticipated reward.

"Baseball, what is that?" Giuseppe used to criticize his sons at high decibels in Italian. "A bum's game!" All this baseball was good for, said someone conscious of sticking to a family budget, was wearing out shoes.[6]

It was a great surprise to him when he was shown that a man could not only make money playing a children's game, but make a solid living. Although three of his sons became major leaguers, and Giuseppe gradually understood the acclaim they received and was proud of them, if they hadn't been able to demonstrate that baseball could be a livelihood he would have frowned at their commitments.

By 1940, Vince, Joe and Dom DiMaggio all held down major league outfield jobs. Joe DiMaggio was often viewed as taciturn and removed. Dom was viewed as friendly, but somewhat shy. Vince was the garrulous one. Although Dom was an All-Star for the Boston Red Sox and Joe became a demi-god in New York, Vince was a ten-year, journeyman outfielder who played for the Pittsburgh Pirates, Cincinnati Reds, Philadelphia Phillies and New York Giants with a .249 lifetime average.

"If Joe could talk like me and I could hit like Joe, we'd both be worth a million bucks," Vince DiMaggio said once.[7]

Joe probably made it to that financial stratosphere without Vince's gift of gab. When Vince returned home at the end of the 1931 summer

1. A Kid Named Joe 15

following a stint playing ball in Tucson for a subsidiary of the San Francisco Seals, he spread his salary and bonus out on the kitchen table in cash. He wanted his father to understand that a fellow could make money in baseball. His father's reaction was to ask where he stole the money.

Upon convincing his father that he had made legitimate pay, Vince introduced him to the owner of the Seals. They became friendly and eventually Giuseppe attended a ballgame in person. Although his brothers became better players than he was, Vince said he paved the way for them at home so they could pursue their dreams.

Given the context of the times, Joe DiMaggio was a better known minor leaguer than most when he was heading to the Yankees that first time in 1936. For decades, the Pacific Coast League, founded in 1903, was the closest thing to a third major league. With the majors concentrated east of St. Louis, teams on the West Coast like the Hollywood Stars, Los Angeles Angels, San Francisco Seals and Seattle Rainiers provided top-notch play. Major league scouts sought the best talent and often found it in the sunshine of the west where mild weather made for long seasons. The Yankees' own Tony Lazzeri graduated from the Pacific Coast League to New York after slugging 60 home runs and driving in 225 runs for the Salt Lake City Bees in 1925. Another DiMaggio brother, Tom, who did like fishing, acted as an agent for brother Joe when the future Yankee signed his first contract with the Seals for the 1933 season at age 18.

The Joe DiMaggio that the world came to know was still a little bit rough around the edges. He was touted as an infielder, a hard-to-believe supposition the way he roamed center field with his long stride and fluid grace that seemed a perfect match from the start with the Yankees.

At the plate, however, he was a nearly finished product as a teenager. DiMaggio batted .340 with 28 home runs and a league-leading 169 RBI, statistics that instantly put him on radar screens as a prospect. Those were impressive, but basic fundamentals in a young recruit. The truly astonishing development of the summer was that DiMaggio hit safely in 61 straight games.

That was an unheard-of accomplishment, a record for any level of professional baseball. It was almost unfathomable and the achievement made DiMaggio a hometown hero, almost overnight one of the most popular athletes in San Francisco. By the time DiMaggio passed 30 games in his streak, the newspapers were following his exploits as if he were a presidential candidate on a campaign swing, not swinging a bat. For ease in fitting his name into headlines, the Frisco papers began referring to the player as "Joe." Just Joe. He was shy and didn't know what to say as he was surrounded by sportswriters each day. He didn't embarrass himself, but he didn't distinguish himself with the Gettysburg Address of baseball, either.

DiMaggio's hitting streak gained bounce beyond the locals, picked up and reported on by the Associated Press wire service. Speculation soon began on what type of a major leaguer he could become. Large sums of money (for the time) were bandied about. DiMaggio was worth as much as $100,000, it was suggested.

But DiMaggio signed for a second year with the Seals. He was going nowhere yet. Then a fluke accident threw off all plans for the immediate future and jeopardized the long-term future as well. On a night following a family celebration that concluded with dinner at his sister's house, DiMaggio was stepping out of a taxi cab when his left knee gave out. Abruptly, with no warning, bones cracked and DiMaggio was in excruciating pain. That was the story he told. A newspaper story of the time questioned details. However, the basic problem was accurate. DiMaggio had messed up his knee and who knew when he would be able to play again?

With almost the equivalent lightning speed with which they had taken such an interest in DiMaggio, scouts for major league teams backed off. In the 1930s, and for many decades to follow, a knee injury for an athlete was often the kiss of death. The wrong rupture or tear meant the athlete never had the same spring in his step again, never could run as fast or jump as high. Some people thought DiMaggio might be finished before he started.

The Chicago White Sox were one of the teams shadowing DiMaggio, but once he hurt his knee they didn't know what to do. They wanted detailed information on the injury and whether DiMaggio could come back. The Yankees had not backed off, but wanted the same information. They had a scout who had previously lived in North Beach, however, and he said he could find out the truth. The scout, Bill Essick, received a favorable long-term prognosis after he arranged for a doctor hired by the Yankees to test DiMaggio. Essick reported to the team that given the limited nature of the injury and DiMaggio's youth, he would be okay.

Essick, whose nickname was "Vinegar Bill," usually steered the front office in the right direction, so if he said DiMaggio still had it, he was believed. Essick spent about a quarter of a century in the Yankees' employ, starting in 1925, but his recommendation that the Yankees hang in with their pursuit of DiMaggio was probably his greatest accomplishment. It was a list of accomplishments that included signing Lefty Gomez, Joe Gordon, Bob Meusel, Frank Crosetti, and Ralph Houk, too. Jacob Ruppert opened his checkbook when Essick spoke, but Essick could be gratifyingly thrifty with the boss' bucks, too, signing Gordon for $500. He obtained Johnny Lindell's name on a contract for only a $150 investment.

The Seals wanted $65,000 for Lazzeri and Ruppert showed his trust in Essick by telling him if the player was worth the money, go ahead and spend it. Everyone knew that the raw, young DiMaggio was worth more than that when healthy, but he turned into a comparative Kmart special after his injury.

Early signs when DiMaggio returned to the Seals' lineup, though, were not so promising. He could be seen limping at various times on the field. But DiMaggio was fortunate. His knee did heal.

Ed Barrow was satisfied that the Yankees were buying a player who could become a starter in the outfield, instead of someone who would sit in the clubhouse soaking his leg, so he authorized a discount deal with the Seals. Attendance had dropped in the minors during the Depression, just as it had in the majors, and the Seals were hungry for cash. However, DiMaggio's knee injury altered the marketplace. Instead of holding out for $100,000, the Seals could cajole just $25,000 and five players out of the Yankees for DiMaggio. They did obtain the rental of DiMaggio for one more year as he gained seasoning, so he was still a Seal for 1935. On the day the deal was announced, DiMaggio was one day shy of his 20th birthday. In later years, Barrow, the man who bushwhacked the Boston Red Sox for Babe Ruth, referred to his acquisition of Joe DiMaggio as "the best deal I ever made."[8]

A year after becoming Yankees property, DiMaggio was headed to New York, a 21-year-old rookie oozing talent. His hair was dark and curly, his smile toothy and self-effacing, his nose aqualine and his baseball instincts some of the finest ever seen in a player so young. He was the shy son of an Italian fisherman, about to be turned loose in the world's most sophisticated and raucous city. In the 1930s, New York was where those with talent came from the hinterlands to prove themselves.

Joe McCarthy recognized the raw talent in DiMaggio and he glimpsed the future in 1936. He just wanted to slow down the train a little bit. He started DiMaggio alternately in left field and right field, but when he saw those antelope strides he knew what role DiMaggio was destined to fill. He was going to be the New York Yankees' center fielder in spacious Yankee Stadium for a long time to come. "Only the great ones can play out there," McCarthy said.[9]

2

Replacing Ruth

Lou Gehrig was Babe Ruth's straight man. If Ruth had a flask of whiskey in his coat pocket, Gehrig drank from a bottle of milk. If Ruth seemed determined to charm every woman in a skirt, Gehrig was content with the company of his mother and wife. If Ruth was made for Broadway's bright lights, Gehrig was a better fit for the suburbs. Ruth was a swashbuckler who might leave you waiting at the train station. Gehrig was as reliable as the Fourth of July. You knew when it was coming and you could count on Gehrig to be there on time.

But Gehrig was younger and when Ruth left, Gehrig was still the clean-up hitter. He may not have had anyone to protect in the number three spot in the order, but he remained a stupendous hitter who tore large holes in pitchers' earned run averages with his constant barrage of runs batted in.

Gehrig never hit 50 home runs in a season, but he hit nearly 500 in his career. He may have gained a psychological advantage over pitchers because they were relieved if they struck out Ruth hitting ahead of him and may have let down, or if they felt extra pressure to get him out because Ruth was on base.

It wasn't as if Gehrig was a mere complementary player to Ruth. His personality was subsumed. He was quiet by nature, shunned the bright lights, and was more homebody than night-clubber. Ruth might show up at the ballpark nursing a hangover. Gehrig was on time and ready to work when he arrived. He was a solid citizen who never made waves or trouble for his managers.

Gehrig was no fool. He understood that Ruth was a human circus act that the people admired more than the trapeze artists and animals in the real circus. "I'm not the headline guy," Gehrig said. "I know that as long as I was following Ruth to the plate I could have stood on my head and no one would have known the difference. It's a pretty big shadow. It gives me lots of room to spread myself. The Babe is one fellow and I'm another and I could never be exactly like him. I don't try. I just go on as I am in my own right."[1]

Yet he was one of the greatest players of all time. Born Henry Louis Gehrig in 1903, Gehrig gained fame not only from his prowess with the bat (his 23 grand slams are still a record), but most notably for his 2,130-game playing streak that most baseball fans thought would last forever, but was eclipsed by Cal Ripken Jr. That Gehrig trait of reliability resulted in his being nicknamed "The Iron Horse."

Even playing in the shadow of Ruth, starting his career before the All-Star Game was invented, and having his career cut short by a terminal illness, Gehrig recorded stupendous numbers during his 17-year career. He batted .340, slammed 493 home runs and drove in 1,995 runs between 1923 and 1939, was twice named American League Most Valuable Player, and seven times was selected as an All-Star. In the modern era of baseball it's questionable whether even the Yankees, who seem to have a bottomless treasure chest to pay players, could have compensated Gehrig and Ruth sufficiently to keep them both away from free agency.

Gehrig grew up in New York of German heritage. He was not especially tall at 6 feet, but his well-distributed 200 pounds were especially powerful on playing fields. He possessed the broad shoulders and thick thighs of a football player, and the muscular arms that aided his power hitting. Being a local boy, Gehrig's baseball ability did not escape Giants manager John McGraw's tipsters, and he summoned Gehrig for a tryout.

Gehrig was already committed to attending Columbia University, at the wishes of his mother, Christina, but he did go through a workout for McGraw. The report was that Gehrig peppered the horsehide quite a distance several times, but that after letting a ball skip through his legs at first base McGraw lost interest in him.

In the fall of 1922, Gehrig was a running back for the Lions' football team, and he was a better football and baseball player than he was a student. Among his courses were contemporary civilization and trigonometry. It is not clear if he ever had the need to use trig in his life, but contemporary civilization was about to embrace him.

The man who discovered Gehrig for the Yankees after he had been

2. Replacing Ruth

brushed aside by the Giants was New York's super scout, Paul Krichell. Krichell spent 36 years in search of talent for the big club and with the backing of a front office that increasingly trusted his judgment became as responsible as any single team official for keeping the Yankees ahead of the pack in the American League.

Krichell was born in 1882 and spent 1910 and 1911 as a catcher with the St. Louis Browns. He had a Jess Willard–type bout with Ty Cobb at home plate after the Tigers star slid home into him and knocked the ball out of his glove. Krichell coached for the Red Sox in 1920 after kicking around the minors again, and joined the Yankees in 1921.

Krichell accumulated great players like some little boys collect baseball cards, although he collected them in flesh and blood. Among his signings for the Yankees: Gehrig, Phil Rizzuto, Red Rolfe, Tommy Holmes, Leo Durocher, Charlie Keller, Tony Lazzeri, Johnny Murphy, George Stirnweiss, Hank Borowy, Mark Koenig, Bill Werber, Marius Russo, and George Selkirk. Krichell kept a personal Hall of Fame display of framed photos of the men he signed who made the majors on an office wall.

On the day Krichell first saw Gehrig play he was sitting in the stands of a Columbia-Rutgers game in New Brunswick, New Jersey, to kill time. If Fordham or New York University had been playing a home game the scout said he never would have left Manhattan. He had not heard of Gehrig, but sized him up quickly.

"I did not even know what position he played," Krichell said. "But he played in the outfield against Rutgers and socked a couple of balls a mile. I sat up and took notice. I saw a tremendous youth, with powerful arms and terrific legs. I said, 'Here is a kid who can't miss.'"[2]

By 1925, Gehrig was the starting first baseman for the New York Yankees, stepping in to give Wally Pipp a day off, ostensibly because the incumbent had a headache, but perhaps just because manager Miller Huggins knew the young player was ready for the job. Fourteen years passed before Gehrig allowed anyone else the chance to handle a first baseman's mitt for a full game. He played through injuries big and small, broken bones and illnesses that carried high fevers. "I had him for over eight years and he never gave me a moment's trouble," said Joe McCarthy. "I guess you might say he was kind of my favorite."[3]

Gehrig smacked 40 or more home runs in a season five times and three times led the AL in that category. He led the league in RBI five times with a high of 184, and had two other seasons over 170. Although Gehrig batted .300 or more 12 times, including three times in the .370s, he won just one batting title with a slightly lesser average.

The destruction wreaked by Ruth and Gehrig back-to-back in the Yankees order for all-around statistics in the home run, RBI and average categories has never been matched. Yet Gehrig and Ruth were not always the best of pals. Consistent with Ruth's character and habits, he probably did not even remember Gehrig's name for a few years. Ruth was flamboyant, Gehrig reserved, and they did not socialize much. Eventually, after Gehrig married his protective wife, Eleanor, she worked to bring him out from under Ruth's shadow and the two players had a falling out.

The key players were civil in the clubhouse and dugout for several years, though they ultimately reconciled after Ruth retired and Gehrig became ill. In 1936, Ruth's playing days lay in the past and Gehrig's tribulations lay in the future. The immediate question for the Yankees was how they could rekindle their glory days when winning pennants was a regular habit, not a sometime thing, and who would lead them.

After a long courtship, Gehrig married girlfriend Eleanor in 1933, and in 1934 Gehrig hooked up with Ruth's promotional agent, Christy Walsh, who began obtaining endorsement deals for the other slugger. Eleanor had pushed for Gehrig to be more proactive in marketing his name and making some extra money. He was the first of innumerable star athletes to appear on a Wheaties box, a tradition that continues today. He also endorsed Aqua Velvet lotion and Camel cigarettes, an early promoter of what used to be a routine connection between athletes and smokes whether they smoked them or not.

Ruth had transformed baseball from the Ty Cobb style of advancing one base at a time with "scientific" approaches like the hit-and-run and stolen base to a style that matched his gluttonous appetites, scoring runs in bunches by taking all four bases at once with home runs. Although prior to Ruth's emergence no one else had hit more than 20-something homers in a year, he proved his home-run power was no fluke. On July 13, 1934, Ruth smashed his 700th career home run in Detroit. The ball soared out of what was then known as Navin Field in the third inning and into the vision of a 16-year-old boy named Lennie Bielski. Bielski was hanging outside the stadium waiting for a friend late for the ballgame when the crowd yelled. The ball cleared the fence, bounded down the street and rolled under a car with Bielski in full-sprint pursuit. He fished out the ball, but didn't get far from the scene. Bielski said he was immediately surrounded by ushers and police officers who carried him into the park.

Ruth was well aware his blast was No. 700 and he wanted the ball, immediately offering anyone within earshot $20 if they could chase it down. The ball was introduced to Ruth in the Yankees' locker room at the same time Bielski was. Ruth cut the boy a deal. Ruth gave Bielski $20 and another ball autographed "To the boy who got my 700th home run, best wishes, Babe Ruth."[4]

Reminiscing about that day in a *New York Daily News* story 39 years later, Bielski said Ruth reached into his pockets and realized he didn't have any cash, so he asked Gehrig to loan him the 20 bucks. Gehrig, aware of Ruth's reputation as a big tipper, said the slugger had paid several thousand dollars to retrieve his 600th home-run ball. But Bielski didn't mind and he saved both the $20 bill and the Ruth autographed ball.

That wasn't the end of it, though. Through the years Ruth stayed in touch with Bielski, sent him gifts, and until he retired gave him box seat tickets when he played in Detroit. Bielski laughed when he said he wondered "if Ruth had a guilty conscience" because he only paid him the $20 for the famous ball.[5]

Ruth spent his final active year, 1935, touring the National League, leaving Gehrig in charge of the clutch hits. Ruth bid adieu to the game on May 25 after swatting the final three home runs of his illustrious career in one game against the Pittsburgh Pirates for the Braves. He was 40 years old and despite this moment in the sunshine, Ruth knew he was finished. On his third jaunt around the bases for the 714th homer of his career, it was as if he was racing the sands to the bottom of the hour glass. "I thought about it going around the bases for the third time," Ruth said of how wild it was that he hit three in a game again.[6]

Gehrig was hardly washed up, but he found it a little bit more challenging to get pitches to hit without Ruth in the lineup. During the 1935 season, Gehrig batted .329 with 132 walks, 30 home runs and 119 RBI. Gehrig once again played in every game for the Yankees, keeping his streak going.

New York did not win the pennant in 1935 and had not won the pennant since 1932. Owner Jacob Ruppert was probably muttering under his breath a phrase not unlike what Leo Durocher later said about nice guys finishing last. Perhaps Ruppert amended it to nice guys finishing second.

Gehrig was the cornerstone of the franchise now and teammates looked to him for veteran leadership. Gehrig had always led by example, not by vocal, rah-rah chants, and he did not change his personality that year. If other players expected him to, they were mistaken. He was still the team's best hitter, but the one-time Murderers Row cast was actually short on power without The Babe and some of his supporting cast.

Gehrig was still anchoring first base, but with Ruth departed to the Braves, the Yankees needed a new right-fielder. Glancing at the years between 1919 and 1935, the Yanks' history with that position was intriguing.

In 1919, the Bronx Bombers tried a young man out of the University of Illinois in right field. His name was George Halas, and by batting just .091 in 12 games realized his future lay in professional football. In 1920 the Yankees inserted Ruth into the spot and Halas got busy founding the Decatur Staleys, which became the Chicago Bears. Halas remained boss of the Bears for 63 years, until his death in 1983, and is a member of the Pro Football Hall of Fame in Canton, Ohio. The George Halas Trophy is presented to the team that wins the National Football Conference championship game. Most people believe he made the proper career choice.

In 1935, the Yankees were hoping for more production out of Ruth's successor. The Yankees went from someone called "Babe" patrolling right field to someone called "Twinkletoes." Twinkletoes was the moniker laid on George Selkirk after a coach, whose own nickname was "Spike," told him that if he ran on his toes it would help prevent all of the Charley horses and cramps he got in his legs.

This was also a rather peculiar nickname for a guy like Selkirk, whose hobby was wrestling. More at home at first as a catcher than an outfielder, Selkirk was not so artful out on the grass. But his wrestling background, Selkirk said, gave him the gumption to be a daredevil outfielder. "One reason why I do not fear running headfirst into concrete walls," he said, "is that I was thrown out of the ring onto the concrete floor more than once."[7]

Selkirk, a rare Canadian in the majors in the 1930s, picked up the Twinkletoes nickname while playing in Jersey City, and through a life of its own it stuck to him for life. Selkirk saw action in 46 games for the Yankees in 1934, batting .313 and impressing manager Joe McCarthy with the strength of his arm. McCarthy anointed him Ruth's replacement the next season.

When Ruth made a curtain-call appearance in left field on August

12, 1934, at Fenway Park against the team he broke in with, Selkirk was playing right. McCarthy removed Ruth so he could receive an ovation from his old Boston fans, and Selkirk abashedly caught himself doffing his cap and clapping for Ruth, too. "There I was, playing as a Yankee, and that was thrill enough," Selkirk recalled many years later. "It was something that came from the heart. I felt a little ashamed of myself, thinking that I looked just a busher, and then I looked around and there were the rest of the Yankee players and they were doing the same thing."[8]

In an era when teams were just starting to put numbers on the backs of uniform shirts, Ruth's number three was not immediately retired, and Selkirk inherited Ruth's position, uniform number and spot in the batting order. If he felt the pressure he didn't broadcast it, but Selkirk started slowly with weak hitting at the plate.

Actually, McCarthy gave Selkirk the chance to avoid wearing number three, but Selkirk went in whole hog in adopting his role as Ruth's successor. "Joe McCarthy asked me if I did not want some number other than the 'Big 3' that Babe had worn on his back," Selkirk said, "but I was just cocky enough to say, 'Wearing Babe's number will not make me nervous. If I am going to take his place, I'll take his number, too.'"[9]

Since he got off to that slow start, maybe Selkirk was just fooling himself when he believed he could slip seamlessly into the Ruth role. McCarthy benched him for a while and when he put him back in the lineup, Selkirk batted fourth behind Gehrig. After that, for a guy who followed a legend, Selkirk performed remarkably well in 1935. He batted .312 with 11 home runs and 94 RBI. If Ruth recorded a year like that it would have been labeled a slump. But for a mere mortal, it was a good year.

The next year Selkirk reflected on what the experience had been like to take over for the most famous player in history. "Was that a tough assignment?" he parroted back to a questioner. "I was expected to make the fans forget all about one of the greatest players in the history of the game, Babe Ruth. Did I worry? Well, I tried not to. Ruth, you know, always had been my baseball hero, but never had I thought I ever would be taking his place."[10]

Of course, no one really ever took Ruth's place. That didn't mean Colonel Ruppert and Ed Barrow weren't always on the lookout.

3

Co-Starring Gehrig and DiMaggio

You bet the Yankees were counting on Lou Gehrig to be the leader. Colonel Ruppert and Ed Barrow weren't going to pay out big bucks like $31,000 a year at the tail end of the Depression for someone who wasn't going to carry the team to a pennant.

Compared to Babe Ruth, Gehrig had never battled management for every dollar he felt he deserved. He accepted the front office offers without protest and showed up on time for spring training. Gehrig clearly had more leverage than he thought he had. Ruth talked his way into an $80,000 deal at his peak and even if many (especially his wife) thought Gehrig was worth just as much as the Bambino, he didn't try holding out for $50,000 until 1937.

In the early 1930s, with the economy in the tank, hordes of Americans out of work, and declining attendance at the turnstiles, major league owners could justifiably argue that business was bad. It was unseemly for a ballplayer, lucky to have a job at all and lucky to be playing a game for a living during hard times, to complain too loudly.

Red Ruffing, like Gehrig bound for a Hall of Fame that was just being created, was paid $12,000 in 1936, and the newcomer, Joe DiMaggio, got a rookie salary of $8,500. It beat crab fishing.

The 1935 Yankees were Ruthless, not toothless. They finished second in the American League, their 89–60 record three games behind the Detroit Tigers of Hank Greenberg and Charlie Gehringer, a one-two Hall of Fame connection in the batting order that was also one of the best ever.

By the time DiMaggio did make it from San Francisco to Florida to New York, in the finest tabloid newspaper tradition of the time his name

3. Co-Starring Gehrig and DiMaggio

and predictions for his achievements greeted the public early in the mornings in type THIS LARGE. *The Sporting News* actually wrote a story telling everyone to calm down and let DiMaggio be DiMaggio, not Ruth.

Barrow became worried that DiMaggio would be crushed by the pressure. He did not yet know his man. When the general manager took DiMaggio aside and told him not to let this glare of publicity get to him, DiMaggio said, "Don't worry, Mr. Barrow, I never get excited."[1]

For all of the hype and glowing reports, no one could have estimated the impact of DiMaggio, who may not have been able to drive a car, but could drive in runs. He was 6-foot-2 and weighed about 195 pounds. His long legs made him look taller, but he was deceptively fast, collecting 15 triples in 1936 taking those sharp corners in the infield.

In his debut season, DiMaggio batted .323 with 29 home runs and 125 runs batted in while stroking 206 hits. He was selected to the All-Star team for the first of 13 straight times. In 2011, 75 years later, *The Sporting News*' baseball annual cited DiMaggio's season as the best ever by a rookie Yankee.

He had a knack for getting the jump on foul balls in the corner fields, and Joe McCarthy knew that DiMaggio was destined to take over the broad expanses of center field at Yankee Stadium. Still, his first year, when DiMaggio played 138 games, McCarthy deployed DiMaggio in center 55 times and in left for 66 games. It was a subtle message. McCarthy wanted DiMaggio to ease into his certain starring role, not be thrust upon a veteran team as a savior and thrown to demanding fans all too ready to compare him to the incomparable Ruth.

As good as DiMaggio was, the talent in the field surrounding him was deep and loaded with versatile, hard-hitting men. Besides DiMaggio and McCarthy himself, there were five future Hall of Famers on the Yankees in 1936. Bill Dickey was the main catcher. Gehrig, of course, still had his games streak going at first base. Tony Lazzeri played second. Pitchers Ruffing and Vernon "Lefty" Gomez, perhaps the funniest man to ever play major league ball, were on the mound.

Thank you, scouts Paul Krichell and Bill Essick.

Also, the defending champion Tigers lost Greenberg with a broken wrist during the first month of the season and future Hall of Fame catcher Mickey Cochrane to a nervous breakdown later in the season. The Tigers still finished second, but it wasn't much of a pennant race. The Yankees were 19½ games ahead on the last day of the season.

Although he was shy compared to many others who came to Manhattan with the goal of conquering Broadway, by the All-Star break of 1936 DiMaggio was featured on the cover of *Time* magazine. If there was pressure on his shoulders he shrugged it off like the drops falling from the shower in the Yankees clubhouse. It was easy to forget he was only 21 when the season began and his San Francisco, Italian immigrant upbringing had been rather sheltered.

DiMaggio never let outside elements distract him from his task at the ballpark. He was always first a baseball player. He recognized that this was the best opportunity he would ever have to make good money. He had no desire to adopt the commercial fishing lifestyle of his father and two of his brothers. He had to make good and he had the goods to make it.

It was not easy to be the toast of New York and pretty much ignore it, but there were elders watching out for him to ensure that he did not get taken in by any scams or make a reckless mistake. In 1936, Frank Crosetti was New York's shortstop. Lazzeri was the Yankees' second baseman. Like DiMaggio, they were Italians from San Francisco, his companions for the 3,000-mile-long car journey to spring training camp. They made sure the innocent was reasonably well protected. At that age, and at that rookie stage of his major league career, DiMaggio was an innocent. He talked to newspapermen when he was cornered, but sometimes jogged right past the sports writers clamoring for comment when he had nothing to say. He was no night owl. He made news simply by being DiMaggio, the kid who hit in 61 straight in the Pacific Coast League and the kid who was stepping into the Yankees outfield recently vacated by Babe Ruth.

Gomez, who earned his nickname of "Goofy" through his sometimes offbeat actions and his often clever remarks, tweaked everyone. Although in public speech the use of the description "Dago" for an Italian was derogatory, among the boys it was a comment of affection. On the team, Lazzeri was called "Big Dago," Crosetti was "Little Dago," and DiMaggio was "Dago."

During a game against the St. Louis Browns, the upstarts had a runner on first. The batter smacked the ball back to Gomez on the mound, who fielded it and promptly threw it well over second base to DiMaggio rushing in from center field to back up the play. Although Gomez pitched out of trouble, his manager was ticked off by the errant throw when he returned to the dugout and asked Gomez what he was doing. "Someone shouted, 'Throw it to the Dago,'" Gomez said. "Nobody said which Dago."[2]

3. Co-Starring Gehrig and DiMaggio

That was Gomez all over, making light of a situation, yet adjusting his pitching for the victory. It was Gomez who ended up rooming with DiMaggio on the road. They made for a strange pair, Gomez always outgoing and joking, DiMaggio the strong silent type and introverted. Gomez said that once on a five-city, two-week trip DiMaggio never said a word in a hotel room. He spent all of his time listening to the radio, reading the sports page and reading Superman comics. "Two weeks, not one word," Gomez said.[3]

Yes, as a rookie DiMaggio did just about all of his talking with his bat. It didn't matter since Gomez did enough talking for everyone on the team.

Immediately, DiMaggio became a fan favorite, invited to dinners and public appearances. He was particularly embraced by the Italian-American community in every city in the American League, but loathed the notion of giving speeches. DiMaggio begged Gomez, who after baseball made his living as an after-dinner speaker as the king of the hot stove league, to go with him.

The same thing happened at every Italian-American banquet or Knights of Columbus feed. DiMaggio was introduced, said thank you very much for having him, and then immediately turned the microphone over to Gomez to tell stories. "Then he would sit down and I would have to entertain them for 20 minutes before we could go home," Gomez said. "Then they would load him down with presents and that would be the evening. He'd come home with a dozen shirts or a golf bag or a watch or a toilet set or luggage or something like that."[4]

DiMaggio learned early in his tenure with the Yankees that there was profit in being Joe DiMaggio away from the ballpark. He was rarely comfortable with the circumstances that would provide him with the perks. Once, said Gomez, after he had gone to more dinners with DiMaggio than he could count, he chose not to accompany his roomie to an event in the Chicago suburbs. He insisted that night he felt like going to the movies instead of cracking jokes for a crowd with chicken on its plate.

Finally, DiMaggio went alone to a dinner. When Gomez got back from his flick, the room was crammed with a golf bag, golf clubs, a travel bag, watch and other gifts. DiMaggio looked him in the eye and told him that there was another set of everything for Gomez, but he didn't get it because he didn't show up. Gomez never figured out if there really was a duplicate set of swag or if DiMaggio was playing a joke on him. Especially as DiMaggio aged and grew in stature, becoming more regal as the years passed, few teammates teased him, but Gomez never shied away from doing so and said the men continued the practice for decades, long after they retired from baseball. "He needles me as much as I needle him," Gomez said 35 years later.[5]

From his earliest days with the Yankees, and in public during his days in New York, DiMaggio always projected a demeanor of seriousness. Gomez said that for years DiMaggio collected all of those golf gifts from dinners and gave the stuff away. Years later, after he left baseball, DiMaggio began playing golf, and his old roommate said it was one thing that relaxed him. "He was too serious about baseball to laugh on the field," Gomez said. "But he could laugh all day long if something struck him funny off the field."[6]

It is difficult to imagine DiMaggio giggling, but Gomez was around him enough to actually witness the kind of silly moment 99 percent of Americans would never suspect of DiMaggio. Once they were traveling on a train and DiMaggio called Gomez, who was in a bad mood because he had lost a tight, extra-inning game in Cleveland, over to him because he wanted to show him something.

To Gomez's astonishment, DiMaggio said, "Lefty, it's something I just learned," and put his thumb and first finger on the end of his nose. DiMaggio didn't quite have a nose an Olympian could ski down, but it was large. "He begins tweaking it — bong, bong, bong," Gomez said. And DiMaggio said, "Don't I sound like a banjo?"[7] Damn, it did sound like a banjo, Gomez thought, and burst out laughing. He doubled over laughing. He almost fell on the floor laughing. It was a moment of levity with stone-faced Joe DiMaggio that he never forgot.

No one who met Lefty Gomez forgot him, either.

Gomez was 27 during the 1936 season, three seasons of 20-plus victories behind him for the Yankees, but one of the players in 1935 who didn't respond well with the absence of Ruth. Although his earned run average was a sound 3.18, his record was only 12–15. Only the year before he had been a dominating 26–5, so Gomez, a left-hander, naturally, was trying to regain his equilibrium in 1936. If the Yankees were going to bury those second-place days six feet under, Gomez had to pitch more like his usual self.

The New York Yankees were a buttoned-down, pin-striped outfit as serious as the highest levels of the federal government or corporate America.

They were not exactly the boys of summer if that connoted being boys frolicking in the sunshine the way they had on the playground back home. In actions and attitude, Gomez was the wayward son, the one tolerated despite his fooling around because he could throw heat that would freeze opposing batters.

Vernon Louis "Lefty" Gomez was born November 26, 1908 in Rodeo, California of Spanish and Irish descent and was often referred to as Mexican-American. Like so many of the 1920s–1930s era Yankees he played sandlot ball in the San Francisco Bay area, in his case in Oakland. And like DiMaggio and Lazzeri, his professional debut was with the San Francisco Seals. The Yankees paid $39,000 to the Seals for his rights, more than they paid for DiMaggio, though of course Gomez didn't have a lame knee at the time.

Gomez was a terrific addition to the Yankees after a short and mediocre start to his major league career in 1930 when he finished 2–5. By 1933 Gomez had recorded his first two 20-win seasons and was selected for the American League squad managed by Connie Mack when the first All-Star Game was played. In fact, Gomez, who was ordinarily such a poor hitter he made jokes about his limitations, drove in the first run in All-Star Game history.

Once, Gomez smacked a double and was so happy to be visiting second base he didn't pay attention to what was going on around him in the field. "I had only one weakness, a pitched ball," Gomez said. "One day I hit a double and then I was picked off second. When I got to the dugout McCarthy asked me, 'What happened?' I told him, 'How should I know, I've never been there before.'"[8]

During spring training of 1935, following his seasons of 21, 24, 16, and 26 wins, Gomez was asked to write a first-person story for a syndicate essentially explaining how he got to be so good. Gomez gave credit to Nick Williams, his manager with the Seals in 1929 for helping him develop, but saved the largest share of gratefulness for former Yankees pitching great Herb Pennock. Gomez called Pennock, inducted into the Hall of Fame in 1948 with a 240–162 record, "the greatest southpaw baseball has seen.... It was not until I had settled down with the Yankees and came under the influence of Pennock that I realized how much I still had to learn. Herb took great pains with me. Unlike other veteran stars he had no selfish streak. He showed me all he knew and criticized my failings unmercifully."[9]

Lefty Gomez rarely looked as stern as he does in this picture of him on the mound. Nicknamed "Goofy," Gomez told stories and jokes that kept the Yankees clubhouse loose as he ran up enough wins to be selected for the Hall of Fame after spending years as a featured after-dinner speaker at baseball events.

3. Co-Starring Gehrig and DiMaggio 33

It was easy enough for Gomez to admit to being an admonished pupil after he became a big winner, but his sense of humor, optimistic demeanor and light-hearted approach to just about everything were the defining characteristics of his personality.

The day Gomez made his major league debut with the Yankees in 1930, it was in relief. He was as nervous as a student who hadn't prepared being ordered to give an oral report to the class. "As I was making the long walk, thoughts kept running through my mind," Gomez said. "'Should I spike myself?'"[10]

Those were the kind of comments that gained Gomez his nickname of "Goofy." Sometimes sportswriters sought to make it more ethnic and their version of the name in Spanish was "El Goofo." "The Gay Castillian" was more of a reach, but Gomez put up with that stuff.

When Gomez was brought to New York by the Yankees he stood 6-foot-2, but only weighed 150 pounds. He was a very tall pencil. He didn't begin the season in the majors in 1931, but when the Yanks brought him up his fastball and curve dazzled the American League. He won 21 games in the last three-and-a-half months of the season, only to be called in to the front office by Ed Barrow and told he was too thin. Gomez wasn't trying out for the National Football League, so he didn't think weight should count as much as his results on the mound. "I asked him how big you had to be," Gomez reported later. In response, the Yankees shipped Gomez to a California health farm to build a strong body in the off-season. "Four quarts of milk a day. In bed at nine o'clock, up at seven. I think I got up to around 155 pounds."[11]

He gained some weight as he gained age and baseball history statistics do refer to Gomez as weighing 173 pounds. He must have gone on a chocolate-milk diet later.

While Gomez was thought to be a playboy type who enjoyed going out on the town and soaking up the night life, he got married in 1933 before he was 25. Of course, he did marry a glamorous woman, actress June O'Dea, a Broadway star whose big splash in the theatre came in "Of Thee I Sing" after her days as a Ziegfield Follies girl. O'Dea gave up her career to raise a family with Gomez, but their marital discord made the same kind of tabloid headlines their hitching up did.

By December 27, 1937, Gomez sued O'Dea for divorce and the *New York Journal* of that day noted his attempts to "strike her out with a Mexican divorce." O'Dea played it coy, saying she would never divorce the pitcher because she was Catholic, but could live with a separation. She tried to take the high road, saying, "He is too fine a boy and I think too much of him to criticize him." Gomez disembarked for Reno, Nevada, to establish a six-week residency to seek a divorce that way. That didn't work, either, and O'Dea and Gomez remained married until death did they part decades later.

The Yankees won 102 games in 1936, DiMaggio's rookie year, and they looked as powerful as they ever had during those Roaring Twenties. The opponent in the World Series was the New York Giants. The crosstown rival had bounced back operating under the great Bill Terry after its slumping final days under John McGraw.

Terry, whose .401 batting average in 1930 represents the last time a National League player broke the .400 mark, feuded with McGraw during the last days of McGraw's 33-year managerial career, sometimes going days at a time with barely more than a grunt passing between the two Giants institutions. But when McGraw's health was failing, he anointed Terry as his successor anyway.

The Giants won the 1936 NL pennant with 92–62 record. On paper the Yankees seemed superior. Outfielder Mel Ott, on his way to setting the National League home run record of 511 by the time he retired, was the Giants' chief offensive weapon. But the man to be feared was the older circuit's ace pitcher, Carl Hubbell. Hubbell, the premier screwball thrower in baseball history, destined to win 253 games and be elected to the Hall of Fame, thought he could master the Yankees' rugged batting order. Indeed, Hubbell handcuffed the Yankees in the first game, beating Red Ruffing, 6–1, at the Polo Grounds by scattering seven hits.

Gomez was the beneficiary of a Yankees onslaught against Hal Schumacher in the second game. The American League club won, 18–4, on 17 hits. Gomez didn't have to be his sharpest, but the barrage helped him compile a lifetime 6–0 World Series record.

While it didn't matter much to the final result, DiMaggio made a spectacular running catch in center field, hauling in a shot hit 490 feet from home plate by the Giants' Hank Leiber with two outs in the ninth inning. His momentum carried him up the clubhouse steps. President Franklin D. Roosevelt, who attended the game, was led to a limousine on the field and saluted DiMaggio as he left the ballpark.

3. Co-Starring Gehrig and DiMaggio

When Hubbell lost the fourth game, 5–2, it seemed apparent that the Giants would not have enough answers for the Yankees' firepower. Gomez got his second turn on the mound in Game 6 and once again the Yankees pulverized Giants pitching. The final score was 13–5 at the Polo Grounds and Gomez was again backed by 17 hits.

It was during this World Series that Gomez pulled one of the casual stunts that he thought nothing of doing, but others seemed to remember forever. On an occasion when the Giants had men on base, when catchers and managers want their pitcher to be highly focused on the next batter, Gomez called time out. What for? In order to watch a plane fly over the stadium. As thousands of fans waited in anticipation, as the Giants poised to drive in runs, as McCarthy and catcher Bill Dickey anxiously awaited his next offering, Gomez amused himself by devoting his full fascination to an airplane as if it were Charles Lindbergh returning from his flight over the Atlantic. "A lot of guys said I was goofy," Gomez said afterwards. "But what's the difference between that and calling time to tie your shoe?"

If Gomez had offered up a meatball swatted for a big home run and lost the game, forcing a Game 7, then there might have been a Yankees gripe. But he closed out the Giants, won his second Series game of the fall, and the Yankees were once again world champions.

Scoring in bunches the way the Yankees did left even DiMaggio agog, with those 18-and 13-run Series games capping his first year. "When I look back over the record of my first season with the Yankees, I'm still amazed that one team could show such power," said DiMaggio.[12]

Of course DiMaggio was part of that slugging group and his inaugural season proved to be worth waiting for after his seasoning with the Seals on the West Coast. There was no rookie of the year award — it was first given in 1947 to Jackie Robinson — but there is little doubt it would have belonged to Joe D. that year.

The World Series winners' share was $6,430.55 for each player, and one sportswriter happened to bump into Lou Gehrig after he collected. In 1936, that $6,000-plus represented an entire year's salary for many players. The writer asked Gehrig, who was accompanied by wife Eleanor in Times Square, what he was going to do with his newfound riches. At the time, no doubt at Christy Walsh's urging, Gehrig was being considered for the role of Tarzan in the movies. He surprised the sportswriter by kiddingly saying, "Me puttem in annuity."[13]

Mrs. Gehrig seemed mortified that Gehrig would rehearse Tarzan's pidgin English on the street in general conversation, and perhaps in other ways since the writer commented that the next thing she said was, "Lou, stop scratching yourself." She also "translated," informing the writer that Gehrig was saying he planned to invest his World Series check in an annuity.[14]

Gehrig did not bare his muscular chest in mid-town Manhattan, nor did he get to play Tarzan in the films, though he did pose with his arms crossed and chest naked for what might have been considered try-out material. It's not clear if that photograph is from Gehrig's actual Hollywood screen test in 1936, but he really did go for it.

For those who think of Gehrig as a dignified hero, the ultimate reserved and perfect Yankee, they would be astonished to see a Gehrig picture that is definitely from the screen test. In it he is lying down, propped up on one arm, facing the camera and smiling sardonically. He is wearing a leopard-skin outfit hanging off one shoulder that makes him resemble Fred Flintstone while grasping a club casually slung over the bare shoulder.

Tarzan author Edgar Rice Burroughs reportedly frowned on the casting of Gehrig as the jungle hero, and the producer turned down Gehrig in favor of Glenn Morris to star in the 1937 movie "Tarzan's Revenge." Tarzan movies never really went out of style, only out of production for periods of years, but probably no Tarzan ever surpassed Johnny Weissmuller, who became so identified with the role that some forget he was an Olympic gold-medal swimmer who had already made a name performing bare-chested.

Gehrig seemed to maintain his sense of humor about the entire incident and he even autographed some of the outtakes from the screen test. A photograph of Gehrig standing, wearing the same leopard-skin suit and pretending to bend a metal bar, was sold at auction for $4,200 in 2009.

Acting was the career that never was for Gehrig, but he was fine with his original choice where he kept his clothes on. The 1936 World Series was his fourth world title and the best player on the best team that year, DiMaggio notwithstanding, he was chosen American League Most Valuable Player.

4

Ruff Was Tough

No one is born with "Red" written on his birth certificate, even if parents start calling him that as a toddler. Charles Herbert "Red" Ruffing may not have talked as good a game as Lefty Gomez (who did?), but he pitched as well.

Actually, it was Ruffing, a 6-foot-2, 210-pound right-handed flinger, who was the ace of the staff more often than not in the 1930s after he was acquired in a trade with the Boston Red Sox (another fleecing) that left him so happy he almost danced to the mound every time the Yankees sent him out. "I was so tickled to death I couldn't wait till I got there," Ruffing said after the deal.[1]

For good reason. The Red Sox were the worst team in the American League during Ruffing's stay and his best pitches were battered all over Fenway Park. Ruffing endured seasons like 10–25 and 9–22. Few pitchers have ever experienced the combination career highs/career lows that marked Ruffing's mound experiences. If any pitcher ever says that he can do it on his own without the run support of his teammates, he should look at Ruffing's statistics as Exhibit A to prove he is over-stuffed with baloney.

The same Ruffing who couldn't escape the big innings in Boston was the beneficiary of them in New York. "The Red Sox of my time weren't even a good Double A team," Ruffing said.[2]

He joined the Yankees partway into the 1930 season with an 0–3 record and in less than a full season finished 15–8. Over the next 12 seasons, Ruffing won at least 14 games 11 times and 18 or more six times. Four of those years produced 20 or 21 wins.

Ruffing was a workhorse. He pitched 4,344 innings in his career with 335 complete games. Although the attitude was typical of the times, Ruffing was a stalwart when it came to taking the ball for inning one and sticking it out through inning nine. He had 498 decisions in his career, going 273–225, while pitching for seven Yankees pennant winners. On days he threw, Ruffing added a bonus weapon to the batting order. He was no Babe Ruth, but Ruffing's lifetime average was .269 and he batted over .300 in eight seasons with 36 home runs, one of the best totals ever for a hurler.

In some ways it was more surprising that Ruffing was a successful pitcher than a solid hitter. Growing up in Southern Illinois coal country, Ruffing had few aspirations that he thought school might help him with, so at 13 he went to work in the mines for $3 a day. By the time he was 15, he was playing first base for his father's mining team, the Reliance Coal Company of Nokomis, Illinois, but also had a part-time job in the coal world.

If Ruffing needed any proof that he didn't want to spend his life working below ground, the message was rammed home in a frightening fashion. Ruffing was working as a coupler between two coal cars when one ran over his left foot, crushing four toes that had to be fully or partially amputated. Ruffing spent nearly a year recuperating. After he lost the digits Ruffing gave up his major league dream of being an outfielder and adapted to the pitching mound at his brother John's urging. He was fortunate to be able to make the switch and spent 22 years in the majors.

Ruffing proved his toughness at an early age, not only recovering from the accident that disfigured his foot, but even before that. His first professional remuneration came in the form of ice-cream cones awarded by his father, John. But although John Ruffing managed the mine baseball team, he really wanted his sons, Red and John Jr., to devote themselves to another sport — boxing.

"We practiced sparring more than we did baseball," Ruffing said. "The old man was great at punching the bag and to toughen our faces he used to have my brother and me play tunes on the bag, letting the bag hit us on the nose, on the rebound, to toughen our features. My brother and I liked to fight well enough and John did grow up to be a whale of a neighborhood scrapper."[3]

Ruffing said tongue-in-cheek that he must have been an awful disappointment to his father because he didn't take as well to beating people up. However, his dad did worry about him after his accident. While John Jr. gave Red the pep talk he needed to start pitching, John Sr. was skeptical and didn't want his son to fail and become depressed. Although Red lost the first game he ever pitched, he struck out 18 batters in his debut. Soon,

4. *Ruff Was Tough* 39

Right-hander Red Ruffing performed yeoman service for the Yankees during his 22-year, Hall of Fame career on the mound that produced 273 victories. Ruffing pitched into his 40s and recorded a 7–2 World Series mark.

he was making $25 a game in semi-pro play and that led to signing a professional contract.

Although his mobility was limited and his foot speed non-existent, the Red Sox periodically used Ruffing in the outfield. One day Yankees manager Miller Huggins talked confidentially to the opposing pitcher and told him the Red Sox were wasting him and if he could he would obtain him for the Yankees and make him into a great pitcher. Huggins died before the end of that 1929 season. Yet Ed Barrow followed through on the trade, giving Boston $50,000 and an over-the-hill player.

With the Yankees, Ruffing developed the type of crisp curveball he needed to complement his fastball and that transformed him into a star eventually elected to the Hall of Fame. His repertoire of pitches grew from there. "I never have received much coaching," Ruffing said. "One day Bill Dickey said, 'You are pitching a slider,' and I said, 'It's all news to me.' I was holding the ball a little different. I have picked up the fadeaway and I can throw a lot of other fancy stuff."[4]

Huggins did not live to see it, but his prediction about Ruffing becoming a great pitcher with the Yankees came true. Ruffing didn't really boast about it. He might have offered less to the sportswriters than DiMaggio did, shunning the spotlight in a casual way, not rudely.

Nokomis was proud to advertise it was the home of big leaguer Jim Bottomley and wanted to add Ruffing's name to a banner. But he declined the honor, saying, "I might move."[5] Droll, at least. It would have been something to see the town fathers' faces upon hearing that response.

Ruffing let his fastball speak the loudest for him, but whether or not he had much truck with making speeches or even issuing one-liners, it was undeniable that Ruffing was a key element in the Yankees' success. As a whole the mid–1930s Yankees roster didn't talk much. A sportswriter looking for the second coming of Babe Ruth had a better chance of finding him on the field than in verbal exchanges. One legendary story about the Yankees of the time had DiMaggio, Frank Crosetti, and Tony Lazzeri sitting in a hotel lobby on a road trip, people-watching. A sportswriter sat down in another chair and clicked a stop watch on them. For 90 minutes, he later reported, none of them uttered a word. Then DiMaggio apparently grunted. Lazzeri asked what he said, but Crosetti said DiMaggio didn't say a thing, and the trio returned to silence, as if it were prayer hour in a monastery.

When it came to the verbosity, or lack of it on the pitching staff, Gomez and Ruffing more or less cancelled one another out. Johnny Broaca, who did not have the arm of either maestro, did make more noise than a passing subway car. Like Damon Runyon's "Guys and Dolls" amalgams of New Yorkers, Broaca was a character. Actually, a few years into his baseball career, Runyon was writing about him.

4. Ruff Was Tough

Broaca was born in the mill town of Lawrence, Massachusetts, in 1909, where he earned letters in four sports and was smart enough to graduate from the local high school, spend two years at Phillips Andover Academy and earn a degree from Yale University. He broke in with the Yankees in 1934 and won 12 games and a spot in the rotation. A year later Broaca won 15 games and in 1936 he again won 12.

As someone who grew up in the suburbs of Boston, Broaca had actually wanted to stay at home to play. He sought attention from the National League Braves, but was rejected. In spring training of 1935, he got revenge of sorts with five innings of nearly perfect pitching against the Braves. "Six months before I opened negotiations with the Yankees, I made every effort to get a trial with McKechnie," he said of Boston manager Bill McKechnie. Then he approached the team owner. "I begged Judge Fuchs for a chance. I told him not to worry about the money angle. I could not even get into Braves Field for a workout."[6]

After the way he handled the Braves during the spring training game in Tampa, it was clear Broaca wouldn't have to purchase a ticket if he showed up at the gates of Braves Field again. "Broaca is a crafty, accomplished pitcher right now," McKechnie said after the game, "and has unlimited possibilities."[7]

Broaca seemed to have a solid niche with the Yankees as a regular in a strong rotation that promised the likelihood of either a World Series bonus every year or the drama of fighting for a pennant. But in the middle of the 1937 season, Broaca jumped the team and vanished from New York and major league baseball. No reason was given publicly when Broaca abandoned the Yankees on July 18 on a road trip to Cleveland, but he did not rejoin the team the rest of the season, or for the 1938 season. Runyon described Broaca as "the first fugitive from a World's Series."[8] The strangeness of the case even perplexed Broaca's teammates, who voted his wife Cordelia, whom everyone described as a beautiful 22-year-old brunette, a $1,000 Series partial share. That was something that Broaca no doubt very much resented because it turned out he and his wife were feuding and about to visit divorce court.

The hearing in the case filed by Cordelia Broaca in Barnstable, Massachusetts, was contentious and replete with contradictions. Yankees teammates were presumably spellbound as Mrs. Broaca testified that her husband hit her in the head with his fist and kept her without food or money in a residence in Orleans, Massachusetts. "I always let her have anything she wanted and I never abused her physically," Broaca testified. "She was very temperamental and at times difficult to control. She cried at the slightest provocation." Broaca said he rented a hotel apartment in New York for his wife, cooked, and did the dishes.⁹

One newspaper report said that twice since the divorce papers had been filed, Broaca had had periods where he still lived with his wife. Back and forth it went. Mrs. Broaca said Johnny left her because he said he couldn't afford to raise their now-four-month-old son. Broaca hinted that one reason he left the Yankees and didn't think he had much of a baseball future was because of a sore arm that he compared to the problems St. Louis Cardinals twirler Paul "Daffy" Dean was having.

There were rumors, never proven, that Cordelia Broaca was having affairs with different Yankees teammates. This would explain why Broaca might leave the team and might be an explanation for why he seemed to harbor bitterness towards her for the rest of his life. But Broaca never explained himself beyond the courtroom, where it was he-said, she-said under oath.

Meanwhile, Mrs. Broaca offered a litany of cruelty allegations, saying that the pitcher raged at her and threatened to physically harm her, drove her outdoors into the snow while she wore a nightgown, and made her sit in a dunce chair in the house. Broaca, who wore glasses and was frequently described as looking scholarly, physically did not match up with the average American's vision of a demon. If there had been a *National Enquirer* at the time, it would have had a field day filling its pages with lurid testimony shocking to most staid Americans far more conservative in the 1930s than in the 2000s.

They were not words that seemed destined to help prevent the divorce and retain custody of his young son, but Broaca testified angrily under oath that he probably spent $28,000 in the preceding two years throwing parties. He was making $14,000 a year from the Yankees. "It was easy come, easy go," Broaca said, portraying himself as a playboy of sorts who spent "a flock of money on a flock of people," including his parents for whom he said he bought furniture, a radio, and other things. At the same time his wife testified that the tweed suit she was wearing was a gift from her husband to get married in, but that he hadn't ever bought her any clothes again in the subsequent 15 months. "I haven't had a thing to wear since," she said.¹⁰

The Probate court granted Mrs. Broaca the divorce she sought and ordered Johnny to pay $632 in alimony. Before the court adjourned, the judge asked Broaca, who had been suspended by the Yankees for leaving the team, if he intended to return to baseball. "Sure," he said. "I intend to go back to baseball at the proper time. I'm not going to quit baseball because of alimony troubles."[11] Yet he may have.

Although Broaca informed the judge his arm was improving and he was going to keep working on rounding it into shape in Lawrence, Broaca never reported to the Yankees in 1938. In April, after the season began, a brief note in a baseball column reported Broaca working out with the high school team in Haverhill, Massachusetts, near his Lawrence home. He said if he returned to the majors he hoped it would be in Boston, but that did not occur. Broaca, who previously had demonstrated some skill in that area, briefly tried to become a boxer, probably not the best way to rehab a pitching arm.

When he was at Yale, Broaca was the school's heavyweight boxing champ. The Ivy League college was not exactly the school of hard knocks, but one that required the lifting of hefty textbooks. As spring training approached for 1938, Broaca seemed more likely to be throwing punches than throwing pitches for the Yankees. He set up shop with a trainer in Lowell, Massachusetts, and worked on his jab, not his fastball.

"I wouldn't be surprised if Johnny bobbed up as a boxer," Ed Barrow said when asked by a reporter what the pitcher's prospects were of resuming his baseball career. "He's an odd fellow, a loner. Nobody can figure him out. As a heavyweight he might do all right. He is solidly built and has had good boxing instruction. Looks as if the Yankees will have to struggle along without him."[12]

That last bit sounded a bit on the sarcastic side, but Barrow didn't sound as if he was mourning too heavily what had not long before seemed like a valuable piece of property. Broaca went through the motions of preparing for a pro boxing career, but it was a short-lived fling with the fight game and he never accepted a bout.

He did bounce back to the majors briefly with the Cleveland Indians in 1939 after the commissioner's office lifted the New York suspension. The Yankees sold Broaca, and he compiled a 4–2 record, but that was the end of his big-league career because his arm troubles flared up again. While Broaca was with the Indians, his ex-wife returned to court to try to obtain an increase in his $72 monthly alimony payments. Broaca said no way, unless he gained partial custody of the now-two-year-old. "I'd like to see him once in a while, to see what he looks like," said Broaca, whose ex-spouse had testified in court that he never wanted the child.[13] There was no evidence Broaca ever saw his son again.

Although he never pitched in the majors after his turn with the Indians, a few years later, Broaca surfaced as a periodic hurler with the Caseys in the Boston Park League, a semi-pro league of decades standing. He was making $5 a game.

For most of the rest of his life, until he died at 75 of a heart attack in 1985, Broaca worked as a union laborer doing hard, physical work, digging and lifting on construction sites. Broaca, who had previously spoken of having ambitions to become a teacher and coach after baseball, never pursued those options. Some said he wanted a low-paying job so he could send his wife smaller alimony checks. He lived alone in an apartment in Lawrence and never tried to get in touch with his son, who lived only 25 miles away. Cordelia had remarried and moved to Boston.

After his death Broaca was described as a loner and recluse by surviving relatives and old acquaintances in an article written by his hometown newspaper, the *Lawrence Eagle-Tribune*. A niece, who helped clean out Broaca's apartment when he died, said the only photographs he had were of Howard Hughes and Walter Winchell, both known in their day for being reclusive at the end of their lives.

It was a peculiar mini-collection. Broaca also had a pile of mail in his home from writers harkening back to his Yankees days asking for autographs, or from some fans that sent his old baseball cards requesting signatures on them. He kept those, but never answered or returned the cards.

Nieces, and old admirers who remembered Broaca as a great athlete with such promise, summed up their emotions about the life Broaca led after he left professional baseball. It was so sad the way it all turned out, they said. So very sad because he just gave up on life.

There is no denying that Broaca was a solid representative in the Yankees' rotation in 1934, 1935, and 1936, but when he went AWOL in 1937 he was 1–4. Either his arm woes were real — he later demanded that the Yankees reimburse him for medical bills — or the mental strain of what really was going on with his wife, her indiscretions, or his fiery blowups were ruining his game.

That was the thing about the Yankees in those days — and for most of the last 90 years. If a player went down with an injury or failed to live up to expectations, the team had the financial wherewithal, the muscle, to find a perfect substitute and keep on rolling. Indeed, that was the philosophy. Use the profits from great attendance, and later, broadcast rights, to keep the product healthy. The goal was always to win another pennant, not to rebuild for next year. The goal was never to be satisfied. Other teams might win pennants so rarely that they rested on their laurels after the achievement of fulfilling a long-time goal. Not the Yankees. The Yankees' goal was to win every year.

The man who set the tone for that approach was Colonel Jacob Ruppert, who by coincidence on his 71st birthday on August 5, 1938, appeared on the radio show "Out of the Past," to talk about his life, including his failed attempts to buy the New York Giants and how he came to own the New York Yankees. Ruppert said that when he and Colonel Huston cut the deal for the Yankees many people said they were buying "a pig in a poke" and that it was a bad investment. "At that time they certainly were a poor team," Ruppert said. "But we believed that by acquiring a smart manager and good ballplayers, we could make the New York Yankees into a top-notch baseball club. We knew that it would be difficult, if not impossible, to draw the fans away from the Giants, but we hoped we could offer New York an answer to the otherwise unanswerable Giants."[14]

By that point in Ruppert's tenure, the Yankees had won six World Series, as his host pointed out, surpassing the Giants. The announcer asked Ruppert what gave him the most personal satisfaction. He could not separate all of the special moments, citing the pennants and World Series won and Babe Ruth's 60 home runs in 1927.

Although Huston had long ago abandoned the scene, Ruppert could reflect that buying the Yankees had been solid investment after all, and as far as he was concerned, he was going to do what it took to win more pennants and World Series.

Ruppert had also brought in the perfect man to run the Yankees, with expert judgment, an eye on the bottom line, but above all, an eye on winning. That was Ed Barrow, business manager, soon to be awarded the more visible and appropriate title of president of the Yankees.

Barrow was old-fashioned in the sense that he didn't mingle with the players and manager on the field. He hired them to do their jobs and he stayed in the front office. He didn't want to grow too close to them because he realized the day might come when he had to trade them or release them. His allegiance was first to the ball club's future.

"What made Barrow so great?" a sportswriter said. "A habit of surrounding himself with the most capable assistants available. He sought only the best and paid them what they were worth. Another vital consideration. He relied on their judgment."[15]

Barrow, who said Ruppert referred to him as "Barrows" for some reason, took note when writers repeatedly called him "The Man Behind the Yankees." He said that's exactly what he was. "I was always happy and satisfied in being just that — the man behind the Yankees," Barrow said. "Because that is where I belonged."[16]

Although Broaca had been an integral part of the rotation, one of the Yankees' top five starters, when he fled in 1937, the Yankees did not even miss him. Barrow had stocked the team with so much pitching that not only were there starters with track records ready to step in, there were guys that fans had practically never heard of ready to take turns.

The Yankees started a bit slowly in 1937, but they actually got better after Broaca departed. Pitchers like Monte Pearson, Bump Hadley, Pat Malone, Spud Chandler, Johnny Murphy and Kemp Wicker aided the Hall of Fame throwers in compiling a 102–52 record, the same win total as the team recorded in 1936.

5

Monte, Pat, Bump and Grandma

The trade that brought Monte Pearson to the Yankees from the Cleveland Indians in 1936 was another Ed Barrow masterpiece, though not everyone thought so at the time.

Pearson was acquired for Johnny Allen, a popular Yankee right-hander born in Lenoir, North Carolina, in 1904, who broke into the New York lineup in 1932 as a 26-year-old rookie. The actual signing of Allen was somewhat preposterous, the type of story Hollywood at its hokiest would dream up. Allen was working as a bellhop at a hotel and when he brought something to the room of Yankees scout Paul Krichell he blabbed that he was a pretty good pitcher and could probably help the Yankees. Krichell, the esteemed talent evaluator, arranged for a tryout and darned if Allen wasn't just blowing smoke. Allen became an instant sensation and his first several seasons with the Yankees were startling. He was so good he hardly ever lost.

Allen went 17–4 in his rookie year and the Yankees topped the Cubs in the World Series when Babe Ruth launched his controversial called-shot homer. Could Allen keep it up in 1933? Yes, he could, though not to the same extent. Allen's record was 15–7, but his earned run average ballooned over 4.00. Arm injuries held Allen to a 5–2 record in 1934, but he looked fine at 13–6 in 1935.

That arm weakness, coupled with Allen frequently badgering the front office for more money, plus his legendary temper that led him to verbal jousts with umpires and manager Joe McCarthy, gave Barrow the impetus to make the trade. It was risky because Allen could easily still develop and haunt the Yankees if his arm regained the form it had shown in 1932, but McCarthy preferred peace and harmony in the dugout, and he and Barrow thought the trade odds were with them. Also, the Indians included Steve Sundra, another pitcher, whom the Yankees thought had considerable potential, though he was of no immediate help on the major league roster.

Pearson, who was born in Oakland but grew up in Fresno, also broke in as a rookie in 1932, but he was four years younger than Allen and had no apparent arm woes. The debut of the 6-foot, 175-pounder was nowhere near as glitzy as Allen's. Pearson went 0–0. But in his next two seasons he went 10–5 and 18–13 for Cleveland. At the worst it looked like a value for value deal. At its best for New York, Pearson's youth and lack of arm problems had more upside, and there was a more than even chance he wouldn't complain to Barrow all of the time about the size of his paycheck. McCarthy, backing his boss and soothing his own heartburn, publicly said he was glad to have Pearson and felt he would do a better job than Allen. He was certain that he would get along better personally with Pearson than Allen.

Pearson, whose first two names were Montgomery Marcellus, had the potential to bring levity to a generally reserved clubhouse because he sang and played the guitar. If he failed at baseball he could fall back on a career as a mechanic, one of his early jobs. Rather quickly, Barrow became disenchanted with Pearson's attitude, too, attributing his feelings to the player's complaints about illnesses and arm weakness. In 1936, his first year representing New York, Pearson finished 19–7 and made the American League All-Star team. However, at one point, Pearson became sick and said he was ordered to go home until a doctor could visit. He figured the team would send a medicine man over. He lay in bed, but no doctor came. "For three days I stayed in bed and no one came to see me," he said later. "Then Barrow called me and asked when I was coming to the ballpark. I told him no doctor had been to see me and he banged down the phone. Pretty soon there were a couple of doctors to see me and they agreed that I had a bad case of the flu."[1]

The Yankees saw Pearson as a workhorse, but he had the unfortunate luck to have genuine health problems. Sportswriters began referring to him as a hypochondriac, their opinions perhaps installed by management. "I didn't even know what the word meant until I looked it up in the dictionary," Pearson said."[2]

Running a high fever was one thing a player could get over in a hurry.

5. Monte, Pat, Bump and Grandma   49

Worries over a sore arm were something else. An arm injury could be the kiss of death to a career at an early age, and management hated it when a pitcher said his arm was bothering him. Often in the manager's and general manager's view, the throwers should be toughing it out.

McCarthy looked askance when Pearson told him he couldn't pitch because his arm wasn't right. The manager ordered him to have it examined, and sure enough the report came back in accord with what the pitcher said. The doctor, Pearson said, told McCarthy, "This man has no more right to be pitching than I have. He has the worst looking arm I've ever examined. It's full of bone chips and calcium deposits and most of the time it hurts like hell. But there are days when he won't have a twinge. Those are the days he can help you."[3]

It turned out that the Yankees had traded one sore arm for another, though neither injury was completely disabling. Although Pearson pocketed his 19 wins and the Yankees won the World Series, Allen made as much news with Cleveland as Pearson did with the Yanks in 1936. Mixing his sidearm and overhand deliveries, Allen finished 20–10.

In 1937, Allen appeared in only 24 games because he underwent surgery for an appendectomy, but he finished 15–1 with a 2.55 earned run average. At that point, the record for most consecutive American League wins was 16, co-held by Walter Johnson, Lefty Grove and Joe Wood, and Allen won his first 15 games in a row before absorbing his only loss, 1–0, in his last game of the year. Allen's major league winning percentage record of .938 lasted for 22 years until the Pirates' Roy Face broke it by going 18–1.

And how was Pearson faring? In 1937 he finished 9–3, with fewer starts because of poor health, and Yankees fans grew grumpy making the comparison between him and Allen, who was stirring up favorable stories nationwide.

Allen began the 1938 campaign in the same sizzling style, but soon ran into arm difficulties all over again and faltered. His season's record was 14–8 while Pearson compiled a 16–7 mark and trumped his long-distance competitor in more ways than one. On August 27, 1938, in a game won 13–0 by the Yankees, Pearson threw the first no-hitter in the history of Yankee Stadium. The hallowed Bronx baseball palace had been open since 1923, but Pearson did the honors 15 years after the gates opened in the second game of a double header.

There were 40,959 fans in the yard and the Yankees were ironically playing the Indians, though Johnny Allen was not pitching for the Tribe that day. Johnny Humphries was the starter and the Yankees had to look like a blast-from-the-past replay of Murderers Row to him.

The Yankees won the first game of the doubleheader, 8–7, and began the nightcap even more explosively. Outfielder Tommy Henrich and second baseman Joe Gordon smacked home runs in the first inning to give New York a 5–0 lead after Joe DiMaggio swatted three straight triples in the opener.

Pearson was superb in this start with Cleveland's hot bats in the first game just a distant memory. For the first three innings, as the Yankees piled up the runs, the Indians were helpless at the plate, not garnering a single baserunner. Pearson faltered only briefly in the fourth, surrendering back-to-back walks. No Cleveland batter came close to hitting safely as Pearson mowed the Indians down and the lead kept expanding to 13–0. Gordon collected six RBI.

While Pearson owned a satisfactory fastball, as almost all hurlers must, his bread and butter pitch, his dazzler, was a curveball that fooled the best of sluggers when he was on. The funny part was that the curve came naturally to Pearson, and while so many of his compatriots through the years had trouble mastering the destination of a knuckleball he did not always know where his curve would land. When he conquered the seams, he became a star.

The other way that Pearson's performance trumped Allen's was in the post-season. In an era well before the creation of tiers of playoff series leading to the World Series, a team had to win the pennant to reach the final match-up with the other league. Pearson's Yankees were back on top, starting in 1936, and Allen's Indians were not in the hunt, finishing 22½ games behind the AL champs that year and 19 games behind in 1937.

Allen could buy a ticket or listen on the radio, but he wasn't going to be pitching in the World Series those years.

The Yankees led the Giants, two games to one, in 1936 when Pearson took the mound in Game 4 against Giants ace Carl Hubbell. This was a pivotal game, a chance for the Giants to knot the Series, and with Hubbell pitching the National League bunch had its spirits up.

There was actually some question about whether Pearson would pitch. He told people he was feeling too sick to go. Sportswriters pestered McCarthy to name a replacement if Pearson couldn't start, but he said nothing. He

5. Monte, Pat, Bump and Grandma   51

didn't really believe that Pearson was incapable of pitching. Later, when the writers asked McCarthy how he knew Pearson could stand up to the rigors of the pressurized Series game, he said he was "psychic" and the writers went along. When asked how he received such messages, McCarthy said, "Prepaid. That's the best part of them."[4]

As Pearson pitched shutout ball, the Yankees got the 66,669 fans roaring at the Stadium with a solo run in the bottom of the second inning and by adding three more runs in the third. The Giants nicked Pearson for one run in the top of the fourth and another in the top of the eighth, closing the gap to 4–2. But on a day when Lou Gehrig clouted two home runs, the Yankees retaliated with one run in the bottom of the eighth for a 5–2 lead that stood up behind Pearson's mixed repertoire. "I had to win to keep us ahead," Pearson said. "I never wanted to win a game so much in my life, and I don't think I ever had more stuff than I had that Sunday afternoon. When I saw Gehrig's home run go into the stands, I knew I would win."[5]

It was a Yankees-Giants rematch in 1937, same two teams, same city, same ballparks, and many of the same players. Pearson was tabbed by McCarthy to throw the third contest at the Polo Grounds, with the Yankees ahead 2–0 in games.

This time Pearson faced off with Hal Schumacher and stopped the Giants, 5–1. As Pearson was blanking the Giants, the Yankees graciously provided him with a more and more comfortable lead, scoring one run in the second inning, two in the third, one in the fourth and one in the fifth. The Giants reached Pearson for a solo run in the seventh inning, but that was all. The Yankees went on to win that World Series in five games.

At no time, apparently, was Pearson intimidated by the Giants. "I was just as effective when I faced them, but toward the end of that game, I tired," Pearson said. "I had experienced a lot of trouble with my arm and had been out for two months and a half. My pitches were missing the corner of the plate."[6]

Johnny Murphy, a relief pitcher before relief pitchers became rich and famous, threw the ninth inning to clinch the Yankees victory. It was decades before the late-inning relief pitcher became an appreciated species, but McCarthy had the wisdom to use Murphy as a closer when the term didn't exist in baseball.

The manager frequently brought Murphy into games in the late going when his starters seemed to falter. Murphy was not as flamboyant as some latter-day relievers, but he had his own quirks. Murphy was so fussy and fastidious on the mound that his teammates nicknamed him "Grandma." The Yankees in the dugout invariably yelled, "Here comes Grandma!" when Murphy made the trek from the bullpen.[7]

Pearson was not in serious trouble, or in desperate need of being rescued, but in the World Series McCarthy was taking no chances. He employed Murphy as an insurance policy and there was no fuss or muss closing out this game.

While scouts like Paul Krichell and Bill Essick were always on the prowl for young talent, Barrow was like a jeweler examining other people's valuables and assessing their worth the way he studied players around the majors. One of his areas of expertise was spotting diamonds in the rough where competitors did not comprehend the possibilities. He was especially good at finding live arms for the rotation or the periodic spot starter who could help out in an emergency.

The Yankees had the know-how and the coffers to buy when they needed to, and the bodies in the farm system to trade when that was what an opposing team wanted. One way the Yankees stayed winners was to fill holes in the roster before they appeared, or at worst patch potholes when they did.

One of those fix-it hires was Perce Leigh Malone, better known in baseball circles as Pat. Born in 1902, Pat Malone showed early promise, but admittedly was playing baseball more as a lark than as a serious profession. He moved from his hometown of Altoona, Pennsylvania, to Juniata College where he played baseball and football. It wasn't until the mid-1920s that he began to apply a work ethic to his skill. Then he developed into a hot-stuff, righty-throwing rookie with the Chicago Cubs in 1928 when he went 18–13. Malone was even better his second season, going 22–10, and in his third year he finished 20–9. His dugout boss with the Cubs was one Joseph McCarthy.

Malone slumped in his fifth year, finishing 15–17, and while he did have many solid mound moments for the Cubs after that, he never reached his earlier heights. When the Yankees went shopping for another arm after the 1934 season, McCarthy's familiarity and belief in Malone's usefulness brought him to New York.

Malone went 14–7 in his last season with the Cubs, but in the off-season was traded for catcher James O'Dea and went to spring training with the St. Louis Cardinals. However, he held out for more money when St. Louis submitted a contract and he never played a regular-season game for St. Louis before the Yankees bought his rights.

Disappointed that he wasn't held in higher esteem with the Cubs for his yeoman work, Malone was shocked when his new team seemed to think even less of him and wanted to slice an already cut salary. "It seemed to me that I deserved consideration," Malone said, "but I was put on the auction block and sent to the Cardinals in a three-cornered deal. There Branch Rickey offered me a contract for so much less than I had been getting that I couldn't consider it. Instead, I asked him for a chance to place myself. Rickey was agreeable, but later, during spring training, he sent me a contract at my old figure. This seemed strange to me."[8]

Malone had been waived out of the National League, every team passing on his services, so he could be sold to the Yankees. He didn't mind that development at all. "This was a fine break for me," Malone said, "for the Yankees were a strong team in the biggest city in the country, and under McCarthy, my old boss."[9] The idea of playing for McCarthy again — the two helped win Chicago a pennant in 1929 — appealed to Malone and he signed a new deal with New York. "His arm is still good," McCarthy said. "A fellow like that can come in a pinch and strike somebody out for you. I think he'll help the club."[10]

Malone wasn't that much help, nor was he needed much, in 1935 when his record was 3–5. But in 1936, Malone looked like his old self. Called on in 35 games, he went 12–4 and served the exact function the Yankees had envisioned when they acquired him. Even Malone admitted he didn't have much of a 1935 season and said he wasn't much needed. That changed completely the next year. "In 1936, when we were not as well-equipped with pitching, I got my chance and I was glad I was able to come through," Malone said.[11]

One reason was that his body was in better shape than it had been the year before. Malone lost weight and had his teeth replaced, so he felt better all-around. He did not think he would ever be the same pitcher he was as a younger man in Chicago, but the combination of experience and the way he chose his pitches still made him dangerous to hitters, he felt. Pitching more often helped, as well, he said. "I need to work to keep my control," Malone said. "I'm in the bullpen an average of three times a week. That means I get a pretty good tryout about every other day. I still have a lot of stuff, though not so much as I once had. I'm learning to depend somewhat on my curve."[12]

The average fan might glance at the numbers and see that other starters had more wins, but those who followed the team closely understood that Malone was providing invaluable service that season. In an August article, famed New York sportswriter Frank Graham discussed this point, noting, "They can talk all they wish about Gumbert and Gabler and Galehouse and Chelini and some of those other young fellows, but if anybody should ask you, you would say that Malone is the pitching find of the year. You would have an idea, too, that if anybody should ask Joe McCarthy he would say the same thing."[13]

Probably Malone's finest moment of the regular season was pitching the last eight scoreless innings of a 4–4, 16-inning tie with the Indians. However, Malone also took a loss in the 1936 World Series against the Giants. A year before he would have certainly been in uniform, but watching from the dugout. Malone relieved in the fifth game and gave up the deciding run in the tenth. But the Yankees won the Series, so only a year and a half after being on the sport's discard pile, Malone was a world champion.

A year later, Malone's third with New York, he returned to being seldom-used and did not appear in the World Series. By the time the 1938 season began, Malone was gone, replaced by younger pitchers, and he retired with a 134–92 record. Only a few years after he left the game, Malone died at age 40.

Another owner of an important arm on the staff during the mid-1930s for the Yankees, also in the shadow of Lefty Gomez and Red Ruffing, and another pitcher with much Major League experience elsewhere, was Irving Darius Hadley of Lynn, Massachusetts. The name was too much of a mouthful to say at the ballpark, so the right-hander became better known as "Bump." Actually, although that would be a likely development, Hadley arrived with the ready-made nickname, acquired as a youth when he was reading a child's story with a Boy Scout character called Bumpus. Hadley, who grew up to be 5-foot-11 and 190 pounds, at the time resembled the short and heavy character.

Interestingly, while the story ascribing the pinning of the nickname on him came directly from Hadley's mouth, at least one other New York

5. Monte, Pat, Bump and Grandma

sportswriter said he was called Bump because of the way he bounced off tacklers as a high school running back. Hadley was a sterling athlete in high school. In one prep game he pitched a perfect game and struck out 26 of the 27 opposing batters.

Hadley's father was an attorney and he aspired to follow his dad with the same legal books, so he enrolled at Brown University expecting to emerge as the next Clarence Darrow. Instead, after two years of study he signed with the Washington Senators hoping to become the next Walter Johnson. Neither happened, but Hadley came closer to Johnson's exploits than Darrow's over the years.

Counting his one-game debut in 1926, Hadley spent parts of six years with the Senators and recorded some fine work, including seasons of 14–6 and 15–11. About that one-game season: Hadley was brought right off the Brown University campus in Providence, Rhode Island, when Senators manager Bucky Harris inserted him into a game against the Yankees with the bases loaded and Babe Ruth at the plate "I ran the count to three-and-two," Hadley said. "And then the Babe hit a drive off the left-field wall for a double which scored three runs. A few days later I got a ticket to the minors."[14]

He returned to the majors soon enough and had those solid years before being shipped to the hapless St. Louis Browns. Games were more difficult to win with the Browns and Hadley's best year in that part of the country was probably his 15–20 campaign of 1933.

Hadley bounced around a bit between the Senators, Browns, White Sox and Senators again before New York secured his services for the 1936 season. Hadley discovered that it is a whole lot easier to win games when teammates pile up the runs. Also, he had been suffering from back discomfort for a few seasons and gave credit to Yankees trainer Doc Painter for smoothing out the kinks. Hadley went 14–4 for New York in 1936 and 11–8 in 1937, and when sportswriters asked what transformed a pitching slump into a winning streak, he said, "Very likely it's having guys like the Yankees come through for me."[15]

Sometimes it was the pitcher doing his thing, too. Hadley gained stature in McCarthy's eyes as the 1936 season wore on, and after Ruffing and Gomez took turns starting the first two games of the World Series against the New York Giants, Hadley got the call to start the third game. This was one day the formidable Yankees batting order did not come out slugging. Hadley had to use his wiles, giving up 11 hits, to best the Giants, 2–1, with ninth-inning help from Malone.

Hadley also got a start in the 1937 World Series rematch against the Giants. Called upon in Game 4, he went head-to-head with future Hall of Famer Carl Hubbell and lost that one, 7–3, although the Yankees won their second straight Series title. In 15 years, Hadley compiled a 161–165 lifetime record, but clearly his best seasons were with the Yankees, a team that could supply hitting support. At his best, Hadley baffled batters with a curveball that drove them crazy. "Bump was one of the greatest curveball pitchers of all time," said Joe Cronin, the future Hall of Fame shortstop for the Senators and Boston Red Sox who played against Hadley.[16]

For those with long memories or who study baseball history, Hadley's name evokes one other game incident from 1937. He was the moundsman that hurled the inside fastball that nearly killed future Hall of Fame catcher Mickey Cochrane in a game against the Detroit Tigers that May.

Cochrane was a greatly admired player who was the American League Most Valuable Player for the Philadelphia Athletics in 1928, and won the same honor for the Detroit Tigers in 1934. He was an All-Star the first two years the mid-season classic was played. Cochrane was on three world champions and his picture was featured on the cover of *Time* Magazine.

Thirteen years into a magnificent career with a .320 batting average, Cochrane was anchored in the batter's box on May 25, 1937, at Yankee Stadium when one of Hadley's fast pitches sailed inside and high and cracked him in the head. The fractured skull Cochrane suffered hospitalized him for seven days and ended his playing career. Hadley was distressed about hitting Cochrane, saying he never intended to do it.

"I can't understand why Mickey didn't get away from the one that hit him," said Hadley, who said he had intermittent trouble controlling his fastball that day. "Some of the Detroit players think he lost sight of it when it came up. He looked as if he would pull away and then it happened. Nobody regrets the accident more than I do, but I have the satisfaction of knowing that nobody thinks I threw that ball as a beaner. I never tried to knock a batter down."[17]

Hadley said he was grateful that McCarthy allowed him to stay in the game and that helped settle him back into his pitching rhythm. What was left unsaid was how erratic Hadley was in his next outings — perhaps still bothered by the pitch to Cochrane — before he went on a late-season winning streak to regain the manager's confidence enough to start him in the World Series.

The man McCarthy had confidence in to finish games, during the regular season and in the World Series, was Johnny Murphy, alias "Grandma." When that great kidder Lefty Gomez was inducted into the National Baseball Hall of Fame in 1972, he thanked everyone and said he never would have made it without Joe DiMaggio's slugging and Johnny Murphy's rescues.

The nickname came about because Murphy was so fastidious about his behavior, routine, and approach to the game during his 13-year major league career, the first 12 of them with the Yankees, the last one with the Red Sox. Murphy was an anomaly, a relief specialist at a time in baseball when there were few and they were not necessarily respected as much as sent into bullpen exile because they were not living up to expectations as starters.

Even Murphy began as a starter, for 20 games, with New York in 1934, but after that Joe McCarthy recognized what the 6-foot-2, 190-pounder, also called "Fordham Johnny" because he had attended that institution, could contribute. But after that season Murphy was used only for spot starts. Mostly, he was a fireman, called out of the bullpen in the late going to douse enemy fires, to halt the opponent's rallies. "Johnny is the one man I can always depend on," said McCarthy, a reputation that anyone would love to have.[18]

Murphy was from New York City and was one of the passle of players from that era signed by Paul Krichell, who didn't have to travel farther than a subway ride to claim this pitcher. The combination of a calm demeanor, a virtually unhittable curveball, and a determination to study hitter tendencies when fewer pitchers kept a book on batsmen made Murphy successful enough to go 93–53 in his career and lead the American League in saves four times, although that was determined retroactively after the save statistic was invented.

"Pitching would be improved if hurlers made a closer study of the hitters," Murphy said. "The good ol' curveball is a lifesaver. When in doubt, always pitch a curve." Murphy, who later became general manager of the New York Mets after a long series of post-playing-day administrative work with a variety of teams, played on seven Yankees World Series championship teams. He was the primary architect of the 1969 Miracle Mets, another World Series winner.

When he reflected on his own playing successes, though, Murphy always returned to one outing. In the 1936 World Series, Murphy entered Game 6 in the seventh inning with a 5–4 lead and the tying run on third base, and got out of the jam to spike Giants thoughts of victory.

"My greatest thrill," Murphy said, "was replacing Lefty Gomez in a 13–5 victory and holding the Giants to one hit in 2⅔ innings of that last World Series game of 1936."[19]

Gomez's grateful comment at the Hall of Fame, said light-heartedly, was more than a joke. Johnny Murphy came to the mound to save the day for Gomez and all of the Yankees starters time after time in the 1930s and 1940s.

6

The Real Italian Stallion

It was hitting more than pitching by the early Yankees championship teams that made the impression on people. It was the formidable batting order, the lineup without a weakness. The pitchers did their jobs, but the batters raised slugging to an art form.

Any minute the Yankees were likely to break out with a bombardment. Just the team nicknames were menacing, threats to clobber an opposing pitcher with little warning. At times the Yankees were called "Murderers Row" or "The Bronx Bombers."

Guys like Johnny Murphy made their contributions doing the little things that helped a team win. But it was Babe Ruth and Lou Gehrig that people remembered. They delivered the knockout punches. Between 1927 and 1936, just about the entire Yankees day-to-day lineup turned over, the transition from one dynasty to another. Babe Ruth was gone and most of his teammates followed. Gehrig was still in the heart of the order, but the only other regular from New York's 1927 frequently-called "greatest team ever" still in the lineup was Tony Lazzeri.

Lazzeri was the Yankees' second baseman on five World Series–winning teams, spanning the dynasties right through the 1936 and 1937 champs. He came from San Francisco, the first of New York's Italian-American stars. Yankees scouts caught more big fish at Fisherman's Wharf than Joe DiMaggio's father ever did.

Anthony Michael Lazzeri was born in 1903 and put up colossal statistics in the Pacific Coast League to gain attention. He swatted 60 home runs and drove in 222 runs for the Salt Lake City Bees in 1925. Two years later he was a murderer in the Yankees' unstoppable row.

Lazzeri suffered from epilepsy, and his periodic fits supposedly scared off many teams that might otherwise have bid for him. Once again, Yankees scout Paul Krichell felt potential out weighed risk and New York benefited. Long after Lazzeri's career ended in the afternoon-baseball era, Krichell dismissed the player's illness with a joke when asked about him. "I found out Tony never had a seizure between 2 and 6 o'clock in the afternoon and that was good enough for me," Krichell said.[1]

It was true, too. During his 14 years in the majors, Lazzeri never experienced an epileptic seizure on the field.

The son of a boilermaker whose family maintained a basic standard of living but was not well-off, Lazzeri left school at age 15. In the Yankees clubhouse he was known for being somewhat taciturn and despite excellence on the diamond, including being named a member of the first All-Star team in 1933, took a back seat on publicity. That was not something he seemed to mind. As a teenager, Lazzeri was known for his temper and in the locker room he was known for only limited cooperation with sportswriters. "Interviewing that guy is like mining coal with a nail file," one sportswriter said.[2]

Lazzeri may not have said much, but he made his comments count. One day in spring training a writer, reflecting on how Ruth was a sports hero to many, asked Ruth if he had ever had an idol. Before Ruth could answer with a name that might well have proved fascinating to readers, Lazzeri, standing nearby, provided one for him. "Sure he has, Babe Ruth," Lazzeri said.[3]

Lazzeri was an early darling of Italian-American baseball fans and was often greeted with cries of "Poosh-em-up, Tony" when he came to the plate. The phrase emanated from a mistaken translation of "hit it out," or hit a home run, originated with fans in Salt Lake City, and stuck with Lazzeri throughout his career.

The great melting pot of America went through phases of immigration as different groups from different countries crossed the ocean from Europe. Once established, each nationalistic or ethnic group melded into American society. As more Italian-Americans settled in the United States, learned English and raised first-generation Americans, more of those young men sought careers in baseball.

The types of things that were written in the mainstream press in the pre–World War II society would appall people now. One description of Joe DiMaggio read, "Instead of olive oil or smelly bear grease, he keeps his hair slick with water. He never reeks of garlic and he prefers chicken chow mein to spaghetti."[4]

6. The Real Italian Stallion   61

Tony Lazzeri was the second baseman on the Yankees' Murderers Row teams of the late 1920s and stuck with the club long enough to win another couple of pennants in the 1930s. He was the first popular star of Italian heritage in New York.

Lazzeri had endured many slings and arrows in many forms from fans, journalists and others about his Italian heritage, even called "Dago" in the newspapers. The 5-foot-11, 170-pound Lazzeri was referred to as "the lanky Italian" in print. Just as they did in the late 1940s and 1950s when black players broke the color line, sportswriters identified individual players by nationality in the 1930s, rather than just as human beings.

Although Lazzeri was a home-run hitter in the minors, once Joe McCarthy took over as Yankees manager he informed Lazzeri he wanted him to field his position, engage in more hit-and-run efforts and collect more base hits to drive in Ruth and Gehrig. Lazzeri was not happy, but he had to recognize that Ruth and Gehrig were better power hitters, so he adapted.

Ironically, Lazzeri, who batted .292 lifetime with 178 home runs and nearly 1,200 RBI, and decades later was chosen for the Hall of Fame, is probably best remembered for a mistake. If "mistake" is really the right word; perhaps "disappointing play" will suffice. In the seventh inning of the seventh game of the 1926 World Series against the St. Louis Cardinals, Lazzeri stepped to the plate with the bases loaded. The Cardinals were ahead 3–2 and this was New York's big chance to take the lead and possibly pull away. When future Hall of Famer Grover Cleveland Alexander, at the tail end of a brilliant career as a starter, walked slowly to the mound to relieve, the magnitude of the moment seemed to escalate. Ol' Pete, had already won two games for the Cards in the Series and, after winning the sixth game the day before, thought he was finished and would be a mere spectator for the last day.

Stories have persisted throughout the years that Alexander, who had difficulties with alcohol, had spent the evening before celebrating his triumph with strong drink and was hung over when he arrived at the park. Either way, using the 39-year-old Alexander, on no rest, was a major gamble. Alexander won 373 games and threw 90 shutouts in a 20-year National League career, but his face-off with Lazzeri at Yankee Stadium was regarded as one of his greatest moments.

Alexander struck out Lazzeri on four pitches and then pitched two more innings to close out the Yankees and hand St. Louis the world title — the only one on Alexander's resume.

Anxious to put New York ahead with a difference-making clout, Lazzeri wanted to swing away the moment he stepped into the box, but

6. The Real Italian Stallion 63

manager Joe McCarthy told him to take pitches and maybe Alexander would walk him. Lazzeri heard the instructions, but still thought more impetuously. He wanted to let go and slam a pitch a long, long way. "The first ball Alex pitched was a bad one," Lazzeri said, "high and wide, and Alex, figuring I would not swing at the next, grooved it, and the call was one ball and one strike. I fouled the third and then made up my mind to crack the next one. The Old Master must have read my mind, for he tossed a tantalizing curve on the outside, and although I did my best to resist, I was set to swing, and I did. I missed the ball by eight inches."[5]

Although he could easily be remembered as a goat by ill-tempered fans, Lazzeri insisted on referring to the strikeout play as one of his biggest thrills in baseball, because of the drama and because it was such a tense moment in the World Series. Years passed, he retired and still people asked about the strikeout. That's when he got a bit weary of the topic, wistfully saying he wished fans would ask him about many of the good things he did on the field instead of focusing on the K. One night, musing in a bar to a sportswriter, Lazzeri said, "Funny thing, but nobody seems to remember much about my ball playing except that strikeout," he said. "There isn't a night goes by but what some guy leans across the bar, or comes up behind me, at a table in this joint, and brings up the old question. Never a night."[6]

On the flip side of the accomplishment coin, in a 1936 game against the Philadelphia A's, Lazzeri had the greatest single batting day of his life. The Yankees won the game by a remarkable 25–2 score and Lazzeri smacked two grand slam homers, a solo homer, and a two-run triple for 11 RBI.

In the third inning of the second game of the 1936 World Series against the Giants, with the Yankees leading 5–1, Lazzeri came to the plate with the bases loaded. Dick Coffman was on the mound in relief and Lazzeri powdered the ball to right-center field in the Polo Grounds for a grand slam. "I never can get anybody to remember the 1936 Series, either," Lazzeri said of trying to change the subject with fans from the strikeout to the homer. (7)

Those were the short-sighted. Yankee fans with long-term perspective, San Francisco baseball fans, and Italian-Americans always considered what Lazzeri did special. He represented a revered Italian-American-Yankees connection that included Frank Crosetti and, of course, Joe DiMaggio. Eventually, Crosetti, DiMaggio, and Lazzeri were inducted into the

National Italian American Sports Hall of Fame. DiMaggio and Lazzeri are in the Bay Area Sports Hall of Fame, too.

When the announcement of Lazzeri's induction into the Bay Area Hall occurred in 1989, DiMaggio said, "That's nice and it's high time. He ought to be in the big Hall of Fame, the one in Cooperstown. Tony was great, one of the best I ever saw."[8] Lazzeri was elected to the National Baseball Hall of Fame in 1991.

Given how limited his conversations were with sportswriters, they wrote about his smarts in the field enough times to portray him as an Einstein of the diamond. Once, during a game, with a runner on first, Lefty Gomez fielded a grounder back to him. Instead of throwing the ball to Crosetti coming in to cover second as he should have, Gomez threw the ball to a non plussed Lazzeri. As soon as the play ended, Lazzeri called time and trotted over to the mound to ask Gomez what he was thinking. "I keep reading about how smart you are," Gomez said. "I wanted to see what you would do with the ball."[9] Lazzeri grumbled his way back to his position.

Lazzeri joined the Yankees in 1926 and was a mainstay during the transition from Miller Huggins to Joe McCarthy, from Babe Ruth to Joe DiMaggio, but in 1937 he batted just .244 and whispers followed his play in the field suggesting that he had slowed down. Lazzeri insisted that he had a couple of years left in his body, but that he was going to retire and pursue a manager's job.

"Tony Lazzeri through as the regular second baseman of the Yankees?" wrote columnist Frank Graham. "Maybe. Many a fellow he caught up with when he joined the Yankees is gone. Many a fellow who came after him, too. From his reviewing stand at second base he has seen a long parade of ball players ... the great and the near great and the lesser figures of the game ... marching towards oblivion in the last eleven years."[10]

The writers all believed Lazzeri that he was going to retire and hang out in San Francisco again for a little while if someone didn't immediately name him manager of a big-league club. The rumor was that the Cleveland Indians would bring him in to replace Steve O'Neill as a player-manager.

That didn't happen and although a few predicted it, Lazzeri did change his mind about hanging up his glove and spikes. The Yankees released him following the 1937 season, ending his association with the club for which he played on five World Series winners because the second baseman of the future, Joe Gordon, was ready for a chance to move in.

6. The Real Italian Stallion

Those whom Lazzeri convinced that he was going to retire may have been surprised when Lazzeri surfaced with the Chicago Cubs in 1938 — another pennant winner. Cubs owner Phil Wrigley eyed Lazzeri during the 1937 Series and the Yankees didn't stand in the player's way of making the shift. Lazzeri played in 54 games and hit .267. A year later Lazzeri split his time between the Brooklyn Dodgers and the New York Giants and batted .289 in 27 games. He was 35 when he did retire.

Lazzeri may have harbored ambitions to become manager of the Cubs when he went over to the other league, and Wrigley paid him well, but the player was given no assurance he would assume command. Lazzeri signed a one-year deal as a player-coach.

"This is just what I wanted," Lazzeri said of the opportunity to play a little bit, as needed, but also to further his baseball education in a leadership position that could pay off with a manager's job soon. He admitted it would feel strange wearing another team's uniform after so long with the Yankees, "But I feel just like I'm starting all over again. I get a kick out of that."[11]

When Lazzeri shifted to Chicago, Charlie Grimm was the manager in what was part of his virtually life-long involvement with the Cubs. Grimm's contract as manager was due to expire in 1938, but Wrigley replaced him in mid-summer. Lazzeri was not the choice to take over. It was long-time Cub Gabby Hartnett, then player-coach, who got the job and led the Cubs to the pennant.

The loss of Lazzeri did not hold the Yankees back from winning the American League pennant, their third in a row, either.

DiMaggio was king at the plate, batting .324, knocking in 140 runs and crushing 32 home runs. There was no doubt DiMaggio was one of the best hitters in baseball. He had exploded on the scene as a rookie in 1936 and only seemed to get better.

And the Yankees were right about Joe Gordon. He was totally prepared to step in for Lazzeri at second, a youngster on his way up who could hit, field and even play several positions as needed. Gordon was born in California, went to high school in Oregon, and attended the University of Oregon. "Flash" Gordon was a 23-year-old rookie in 1938 who gained notice for slugging 25 home runs and driving in 97 runs, even though his average was a so-so .255.

When the Cubs met the Yankees in the Series, Lazzeri probably had more friends in the opposing dugout than his own. Lazzeri made it into just two games as the Yankees won their third consecutive world championship with a four-game sweep.

There were inevitable comparisons between the long-time Yankee incumbent second sacker, who remained wildly popular in New York, and his successor. For one thing, although Lazzeri was playing halfway across the country for the Cubs, the *New York Daily News* continued to run an advertising comic strip for the cereal "Huskies" which Lazzeri endorsed. The strip kept Lazzeri in its story line as a character even if he no longer wore pinstripes. Lazzeri was portrayed as a super-hero of sorts because he ate his Huskies.

He was no longer a super-hero in the field or at bat, however. "Youth and age, experience and inexperience faced each other at the Yankee Stadium in a drama that was not lost on veteran baseball followers or the players themselves," one newspaper reported, comparing Lazzeri and Gordon. "For the first time Tony Lazzeri came face to face with Joe Gordon in action — and youth was served."[12]

Once Lazzeri's youth was served out on the field, he turned to managing, not as he hoped as a major league field boss, but in the minors. In 1940, he managed Toronto in the International League, followed by Portsmouth in the Piedmont League and Wilkes-Barre in the Eastern League. He stayed in baseball, but he was either hundreds of miles, or light years away, from Yankee Stadium, depending on perspective.

When Lazzeri was shut out of dugouts in 1944 he opened a bar where he could entertain as a raconteur telling stories about his baseball experiences. Before he could end up as a manager anywhere, on August 6, 1946, Lazzeri was found dead in his Millbrae, California, home at the foot of a staircase.

There were mixed reports about the cause of Lazzeri's death. Despite an autopsy that showed he suffered a heart attack, there were suggestions that he hit his head on the staircase railing, and another theory was advanced that an epileptic seizure had contributed to the fall. Lazzeri was only 42 years old.

Reflecting on Lazzeri's death, a newspaper columnist said Lazzeri was no worse than the second-best second baseman of his day, perhaps behind Detroit's Charlie Gehringer, and that no one during his stay with the Yankees was more appreciated by the fans. "Not even the great DiMag achieved popularity that was Lazzeri's with Yankee Stadium fans," the story went.[13]

6. The Real Italian Stallion 67

Long after his death, Lazzeri was voted into the National Baseball Hall of Fame by the Veterans Committee. He was inducted in 1991, and *Newsday*, the Long Island, New York, newspaper, ran a classic headline reporting the news: "Poosh 'Em Up: Lazzeri becomes an immortal 45 years after death."[14]

The story that followed summarized much of Lazzeri's demeanor and impact. "While alive, he never said much in his own behalf. And he has been dead so long that the memory of his accomplishments has faded. But now Tony Lazzeri's place in baseball history has been preserved and the legend of Murderers Row enhanced."

Frank Crosetti, then 80, and Lazzeri's old double-play partner, was still living when the honor was announced. "It should have happened a long time ago," Crosetti said. At the time, Lazzeri's record of 11 RBI in an American League game had been on the books for 55 years. On May 24, 2011, the record turned 75 years old.

7

Dickey Linked Them All

The guy on the Yankees who sounded the least like he came from New York was Bill Dickey. Broadway where he came from was a particularly wide dirt road. The tallest buildings were barns. But whether Dickey's words were stretched out as if they had extra syllables while New Yorkers were cutting theirs short by leaving off a "g" or an "r" at the end of them, he translated just fine.

Dickey was one of the wise old heads of the Yankees during these years, a player who bridged the powerhouses of the 1920s with the powerhouses of the 1930s. He was like another coach, or back-up manager, on the field, a take-charge guy who not only understood the nuances of the sport, but could impart them to teammates.

The backstop is often a team leader. He helps pitchers call the game. He has an uninterrupted view of the entire field, facing it while his other eight fielders either have their backs to it looking to the plate, or have a sideways angle. The catcher keeps track of the outs, can position fielders, and in the case of Dickey, who not only knew all of that stuff, also brought a heavy-duty offensive game to the park, too.

Dickey was born in Louisiana, but by elementary school was living in Little Rock, Arkansas, where he stayed when he was not wearing Yankee pinstripes. He liked the lifestyle, hunting and fishing and playing golf when time permitted. Dickey talked a lot about bird hunting with his teammates, one of his favorite pursuits.

Dickey began playing baseball locally in Arkansas, in high school, and even one year in junior college before signing a pro contract. Between 1925 and his placement on the Yankees' roster in 1928, Dickey saw the country, suiting up for minor-league teams in Little Rock, Muskogee, Oklahoma, Jackson, Mississippi, Minneapolis, and Buffalo. For the next 17 years he

7. Dickey Linked Them All

never went anywhere else where he did not represent the New York Yankees. Little Rock and Dickey not surprisingly found each other on their own, but the well-known scout Johnny Nee found Dickey for the Yankees when he was competing in the Cotton States League in the state capital.

Nee was pretty confident that he had a can't-miss-player in his sights

All-Star catcher Bill Dickey was the bridge between the Yankees of Babe Ruth and manager Miller Huggins and the Yankees of Joe DiMaggio and manager Joe McCarthy. The Hall of Famer played for the Yankees from 1928 to 1946 and then coached for the team.

when he contacted the Yankees about signing Dickey. "I'll quit scouting if this boy does not make good," said Nee in a telegram to New York.[1]

At age 6-foot-1 and 185 pounds, Dickey was a sturdy specimen behind the plate, but one of his characteristics was that he stayed calm. He was not a loud complainer to umpires and he exhibited cool in tense situations. Except for the one time in 1932 when he went ballistic covering home plate against charging Washington Senators runner Carl Reynolds.

This was one of those situations when the dust really flew, and when it cleared people were astonished at the result, for the placid Dickey punched Reynolds. Reynolds had been called safe at first, but he rose, and circled back to the plate to touch it again because he wanted to make sure. That's when Dickey popped him, breaking Reynolds' jaw. Dickey later said he thought Reynolds was coming at him to start a fight and he deeply regretted throwing the punch. That was an egregious enough transgression to earn Dickey a 30-day suspension.

After a first season learning what catching in the big leagues was all about, Dickey made home plate his home. He caught more than 100 games a season for 13 years in a row in a 17-year career and batted .313. Contemporaries and historians rate Dickey among the top handful of catchers in baseball history.

Those who worked most closely with him had fine compliments to offer, though often they focused more on game savvy and leadership than on his hitting prowess. "I never shake Dickey off," said Yanks pitcher Ernie Bonham in admitting he bowed to the catcher's know-how in calling a game. "I just let him pitch my game for me."[2] Ironically, Red Ruffing, the stalwart Yankee hurler, loved working with Dickey, too, but for the completely opposite reason. "Dickey has never bothered me, never has shaken me off," Ruffing said. "He just lets me pitch my game."[3]

For such completely diametrically opposed statements to be uttered about a player, both as compliments, should indicate how Dickey manipulated his pitchers, recognizing and providing what they needed most. The psychology was superb.

Dickey was a newcomer in the tail-end days of the Babe Ruth dynasty. He was a cornerstone of the club, filling a role so well that manager Joe McCarthy didn't have to worry about the position. Dickey's longevity, and the timing of it, meant that he played in eight World Series for the Yankees, winning seven of them.

7. Dickey Linked Them All

The Arkansas import was so good behind the plate he once went an entire season without committing a passed ball. The only thing that seemed to bother Dickey 'and given that the pitch was illegal, he shouldn't have had to worry about it' was staying on top of the spitter. The spitter and other trick pitches had been outlawed by major league baseball in 1920, but players who relied on them were grandfathered in and could use them for the rest of their careers.

The last remaining legal spitballer was 270-game-winner Burleigh Grimes, who ended up in the Hall of Fame. In 1934, the final season of his career, he made a brief stop with the Yankees, getting into ten games. Dickey caught him, or tried to, without allowing those lousy passed balls to overrun his life.

In Grimes' first game, a runner reached first base. He threw a spitter and Dickey couldn't tame it. The runner went to second base. Another spitter, another ball rolling to the backstop, and now the runner was on third base. Irritated with himself and the situation, Dickey trudged to the mound for a confab with Grimes, who was angry about the ball not being caught and demanded that Dickey tell him what to throw. "The damned spitter again," Dickey said. "But be ready to cover home plate."[4]

Grimes may not have appreciated Dickey's talents, but the Cleveland Indians' Hall of Famer Bob Feller did from afar, and sometimes in All-Star Games. The remarkable fastballer, who broke into the majors in 1936 at 17 (and won 266 games despite spending years in the service during World War II), fantasized about what it would be like with Dickey as his catcher. "If I could pitch to Bill Dickey, I believe I could win 35 games a year," Feller said.[5]

Grimes may have been steamed because Dickey couldn't handle the spitter, but McCarthy always trusted Dickey's ability and judgment. "He was a great catcher, great hitter, and a great man to have in the ballpark," McCarthy said. "The records prove Dickey was the greatest catcher of all time."[6]

Dickey was eased into the Yankees lineup. He played just ten games in 1928 and watched and learned, absorbing the aura of Ruth and Gehrig. He once said that Gehrig was the greatest Yankee of all, and he had a deep friendship with him, but Dickey was pals with Ruth and looked at him as much like a brother you could fool around with as one of the game's all-time greats.

Dickey once played a practical joke on Ruth by breaking an egg into his shoe. For a moment he thought he had gone too far and Ruth was going to slug him, but after a brief pause Ruth laughed. Most people remember Ruth as a heavy-set man with a big belly who ran with mincing steps. But before he took on weight and aged, Ruth was as thin as the usual athlete and had good running ability. Whether for eating too many hot dogs, drinking too much Prohibition-banned booze, smoking cigars and sleeping little, Ruth was not in the type of condition he had been in when he moved to New York from the Red Sox. He still took pride in his ability to get around more swiftly than expected, however.

One day, playing against the Washington Senators, Dickey slammed a triple after watching Walter Johnson, the pitching great who had turned manager, re-position his center fielder. Dickey's next time at the plate, Johnson shifted the center fielder again and again Dickey smacked another triple. Almost unbelievably the scenario unfolded for a third time. Dickey came to the plate, Johnson maneuvered the fielder and Dickey hit the ball so hard it seemed it might imbed a hole in the wall.

The circumstances seemed so ridiculous to Dickey, who was not known as a fast runner, that as he chugged towards third base for what would have been his third triple of the day, he could not stop laughing. That distraction was just enough wasted time to enable the fielder to retrieve the ball and throw Dickey out at third.

Back in the dugout, Dickey took some heat. Ruth, who was never any good with names, anyway, even among teammates he played with for years, gave Dickey some grief for squandering the triple. "Pittridge," said Ruth, who called Dickey that in a reference to the catcher's partridge or quail hunting, "I can outrun you."[7]

Dickey did not calmly accept his verbal lashing from the gaffe, however. He retorted. The Babe escalated his commentary. Dickey replied. And they agreed to a match race at the ballpark the next day before the resumption of the series with the Senators at a distance of 75 yards. The younger Dickey wanted the distance set at 100 yards, but Ruth, who cajoled Dickey into betting $100 he couldn't really afford on the outcome, insisted on a shorter race.

At this point in their lives, Dickey was in his early 20s and Ruth was in his mid–30s. Naturally, other Yankees got in on the bets, with the older Yankees putting their money on Ruth, either out of loyalty or because they had seen Ruth's athleticism on display many times.

7. Dickey Linked Them All

Youth prevailed in this contest, Dickey coming from behind to pass Ruth about three-fourths of the way through the race. "I couldn't have beat him when he was younger," said Dickey, "but I was happy the way it came out."[8]

Dickey could hit as well as just about any catcher who ever played, and that too set him apart. Dickey hit between .310 and .339 every year between 1929 and 1935 and then hit his career-high .362 in 1936. He hit 202 home runs and drove in 100 or more runs in a season four times, with a high of 133 in 1937. Dickey was at his best during the 1930s stretch when the Yankees were at their best year after year.

Apparently emerging into a more serious slugger in 1937, Dickey grabbed the sportswriters' attention with late-inning heroics, hitting an extra-inning walk-off homer and dragging the Yanks to victory repeatedly. They began writing about how he, even more than Gehrig and Joe DiMaggio, was the bellwether of the team.

That year, Dickey stoically caught the World Series with a broken wrist. That no-nonsense, no-excuses approach gave him even more esteem among his teammates. One writer compared the statistics of Dickey and Mickey Cochrane, trying to determine which one was the best and concluding they were just about even. Another asked if the Yankees would have more trouble replacing Dickey than DiMaggio.

Grantland Rice, the dean of American sportswriters, whose vivid style and poetic soul enlivened the reputations of the Four Horsemen of Notre Dame, wrote a poem about Dickey in his syndicated newspaper column. That was about as big-time as you could get.

There was an oft-repeated story about Dickey that every newspaperman got a giggle out of that seemed to illustrate a near-photographic memory when it came to pitch calling. Dickey remembered everything, and imparted that information based on past experience to his hurlers so they could have an easier time getting foes out.

On the night the 1943 World Series ended in St. Louis, the story goes, Dickey was in an elevator in the Chase Hotel with a man in an Army uniform. The fellow leaned over to Dickey and said, "I bet you don't remember me." Dickey gave him the once-over and said that he surely did, even if he couldn't recall his name just then, but that Dickey called for this pitch and that pitch when he played for the Philadelphia Athletics to get him out—and they worked. He was right.

During their run of titles in the late 1930s, Dickey did have some help behind the plate, and the roster did carry the names of others at the position of catcher. However, given how much of the catching load Dickey carried, it seemed as if his backups, Joe Glenn and Art Jorgens, did little more than work out pitchers in the bullpen. It was a 154-game schedule and Dickey caught 120 games in 1935, 140 games in 1937, 132 games in 1938, and 128 games in 1939. Glenn and Jorgens were lucky even Joe McCarthy and Ed Barrow knew their names, never mind fans that weren't related to them. They were insurance policies in case Dickey got hurt. Even then they didn't always get into games because Dickey played hurt, with broken fingers, ace bandages and adhesive tape holding his limbs together.

Glenn, who played in the majors from 1932 to 1940, never appeared in more than 44 games in a season for the Yankees and never at a position other than catcher, but three times hit in the .270s or .280s before moving on to the St. Louis Browns and then the Boston Red Sox.

Jorgens batted .238 with the Yankees between 1929 and 1939, averaging just below 31 games a season, and never playing any position but catcher, either. It might be said his primary position was bench-warmer, though.

An upgrade on the Dickey back-up front was the promotion of Buddy Rosar from AAA Newark in 1939. Rosar had destroyed minor-league pitching, hitting .332 and .387 for the Yankees' top farm club. There was still not much wiggle room for playing time when he arrived on the New York roster, but as a rookie Rosar got into 43 games and batted .276.

Rosar, born in 1915, was from Buffalo and as soon as he exited high school he was signed by Binghamton in the New York-Penn League. Between 1934 and 1936 his minor-league travels took him to Wheeling, West Virginia, and Norfolk, Virginia, as well, where already a renowned glove man, he showed he could hit. There was no doubt the 1937 Newark team, which won 117 games, had some major league-ready players, but the Yankees were so good they couldn't offer much opportunity to young players.

It became clear quite quickly that Rosar deserved more than a reserve role behind Dickey, but there was little chance that he was going to start for some years. Rosar spent four years in the back-up role and nine more in the majors, through 1951, and fully blossomed into a five-time All-Star who set catcher fielding records. He went errorless in 117 games one season for a 1.000 fielding percentage, a record cited by the Guinness Book of World Records. The same streak continued into another season and didn't end until Rosar put 147 error-free games in the books.

Rosar, whose job required him to know pitchers well, formed some strong opinions about them and what he would require of them if he became a manager. The first part of his master plan would be to make them wear loose-fitting baseball jerseys so that in the elbow area or someplace on the arm, cloth would flap and possibly distract batters' concentration. Then he would train them to field better. Little things counted, Rosar seemed to be saying. "You know, pitchers are very special people in baseball," he said. "They have more to worry about than a catcher, an infielder, or outfielder. If they do not have a blazing fastball, they must have a variety of pitches. They must develop something new when they start to lose their 'blinder,' or else it's back to the minors."[9]

Following the 1920s championship run and once the 1930s championship rejuvenation began, the Yankees developed an aura. They were intimidating. They were unbeatable. They might fall behind early, then compile a big inning and demoralize an opponent. The message that the Yankees were the best was so ingrained it worked on other teams' psyches, and in those rare years when New York did not win the American League pennant and the World Series, fans were surprised. "You know the Yanks are supposed to beat everybody all the time," Dickey said. "Nobody thinks it strange or remarkable when we win. If we lose they figure it was accidental and something must be wrong."[10]

That was an image McCarthy and Barrow very much wanted to cultivate. The Yankees of Ruth's time were more fun-loving. Gradually, the Yankees under McCarthy morphed into a more serious outfit. As the Yankees grew more corporate, they became more conservative, at least in terms of how it was hoped the public perceived them.

This outlook suited Joe DiMaggio, Bill Dickey (despite being a clandestine prankster in the clubhouse) and McCarthy. McCarthy tended to frown on players who laughed too loud or spoke too loud. He thought they were goofballs that didn't pay as strict attention to the game as he wanted. McCarthy thought players should linger in the locker room after games to talk baseball.

McCarthy supposedly ordered his wife to pray for the Yankees every day when she attended Mass. But not even McCarthy could will a team to win every day, or even, although it was surprising and did seem accidental as Dickey said, win the pennant and World Series every year. One bad day when the Yankees were defeated and played sloppily, McCarthy was moody when he got home. He got back onto the prayer topic with his wife, who assured him she was praying, but if the world seemed against them, she said, "Joe, we still have each other." "Yes, dear," McCarthy said, "but in the ninth inning today, I would have traded you in for a sacrifice fly."[11]

Working hard and playing the game hard are usually endemic to winning teams. But young men together on a sports team as they travel the country have considerable free time and disposable income and soak up adulation, and they are not going to pretend to be in a monastery. They're going to play ball and play around at night, most of them, at least. Even if they're young, in their 20s, they don't want to be treated like children and second-guessed.

So while McCarthy did his best to play the role of headmaster and some of his players did not lap up the night life or party often, it was a losing battle to think that every minute on the road, in hotels, on a train, was going to be like staying after school. Boys just wanted to have fun.

Sometimes, words speak louder than actions, too, and Lefty Gomez's insouciance got on McCarthy's nerves. He would have preferred "Yes, sirs." But Gomez was a veteran that could teach the youngsters and entertain a little bit. Besides, he was on a path to a Hall of Fame plaque.

Dickey, who liked to have his fun outside of games, had little tolerance for wackiness on the field. One day, with Gomez on the mound and Dickey calling the signals, the opposing team worked the bases loaded. Gomez called time out and beckoned to Dickey to come to the mound. Dickey had just one thought on his mind at the time — how to get the batter out and not give up a run. After his 60-foot, 6-inch jog to the mound, Dickey said, "Yes?"

He about fell over on the dirt when Gomez asked, "Hey, Bill, do you have any extra bird dogs?" They were not talking in code. Dickey answered "Criminey, why do you ask a question like that at a time like this?"

Good question. Ordinarily, Dickey would be pleased to talk about his bird hunting and the dogs he trained to fetch and follow. Not at this moment, however. Gomez casually mentioned that he had met a guy the night before who wanted to buy some bird dogs and he had given the fellow Dickey's name. "So he said to ask you about it if I ever thought of it," said Gomez. "Well, I just happened to think of it."[12]

One might have thought Dickey would have burned into a pile of ash, he was so hotly enraged by the conversation. Another time Dickey called for a fastball and Gomez threw him a curve. After that Dickey dispensed with the signs, figuring he should prepare for the fastball, but adapt for a curveball, mostly so he didn't get caught off-guard and get hit in the head with a pitch.

Only with Lefty Gomez. But those types of interludes came with the territory when catching the southpaw.

8

The Crow Makes a Mark

They didn't invent the "good-field, no-hit" description for Frank Crosetti, one of the Yankees' Italian notables from the San Francisco Bay Area, but it fit. On the Yankees, however, that didn't matter much. The rest of the lineup was filled with "Bronx Bombers," so they could get away with using a player with a lifetime .245 average like Crosetti if he made other contributions.

Crosetti was a good enough fielder at shortstop from the time he came up in 1932 through a 17-year playing career to be named to two All-Star teams on the strength of glove work. Nicknamed "The Crow," Crosetti was also an intangibles guy, the kind that every team needs in the clubhouse, a leader with smarts and attitude. One could also say that Crosetti was ready to sacrifice his body for the good of the team, leading the American League in being hit by pitches eight times.

The circumstances were a bit weird, but appropriate for Crosetti to be called "The Crow." Letting out a cry similar to the bird's call, Crosetti used it as his own form of whistling to signal teammates in the field and runners on the bases.

Never has the phrase "he's a winner" been more accurate in the game of baseball than when applied to Crosetti. He is the record-holder for appearing in World Series. As a player, Crosetti was on eight World Series winners. After retiring, Crosetti became a New York coach and spent another 20 years in uniform. During that time the Yankees won nine more World Series. When Crosetti changed to civilian clothes for good he had been a member of 17 World Series championship-winning teams. Anyone who called him "Mr. Yankee" would not be corrected. Someone once calculated that Crosetti made $150,000 in World Series shares alone, much of that during an era when the payoffs were only in the low-to-mid single-digit thousands.

8. The Crow Makes a Mark

Crosetti was around so long he not only was a full and active participant in the Yankees' second dynasty, he was still coaching as a member of the third Yankees dynasty after World War II and into the 1960s. Although he evolved into an institution as familiar as Yankee Stadium's grounds, Crosetti was actually young once.

Crosetti was born in Stockton, California, on October 4, 1910, and he was a 5-foot-10, 165-pound infielder as a rookie for the Yankees in 1932. Crosetti's role was clear from the start. He only batted .241 that year (though he drove in 57 runs), but he scooped up every grounder hit in his neighborhood. Also from the beginning it was apparent that when Crosetti played, pennants followed. The Yankees won the American League crown in 1932 and beat the Cubs in the World Series.

By the time the Yankees were fully rebuilt in the mid–1930s, Crosetti was a fixture at short and part of the group that made history by setting a record of four straight World Series titles in 1936, 1937, 1938, and 1939. The Detroit Tigers (1907–1909), the Philadelphia Athletics (1929–1931) and the Yankees themselves twice (1921–1923 and 1926–1928), had won three pennants in a row before that.

During that cross-country drive to spring training in 1936 with Tony Lazzeri and Joe DiMaggio, it was Crosetti who suggested throwing "the bum" out when DiMaggio said he didn't know how to drive. Although it translates as a joke years later, Crosetti was seen by some of his contemporaries as mean-spirited and occasionally a bit too hard-nosed. He was considered more serious-minded and internally oriented than outgoing and fun-loving. He wasn't a talker, even in the dugout, rather someone who during a game was watching every bit of action to learn and remember.

Crosetti's personality was not warm and fuzzy. He was a student of the game, trying to absorb every bit of knowledge. This clearly paid off for him during his lengthy coaching career. These aspects of Crosetti's personality were consistent off the field, as well. Although as a long-time figure in the Yankees' organization he was invited to appearances, Crosetti chose to turn down offers to attend off-season banquets, give speeches, or do radio interviews. He went his own way.

"Why does everybody insist about making such a fuss over baseball people?" Crosetti said. "We're just doing a job, like the butcher, baker, or plumber. Doctors, scientists and people who really do important work aren't bothered this way. I can't see it at all."[1]

Once again the Yankees had no trouble disposing of all meaningful challengers in the American League during the 1938 season. New York finished 99–53 and won the flag by 9½ games. The Red Sox, beginning to see the fruits of young owner Tom Yawkey's investments in the team, finished in second with slugger Jimmie Foxx and shortstop Joe Cronin juicing up a previously moribund lineup.

But the Yankees had more depth and pitching. Foxx led the league in batting at .349, but for the Yankees Red Ruffing won 21 games and Lefty Gomez won 18. As an aside to the pennant race since the Tigers finished fourth, Detroit's massively muscled first baseman Hank Greenberg gave Babe Ruth's single-season record of 60 home runs a run for the money. Coming down the stretch it was as close as a Kentucky Derby photo finish with Greenberg slamming 58.

Teams stayed close to the Yankees until about July 1. Then New York owned most of the rest of the summer, going 48–13 in July and August to put everyone in the rearview mirror. The Yanks notched their record-tying third straight pennant.

Crosetti had come a long way by 1938. He was not a natural talent, but a self-made man at short. One reason that Crosetti might have been so taciturn in the beginning, although it was clearly in his nature, was that when he made the Yankees roster in 1932 he was insecure. He described himself as "a scared kid out of San Francisco."[2]

Crosetti played with the Seals in the Pacific Coast League from 1928 to 1931 and his sale commanded $75,000 of Jacob Ruppert's beer money. It was manager Joe McCarthy who sensed the potential in Crosetti and helped him gain self-assurance and become a slicker fielder, as well as an adequate batsman, if no star wielding the wood.

"I owe everything to McCarthy," Crosetti said years later. "I wasn't much of a ballplayer when I came up. Most managers wouldn't have stayed with me as long as he did. He had a wonderful way with players. He had the knack of giving you confidence and bringing out the best in you. He could handle any situation on or off the field and always commanded respect."[3]

By 1938, it was clear that Joe DiMaggio was the real-deal successor Yankees star to Babe Ruth. From the start, DiMaggio battered big-league pitching as if he were still playing elementary school sandlot ball. He led the AL in home runs in 1937 with 46 and in 1938 DiMaggio smashed 32 long balls, drove in 140 runs and batted .324.

8. The Crow Makes a Mark

DiMaggio played his rookie season for $8,500 and asked for $17,500. He was one of several Yankees looking for more cash from the Colonel than he was offering. After the leanest years of the Depression, they hoped that a 1936 World Series title would earn rewards. This was DiMaggio's first skirmish with the front office over money. He ended up getting more or less what he wanted, but it was foreshadowing for upcoming battles.

After leading the league in home runs in 1937, DiMaggio, advised by business expert brother Tom DiMaggio, asked for $40,000. The Yankees countered with an offer for $25,000. In a famously publicized contract negotiation, Ed Barrow asked DiMaggio what he would say if he learned that not even Lou Gehrig made $40,000. "I'd say, Mr. Barrow, that Gehrig is grossly underpaid."[4]

Gehrig had been one of the best players in the world for years, but he was not a boat-rocker. He didn't fight with the front office over money. He, too, was holding out this time and when he signed for $36,000 it was obvious that DiMaggio was not going to make more than the "Iron Horse." The Yankees went off to spring training and DiMaggio hung out in San Francisco, working at the family restaurant, "DiMaggio's Grotto," on Fisherman's Wharf and trying to stay in baseball shape by working out with the Seals. Newspapers published photos of DiMaggio with an apron on cooking spaghetti instead of him in pinstripes cooking up ways to beat American League teams as there normally would have been at that time of year.

On and on the holdout dragged. Barrow, a master of such tactics, worked to turn the fans against DiMaggio through the newspapers. The U.S. economy was somewhat on the rebound, but many average workers were still suffering, so a holdout for a higher salary than most Americans would see in their lives did not play well in the public relations arena for DiMaggio.

Ruppert even had McCarthy say that the Yankees could get along fine without DiMaggio, which wasn't true. But Barrow, Ruppert, McCarthy and the public lined up against DiMaggio and ultimately wore him down, although not until April 30 when the season was under way. The goodwill DiMaggio had stockpiled in his first two seasons dissipated and fans booed him at Yankee Stadium. DiMaggio was hurt, but did not say much. It was a good time to keep his mouth shut. He let his bat and glove do his talking and that was a wise approach, especially since he immediately showed top form and promptly helped the team win games again.

The Yankees were the Yankees, and their imperial approach to the game's best players, controlling Gehrig's salary and beating back DiMaggio's demands, did not seem to hurt the team, except in DiMaggio's personal estimation. It would be hard to argue that he wasn't worth the money he asked for, that year and in later years, but ballplayers had no leverage in those days. Free agency did not exist. Playing out one's option to go to another team wasn't an option. The seeds of future baseball labor wars were rooted in these days of the 1930s, 1940s, 1950s and beyond when owners tried to squeeze every penny out of their teams, and to keep salaries low enough that most players had to take off-season jobs.

Newspaper columnists were nasty to DiMaggio at this time, portraying him as greedy and selfish among other things. The idea of player freedom was not an idea whose time had come, or was even thought of, and the sportswriters more often took the side of management in disputes like these.

On the field, the bitterly angry DiMaggio remained exemplary. He hit two home runs in his first three games back in the lineup, and was again an All-Star. But he had to defend his actions — and did — to the same sportswriters who lobbied against him. "All I was trying to do was to get as much as I could," DiMaggio said. "Is that so terrible? I had a great season and some of my friends said I ought to be worth $40,000 to a team like the Yankees. I guess they were wrong. I know I was wrong holding out as long as I did. I hear the boos and I read in the papers that the cheers offset them, but you can't prove that by me. All I ever hear is boos ... and the mail. You would have thought I had kidnapped the Lindbergh baby, the way some of the letters read."[5]

There was certainly a lesson for DiMaggio in the disappointing experience about the fickleness of fans and even how his employer viewed him as a commodity. This was also demonstrated when the Yankees declared they didn't really need DiMaggio to keep winning pennants since Myril Hoag was hitting .352 in spring training. Myril Hoag? While DiMaggio was supervising the wait staff's distribution of lasagna in Frisco, Hoag was holding down center field in St. Petersburg. His bat was making a good case for the Yankees to keep him on the regular-season roster one more year. Hoag had been a member of the Yankees since 1931 and anyone who watched the team realized he was not going to be the second coming of Joe DiMaggio. He was not even the first coming of Melky Cabrera.

8. The Crow Makes a Mark 83

As a minor leaguer, Hoag showed considerable promise. In 1930, Hoag hit .337 for Sacramento in the Pacific Coast League and the Yankees bought him for $75,000. Usually a star in the PCL had the skills that translated to the majors, but Hoag was never more than a fourth outfielder for New York. He had such a strong throwing arm that there were times the Yankees discussed making him a pitcher, but that never happened.

A somewhat streaky hitter, Hoag's greatest moment in the majors occurred in 1934, when he collected six hits in a single game. Only twice have players stroked seven hits in a nine-inning game.

Hoag was a 5-foot-11, 180-pound right-handed hitter who was a useful back-up, but who was 29 the first he before got into 106 games, his most with the Yankees, and batted .301. The only way Hoag was going to replace DiMaggio was if he had a long-term injury. In 1938, once DiMaggio returned, Hoag did work his way into 85 games and he batted .277.

There was some irony in the DiMaggio-Hoag dynamic. In July of 1936, with DiMaggio and Hoag playing at the same time, they had a brutal collision in the outfield chasing a fly ball and Hoag was seriously hurt. This was DiMaggio's rookie year, before McCarthy moved him permanently to center field. DiMaggio was playing right against the Detroit Tigers and Hoag was in center. Goose Goslin whacked a line drive to right-center and both men tracked it. Running full speed, each player believing he had the ball, they collided, knocking each other flat as their heads banged. While they lay in the outfield grass the ball bounded away for an inside-the-park home run. That was not nearly the most serious consequence of the accident.

Initially, DiMaggio and Hoag seemed okay. Hoag played the next day. But two days after the collision Hoag was found unconscious in his Detroit hotel room and rushed to the hospital for immediate brain surgery to alleviate a clot. The damage emanated from Hoag smacking his head against DiMaggio's, but the seriousness of the impact was underestimated. At first doctors strangely asked manager McCarthy for permission to do the surgery, but McCarthy said he did not want that responsibility and urged them to get in touch with Hoag's wife. There was some talk that Hoag's wife would have to fly to Detroit from Sacramento to give approval for the surgery, but the on-site doctors refused to wait and drilled holes in his head to relieve the pressure.

As the Yankees moved on to their next destination on their road trip,

Hoag was left behind in the hospital. Pitcher Johnny Broaca stayed with him as a representative of the team and later phoned McCarthy to update the gloom-shrouded team on details.

What the doctors could not predict was how Hoag would react to the stress on his body and brain. It was possible he might die from the injury and the operation. It was possible he might suffer permanent brain damage. The initial prognosis was that Hoag would never again play baseball. But Hoag rehabbed well.

The next April, when McCarthy put Hoag back in left field for games against the Red Sox, it was considered a gamble, but one that had to be taken for Hoag's confidence to be boosted and for the team to find out what he could do. Hoag played well and that 1937 season was Hoag's most active for New York.

"With Myril Hoag in the heroic role, one of the most courageous and determined comebacks yet organized by a ballplayer today held the attention of the Yankees as they faced an over-the-weekend series with the Red Sox," one New York sports columnist wrote. Teammates, the writer noted, described Hoag "as game a guy as you will ever see on a ball field."[6]

Although unlucky to have suffered the injury at all, Hoag was lucky in his recovery. He fully regained his health and baseball abilities and renewed his career. His best seasons with the Yankees came after the collision, and Hoag played 13 seasons in the majors.

Beating the odds, Hoag did make it back to major league form, but he was never more than either a weaker link in the starting outfield lineup for the Yankees, or a periodic fill-in or pinch-hitter. After the 1937 season, Hoag became a St. Louis Brown, where he had more of a chance to start, and then a member of the Chicago White Sox. For both teams he played in more than 100 games a season.

The Yankees of that era, though, were not hurting for outfielders. Ben Chapman was completely overshadowed by DiMaggio and his own personality flaws, but was an All-Star. Newcomers George Selkirk and Jake Powell were hungry for playing time, too, and then, by 1937, Tommy Henrich was in the mix. Hoag shared in the capture of two World Series championships, but was gone before the third in the string was earned.

It was in 1938 that the Yankees took that next step to stamp themselves as a fresh dynasty. They won the World Series in 1936 and 1937, alleviating Jacob Ruppert's irritability about finishing second. Winning a trifecta

8. The Crow Makes a Mark

elevated New York into elite status. On the eve of the National League owners meeting immediately following the 1937 World Series, President Ford Frick declared that his league had to do something to prove it was the equal of, or superior to, the American League. "I don't doubt several of our club owners will insist that we investigate all possible ways and means to correct the existing condition," Frick said without mentioning that the existing condition was losing.[7]

At that point the American League had won eight of the previous ten World Series, and not all of the damage had been done by the Yankees. The Tigers and Athletics had contributed to harming the NL's self-image, too. No doubt, the old Giants boss John McGraw, who despised the American League in its early years, was rolling over in his grave upon hearing such defeatist talk. "The Yankees, for our league, happen to be one of the super teams, and perhaps one of the greatest of all," Frick said, "that pop up once in every 10 or 15 years."[8]

Frick was correct in his analysis that the Yankees were one of those "super teams," but they hadn't yet run their course, either. It was going to get worse for his National League. And, as it so happened, the Yankees were more like one of such super teams that showed up more like three times per century, not just every decade or so.

Exactly a year after Frick's call to arms, the Yankees did it again, sweeping the Chicago Cubs in the 1938 World Series. New York won 3–1 and 6–3 at Wrigley Field and 5–2 and 8–3 at Yankee Stadium. It was not the Cubs' year. In fact, it was not the Cubs' century, but that wouldn't become apparent for a few more decades.

The winning pitchers were Red Ruffing, twice, Lefty Gomez and Monte Pearson. In the second game, Gomez's victory, it was 3–2 Cubs going into the eighth inning. But then Crosetti (top of the eighth) and DiMaggio (top of the ninth) each hit a two-run homer to clinch the win.

Not even a slightly rejuvenated Dizzy Dean could save the Cubs that game. Back from his injury-shortened years with the Cardinals, Dean showed flashes of what made him the last National League 30-game winner in 1934. The light-hitting Crosetti was the Yankees' hero of the moment. Crosetti's swat cleared the left-field fence.

As Crosetti trotted around the bases, the always-talkative Dean yelled to him, "Hey, Frankie, betcha couldn't have done that when I was good." And Crosetti responded, "You're damn right I couldn't."[9]

In the first game, Crosetti had lifted pressure from Ruffing's shoulders with terrific fielding plays, including throwing a man out at the plate after making a running stop on a ground ball. That was one of the examples of why Crosetti was a fixture with the Yankees and an All-Star shortstop, even when he didn't hit at all.

Dean's shout was a poignant one. He would never be as good as he had been in 1934, when he finished 30–7, and right then the Yankees were the ones who were good. Very, very good.

9

The Yankee Way

Replenish, not rebuild. That was Ed Barrow's philosophy and the Yankee Way. Rebuilding implied things gone awry. Replenishing meant adding to the roster, not starting all over again. No need for that when the team was winning the pennant and World Series again and again.

Fine-tuning was needed, yes, because some players got older and their skills diminished, some players got injured and had to miss games. It was a never-ending job keeping the team at its peak.

Sometimes that meant making a trade or buying an established player to fit in and fill a role. Other times—and this was the most satisfying—young talent on the farm was bursting through, waiting to be summoned to the majors from AAA Newark. You could see some guys coming a couple of years away and you could only keep them down so long or you were wasting your investment. They either had to be promoted to the big-league team or traded elsewhere for a player who could fill another need.

If you could groom one guy a year like that who was ready for the top team's starting lineup you were doing well, and in 1938 Joe Gordon was that guy for the Yankees who had nothing to gain by playing another summer in the minors.

Gordon was born February 18, 1915, in Los Angeles, but his family moved to Portland, Oregon, where he attended high school. Yankees scout Bill Essick found Gordon playing at the University of Oregon in 1936 and talked him into attending an Oakland Oaks tryout camp. He made the Oaks roster and by 1937 Gordon was headed to St. Petersburg for his first training camp with the Yankees.

"As long as I can remember, I have always had a baseball and a bat in my hands," Gordon said. "When I was a kid, things were not so easy financially. A nickel was a lot of money. As for $2, the price of a ball and bat, that was an unheard of sum."[1]

Gordon, still a shortstop, learned the finer points of the professional game in Oakland. He was nervous about joining the Yankees in spring training, feeling very much like a rookie, before being sent to Newark for seasoning as a second baseman, where he also shined.

"Not until I had got into a Yankee uniform and gone out on the field did I believe it," Gordon said. "Instead of the cold shoulder I had expected, I got a warm welcome from the world champions. I was introduced around and at once treated like one of the boys. That was a big boost, a kick for my morale."[2]

Only he wasn't yet one of the boys. Gordon played the 1937 season at Newark and he wasn't officially deemed the heir apparent at second base for New York until the Yankees released Tony Lazzeri after the 1937 campaign. Then the job was Gordon's to lose. He didn't.

"Flash" Gordon, nicknamed after the comic strip hero, was heavily hyped in the New York press as the 1938 season dawned. He was projected as an instant sensation by an organization used to being so blessed. The only problem once the season started was that Gordon got hurt by colliding on a play with Joe DiMaggio and his confidence lagged when he wasn't hitting the curveball so well. Deep down he still wondered if he belonged with the great New York Yankees.

Although heralded as the next second baseman for the Yanks, and with his path cleared by the front office with the dismissal of Lazzeri, Gordon wasn't so sure he could do what was expected. "If McCarthy wants me to go back to Newark, I won't be disappointed," Gordon said at the start of 1938 spring training. "I know that making the grade in this league is tough business."[3]

McCarthy seemed to have more confidence in Gordon than the player showed in himself. McCarthy wanted and needed Gordon to succeed, and he couldn't afford for the rookie to talk himself out of playing at a top level. "Gordon is overawed by the picture in this league," McCarthy said. "He doesn't know that he has the makings of a greater second baseman than we have seen in the majors in 20 years."[4]

If that type of praise didn't leave a young man glowing, then no psychological pep talk would help. Like all managers, Joe McCarthy had his personal style and quirks in the way he handled a ball club once a game

9. *The Yankee Way* 89

Joe Gordon was acclaimed as an acrobat in the field for his work at second base and he had a strong bat to complement his glove play.

began. McCarthy preferred to sit alone in the dugout rather than next to players. But during Gordon's recovery period he had the rookie sit next to him. It was an unusual gesture by McCarthy, but it soon became clear that the simple idea was part of a grand strategy. McCarthy did not want Gordon to get mentally stale and to worry while he was out of the lineup.

One day during a game against Detroit, the Tigers' future Hall of Fame second baseman Charlie Gehringer made an error. McCarthy turned to Gordon and said, "Don't they say that's the best second baseman in the game?" Gordon nodded his head yes. McCarthy looked at Gordon and said, "You'd've fielded that ball with a catcher's mitt."[5]

This sort of live instruction filtering from McCarthy to Gordon went on until Gordon was ready to play again. Just before he was inserted into the starting lineup, Gordon told McCarthy he wanted to get married. Gordon and his girlfriend from college eloped and married in Maryland. He moved into the lineup June 9 and the second base job was his, with time out for World War II, through 1946.

After his shaky start Gordon began playing as advertised and sportswriters became increasingly enamored of him. The Yankees had not received much hitting out of the second base slot the year before and Gordon exceeded the previous production while introducing a dazzling fresh glove to the infield. While his season's average was only .255, Gordon hit 25 home runs and drove in 97 runs, the latter two statistics being notably high for a middle infielder. For all of that, it was Gordon's fielding that gained him the most raves. "Gordon is fast," wrote one sportswriter. "He is a great hand at the double play. The Yankees are getting defensive skill around second they had not boasted in years."[6]

In those days, the league's other seven teams always tested rookies one way or another when they got on the field. Gordon said he thought the era had passed, but found out that was not so. He took verbal lashings and runners sliding into second with spikes up, and even experienced some opponents spitting tobacco juice on his uniform. Initially caught by surprise, Gordon was slow to retaliate, but then realized he had to in order to gain and hold respect.

"I had been hearing a lot of yarns about how they were too gentlemanly in the big leagues to ride rookies anymore, but I only know they didn't let up on me," Gordon said. "I had to strike back to live. "The way I look at it, I was finding my way around when I was a freshman. The runners came sliding into me at second base, kicking the ball out of my hands. But the next time I got on and went down I'd do a little of that kind of kicking myself. I couldn't let the veterans get anything on the kid. After a while they quit their tricks. I always had a comeback when they took to ribbing me verbally, too. Perhaps it wasn't always a bright saying. It would probably look silly in print. But it shut up the wise guys. That was all I wanted."[7]

Sitting next to McCarthy for those precious minutes or hours at a time that year was invaluable for Gordon, he said. It was like taking graduate school courses in the subtleties of baseball. When someone asked him what he learned, Gordon said, "Everything.... (I) never knew there was so much baseball in the world before."[8]

The Yankees won their third straight World Series in 1938, defeating the Cubs, and Gordon was the most significant addition to the lineup. The next year, Gordon was a given in the lineup and his reputation as a hot fielder spread. When the All-Star team for 1939 was announced, the Yankees presence was overwhelming. Pitchers Lefty Gomez and Johnny Murphy were joined by reserves Lou Gehrig and Frank Crosetti. New York American League starters were pitcher Red Ruffing, catcher Bill Dickey, outfielders Joe DiMaggio and George Selkirk, third baseman Red Rolfe ... and Gordon at second. Appropriately enough the game was played at Yankee Stadium.

Although he had already been in a World Series as a rookie, this was a kind of national coming out party for Gordon. Joe Cronin, the American League manager and shortstop of the Red Sox, like everyone else who watched, lavished praise on star pitcher Bob Feller. But after his up-close-and-personal look at Gordon's work around second base, he gushed about the young infielder, too.

Yes, the Cleveland Indians hurler was outstanding in the 3–1 victory, Cronin said, but Gordon "was the difference. He saved the ballgame. There isn't anything around the bag Gordon can't do. He's the best second baseman I ever saw."[9]

Gordon stopped a Mel Ott single from zinging into the outfield in the sixth inning to save a run thanks to a double play immediately afterwards. Then Gordon made a spectacular grab of a Joe Medwick rip in the eighth inning that had Cronin uttering comments about Gordon having acrobatic training. Those are the types of plays that Gordon made routinely.

Add a player here, add a player there and never weaken the lineup, only strengthen it. That was how the Yankees stayed on top. The core would change over ever so slowly, ever so slightly. When Babe Ruth departed, that was monumental. When Joe DiMaggio stepped in, that was big stuff. But there were some rocks in the lineup, from Lou Gehrig to Bill Dickey to Tony Lazzeri and Frankie Crosetti, that made people think the Yankees never changed, only continued. They would look around at those guys and think, "Hasn't he been there forever?" The release of Lazzeri in favor of the incoming Gordon was one of the big changes that generated more attention than most.

One position that was problematic for the Yankees was third base. They had a rotating cast until Joe Sewell spent the last three years of his Hall of Fame career (1931–1933) holding down the hot corner. Sewell was one of the most difficult men to strike out in baseball history, was a good fielder and retired with a lifetime .312 average. But by the time the Yankees got him he was slowing down, and although he hit .302 for New York one year, he also hit in the .270s twice and provided little power.

Once again, however, the Yankees scouts and farm system developed a ready replacement for Sewell with Robert Abial "Red" Rolfe, a native of Penacook, New Hampshire, who had attended Dartmouth College of the Ivy League. Rolfe was 25 when he gained possession of the job with 89 games of play and a .287 average in 1934. Within a few years he became an All-Star regular, and eventually was selected for the American League team four times.

Rolfe graduated from Dartmouth (following his high school experience at Phillips Exeter Academy, both schools demanding brains) and got into one game for the Yankees in 1931 before being shipped to the minors for two more seasons. He kept thinking, and occasionally saying, that the New York Yankees should have at least one genuine New England Yankee on their team. His family did not come over from Europe on the Mayflower, he said, but after missing out on that journey, they did make the next ship.

"If I had been sure I had been related to the John Rolfe who married Pocahontas way back when (in 1614), I supposed I would have signed with the Cleveland Indians instead of the Yankees," Rolfe said. However, he was enticed to New York by scout Gene McCann with the spellbinding phrase, "How would you like to sign a New York contract and play on the same team with Babe Ruth and Lou Gehrig?"[10]

Rolfe was neither shy nor cocky. He might chatter about his heritage, but when it came to baseball he was as engaged as he had been with his other studies in college. He took notes about everything, as if a final exam were scheduled. In a way, perhaps, it was, if one counts performance as a test instead of a written quiz.

"Rolfe has personality," said Joe McCarthy, "He has color and I don't mean just his hair. And he asks plenty of questions and writes down the answers. He also has a lot of other information in his little black book. For instance, he writes down just what every pitcher throws him in the clutch, so he can be set in the pinch."[11]

In '35 and '36, Rolfe, who had always been a shortstop, split time between short and third base. Originally he didn't care much for the change, dabbling at third, and McCarthy had to massage his psyche a bit with periodic talking-tos.

"It's a cinch," McCarthy told Rolfe about the switch. "You'll be a great third baseman. Why, the balls come straight at you. They come faster and you'll have more time to throw. You can do it. It's the easiest job on the field." Rolfe played the position, got a few easy hops and started to agree with McCarthy about the comparative difficulties of the two positions on the left side of the infield.

Until the hit came that was bound to happen sooner or later. The struck ball took a surprise hop, hit Rolfe in the face and smashed his nose, loosened two previously perfectly fine teeth, and stained the entire front of his uniform with blood. Infuriated, Rolfe had an answer for McCarthy then. "Easy is it?" he steamed. "A cinch to play, eh? You can have third base. I don't want to get killed!"[12]

Of course when the emotions calmed, Rolfe stuck with third, partially because that's what McCarthy wanted and partially became he wasn't going to back down from a challenge.

Rolfe grew into his job in 1935 when he hit .300, but blossomed into a star in 1936 when he batted .319 with ten homers and 70 runs driven in and led the league in triples with 15. Actually, that star label wasn't officially "All-Star" until 1937, though it seemed more payback for Rolfe not being chosen in 1936 with a far superior performance. He played in every game, but hit just .276.

Just about everything about 1936 was delicious for Rolfe. He got hot even before the season started in spring training, and by the time the Yankees worked their way north to start the regular season with their normal complement of traveling exhibition games, he was on fire. After an exhibition game in Jacksonville, Florida, headed to Atlanta, players were still in uniform as they headed back to their hotel rooms.

Rolfe was heard announcing to infielder roommate Don Heffner, "Hot dog! Three hits for the room this afternoon!" Rolfe, who had two of the hits, attributed it to having the right room, number 412, which added up to lucky seven in his mind. "We're just a couple of lucky stiffs, Don, getting assigned to a room that's good for base hits." Heffner tried to give Rolfe more of the credit, but Rolfe said that was the baseball way probably since Abner Doubleday's day, for roommates to share equally. Still, at the time Rolfe was batting .407 in spring training.[13]

Although he did not hit quite as well throughout the 1937 season, Rolfe was coping with an early-season physical problem. A growth on his leg was spotted and Rolfe played the entire season with it. Just after the Yankees'

Ivy Leaguer Red Rolfe wielded a mean bat for the Yankees after he signed with the team out of Dartmouth, and while not a superstar, Rolfe was a four-time All-Star who later returned to his alma mater and became athletic director.

victory in the World Series, dispatching the Giants for the second year in a row, Rolfe went into the hospital for surgery.

By that time he had proven himself a clutch customer in the games versus the Giants, representing his second appearance in a Series. He collected six hits in the five games, batted .300, ran the bases well and fielded superbly, and became a two-time champion. After his adjustment from short to third, Rolfe wasn't going anywhere, and he stayed rooted in the starting lineup as the Yankees won their third and fourth straight World Series championships in 1938 and 1939.

It was a battle for Tommy Henrich to make it into the Yankees' starting outfield. Born in Ohio in 1913 (for years he lied about his age, saying he was born in 1916), Henrich became property of the Cleveland Indians. But later he and his family appealed to Commissioner Kenesaw Mountain Landis, saying he was being held down in the farm system rather than being given a chance to play. Landis, who was liberating players in other farm systems, too, set Henrich free in 1937. Then he joined the Yankees as a free agent.

Henrich said when he was checking into the Hotel New Yorker to hook up with the Yankees, the bellhop figured out who he was. "So you're the new Yankee outfielder," the man said to Henrich, who took it that the individual carrying his suitcase didn't think he had much chance to make it. He listed Joe DiMaggio, George Selkirk, Jake Powell, Myril Hoag, and Roy Johnson, the incumbents, and asked, "Did you ever see those guys hit?" Henrich's retort was simple: "Not yet, but they never saw me hit, either."

"They didn't get a chance, I might add," Henrich said. He sat on the New York bench for a couple of weeks, and then was dispatched to Newark. The story he heard of his call-up went like this. The Yankees lost a close ballgame and McCarthy was red-faced angry about what he saw on the field. In an ill-advised whisper that traveled more loudly than planned, Roy Johnson said, "What does he expect to do, win every day?" That, of course, was exactly what McCarthy and the Yankees expected.

McCarthy went to the front office, demanded that Johnson be dumped, and asked Ed Barrow "to bring up the kid from Newark."[14]

The deed was done. Johnson, part–Cherokee Indian, spent just 1936 and part of 1937 in the Yankees' outfield mix, but had a respectable career, playing ten years, batting over .300 four times (though not for the Yankees) and posting a lifetime average of .296. He did play for New York in the 1936 World Series, but Henrich definitely had more upside by 1937.

That year, the left-handed-hitting Henrich made himself useful by batting .320 in 67 games, though he did not get into the World Series because of a knee injury. It was the first time, but not the last, that Henrich's knee woes interrupted what he wanted to accomplish on a baseball diamond, and many years later, when he retired, bad knees were mentioned as a cause.

In 1938, Henrich became an outfield regular, eventually squeezing out Selkirk. Although the player who came to be known as "Old Reliable" because of his clutch hitting dropped to .270 in average, he cracked 22 home runs and drove in 91 runs. It was Yankees broadcaster Mel Allen who bestowed the nickname. Henrich's record of making big hits at the right time prompted Allen's memory of a train of that name that ran from Cincinnati to Alabama when he was a youth in that Dixie state.

Henrich was a religious man, and his commentary and stories about him showed up not only in the New York press, but in religious publications. He once wrote a first-person story for "Guideposts," saying, "From boyhood I've practiced my religion to the best of my ability. In fact, it is as much a part of me as breathing. My faith is the core of my living and thinking."

He cited an experience of his youth that he always remembered and applied to his professional baseball career. Henrich wrote that he always lost games to his brother Eddie when pickup teams were chosen and "that was hard to take. I learned to think about how victory would taste the next time we played, rather than brood over today's setback. To me there is such a thing as losing too gracefully. I hate to lose. By thinking victory, somehow it, in turn, will come about."[15]

Playing for the Yankees also meant that victory would usually come about.

10

Joe D. Gets Hitched

A couple of years in New York cured Joe DiMaggio of naiveté, if not shyness. After leading the Yankees to four straight World Series titles by 1939, DiMaggio was just about the biggest thing going in the biggest city in the nation.

Jack Dempsey, the former heavyweight champion, was still one of the kings of the nightlife, and his restaurant was a place to be seen. DiMaggio's place to be seen was center field at Yankee Stadium. He didn't crave celebrity, but it fell to him.

Yet he was no late-night partier. Deep down DiMaggio was the boy from an Italian immigrant family who thought he wanted his own family. He enjoyed the company of glamorous and beautiful women, but sought a traditional home life, even if he didn't know how to live one.

In 1937, DiMaggio, his fame burgeoning, was invited to participate with a minor speaking role in the movie "Manhattan Merry-Go-Round." Dorothy Arnold, who had been in show business as a dancer, and played a dancer who didn't have a speaking part in the movie, was on the set. They met there when she was 19 and he was 23. They began dating and married on November 19, 1939, in San Francisco at a Catholic church after an engagement that involved the presentation of a four-and-a-half-carat diamond ring from DiMaggio. Thousands of people, invited or not, friends and family and not, descended on the church, filling the pews and the area surrounding the church.

Arnold was born Dorothy Olson in Duluth, Minnesota, and thought she had the goods to make it big-time in show business. Modeling, singing and dancing opened doors, but she wanted to be a movie star, at least until she met DiMag. He wanted her to give up her career and become a housewife, and despite her long-held ambitions, she was game for trying it — to a degree. Not that the one comparison they could make with a Yankee player married to an actress was very encouraging. Gomez and June O'Dea had split.

Although Arnold made movies between 1937 and 1957, with some minor interruptions acting as a housewife, she is not as well-remembered as some of the other bombshells of the day. She had decidedly voluptuous legs, no doubt built from dancing, and in at least one color studio publicity shot her platinum blonde hair made her resemble Jean Harlow. Apparently, this gentleman preferred blondes.

Following the marriage, DiMaggio kept many of his single habits, and of course traveled extensively in spring and summer with the Yankees and spent some of his free time with family in San Francisco. Arnold worked in Hollywood. They both kept up energetic paces. While there was clearly affection for one another, they were both always so darned busy.

Arnold gave birth to Joe DiMaggio Jr. in 1941, but the couple temporarily split up in 1942. Then they reconciled, right before the prying eyes of the press. The divorce became a reality in May 1944. DiMaggio was disturbed by the demise of his marriage, and he and Arnold had periods where they visited and stayed in touch, notably Christmas of 1945 after they were divorced. But Joe was not one of those guys who was going to bare his soul, either in a bar under sedation of alcohol, or in the tabloids, so there were limits on what people ever knew about the relationship.

Although New Yorkers surely would have lapped up every juicy tidbit of his marriage's high and low points, mostly they cared how he performed on the field, and there DiMaggio had few equals in the game. DiMaggio's first four seasons were like a dream. He was chosen for the All-Star team in 1936, 1937, 1938, and 1939 and the Yankees won the World Series all four of those years, setting a new milestone for excellence.

DiMaggio's eagle eye at bat was easy to catalogue with his statistics. What was appreciated more by those who knew the inner game was his fluidity in the field and ability to chase down balls hit to the deepest areas of center field. Hank Greenberg, the Tigers' home-run basher, paraphrased Wee Willie Keeler's famous statement about hitting when talking about DiMaggio. Keeler, the early Orioles star, popularized the oft-used statement about the secret of hitting, "Hit 'em where they ain't." Greenberg said the American League opposition had to "hit 'em where Joe wasn't."[1]

One of the nicknames that stuck to DiMaggio was bestowed on him

10. Joe D. Gets Hitched

by radio announcer Arch McDonald at the start of the 1939 season when a new Pan-American airplane was in the news. The plane was called "The Yankee Clipper." And so was Joe from then on. McDonald repeated the name until it caught on.[2]

DiMaggio was a star from the moment he set foot in the batter's box in 1936, but in 1939 he became something more than that. Newspapermen and fans didn't use the term "superstar" back then, but DiMaggio, through sheer force of performance, had become king of the Yankees.

After Ruth left in 1934, Lou Gehrig, still probably the greatest first baseman of all time, and certainly the greatest second banana ever in baseball show business, was still walloping hits off the wall and over it at Yankee Stadium. No rookie was going to usurp Gehrig's status. But by 1939, two things were going on. Gehrig was through and DiMaggio was ascendant.

While he never again made quite the hullabaloo he had with his 1938 holdout, DiMaggio was usually unhappy with the salary offered by the front office. He had little leverage, so settled for less than he thought he was worth. Ruppert was not shy about discussing DiMaggio's disgruntlement in the papers. "I should say that he is a well-paid young man and I can't see where he has any cause to be dissatisfied," the Yankees owner said after one $25,000 offer.[3]

President Franklin D. Roosevelt was making $25,000 in 1938. But not as cheeky as Babe Ruth, DiMaggio did not announce that he had a better year. St. Louis Browns President Donald Barnes made his own announcement, saying he offered Ruppert $150,000 for DiMaggio, but Ruppert replied, "DiMaggio is not for sale at any price."[4]

In 1939, DiMaggio hit 30 home runs with 126 RBI, and led the American League in batting with a .381 average. He was voted Most Valuable Player, sort of an official stamp placed on his rise. It was DiMaggio's first of three MVP awards.

As late as September 9, DiMaggio was batting .409 in his quest to become the first American League .400 hitter since 1923. But the opportunity was lost when DiMaggio came down with an eye injury and Joe McCarthy wouldn't rest him.

"I remember I was batting more than .400," DiMaggio said. "Then I got this terrible allergy in my left eye, my batting eye, and I could hardly see out of it. Joe McCarthy didn't believe in cheese champions, so he made me play every day. I went into a terrible slump. McCarthy had to know the agony I was going through, but I'll never understand why he didn't give me a couple of days off. I guess it was the rule of the day — you played with anything short of a broken leg."[5]

The Yankees were more dominant than they had been during the first three years of this dynasty, going 106-45 in regular-season play, one of the best records of all time. Their winning percentage was .702 and they finished 17 games ahead of the second-place Red Sox.

This was actually marked improvement for the Red Sox, for so long cellar dwellers or near the basement in the AL. Tom Yawkey's bigger spending habit was beginning to pay off. This was personified by the introduction of a rookie left fielder named Ted Williams in 1939. The "Splendid Splinter" was tall and thin, but could hit the ball as far and as high as could be seen. He would soon emerge as DiMaggio's rival for individual supremacy in the American League.

The surprise pennant winners in the National League were the Cincinnati Reds, who had not won a pennant for 20 years. Their last appearance in the World Series was 1919, the year when eight White Sox players conspired to throw World Series games and were eventually blackballed for life by Commissioner Kenesaw Mountain Landis.

The rise of the Reds was unexpected. They placed eighth and last in the National League in 1937 and fourth in 1938. They out-ran the field during the second half of the 1939 season to capture the flag.

New York overwhelmed Cincinnati in the Series, winning 4-0. The winning pitchers were Red Ruffing, Monte Pearson, Bump Hadley 'in relief of Lefty Gomez,' and Johnny Murphy (in relief of Oral Hildebrand), acquired that season in one of Barrow's coups, after eight seasons with the Cleveland Indians and St. Louis Browns.

Despite his MVP season and his desire for bigger bucks, DiMaggio's negotiation with Ed Barrow was of much lower profile than his holdout year. The outfielder stayed in San Francisco and made no statements about what he wanted, and Barrow stayed mum in New York. DiMaggio signed for $27,500 for 1940, a pittance of a raise really, and one that could not have pleased him after becoming the cornerstone of a four-time world champion ball club.

There have been many cases of baseball players of a certain fame doing their best to keep a reasonably low profile in public, but they usually lightened up in the locker room. DiMaggio didn't even do that. You could be

10. Joe D. Gets Hitched

From the moment he broke into the Yankees lineup in 1936, Joe DiMaggio, here crossing the plate after a home run in front of Brooklyn Dodgers catcher Roy Campanella in the World Series, was the heartbeat of the team, first teaming with Lou Gehrig and then taking over leadership of the club.

his teammate and not exchange a word with the guy at the locker a few doors down for weeks at a time.

Babe Ruth was legendary for not remembering teammates' names, but he was always friendly to them. He would greet them generically as pals because he recognized their faces. DiMaggio kept to himself in the clubhouse, and teammates who had been around him for a while respected his wishes not to be bothered. They also told newcomers to the team what DiMaggio's habits were.

That's just Joe's way, they would tell new players on the team about DiMaggio's reticent nature. It doesn't mean he doesn't like you if he doesn't talk to you. With DiMaggio, like Ruth, there was no proof that he knew the names of players who were later arriving Yankees than he was, either. He didn't even say hello to many of them, apparently, never mind give them a big how-do.

By 1939, in his efforts to keep things fresh, Barrow had brought in many substitutes for the bunch that held the fort in 1932 when the Yankees won the World Series contest with the Chicago Cubs. The changes were piecemeal, but there were many players that were out of the picture now and many new ones Barrow fit into their holes.

Tony Lazzeri was one of the first to go, after the 1936 season. The frontline rotation stayed steady, with Ruffing, Gomez and Pearson holding down the top three slots. Johnny Murphy was as reliable as Old Reliable Henrich. Some of the peripheral outfielders were shipped elsewhere to make room for Henrich, Charlie Keller, upgrades among the guys around DiMaggio.

But the single biggest change, after the Yankees had won their third straight title in 1938, was not on the field, where McCarthy still held sway and DiMaggio, Gehrig, Bill Dickey, Red Rolfe and Frank Crosetti still performed.

It was at the top of the company. Colonel Jacob Ruppert died.

Ruppert and his partner, the other Colonel, Tillinghast Huston, had long before parted ways in their shared ownership of the Yankees. Ruppert paid $1,250,000 for Huston's half-interest in 1923, a nice profit from Huston's $225,000 investment of 1915.

In March of 1938, Huston, who was nicknamed "The Man In The Iron Hat" because he wore a derby even in summer since he thought it brought the Yankees luck, passed away at the age of 71. Less than a year later Ruppert followed him into a grave.

Although he could be bombastic when he felt he was fighting for the rights of his team, Ruppert tried to maintain dignity in public. Ruppert put such a premium on winning that he wanted the Yankees to win by several runs so he wouldn't be nervous in the late innings of close games. He assembled the team to do it, too. Ruppert died January 13, 1939, also at age 71, primarily from the effects of phlebitis, which had bothered him for nearly a year.

His final days were spent in a hospital, and one of his last visitors was Babe Ruth. During the years the two men knew one another, Ruppert always called his most spectacular player "Ruth," by last name only, spoken with a slightly German accent so it more often sounded like "Root."

A few days before Ruppert expired, Ruth came to see him at Lenox Hill Hospital. Ruppert was being sustained by an oxygen tank and he waved to a nurse to remove it, saying, "I want to see the Babe." The nurse

10. Joe D. Gets Hitched

answered, "Here he is, right beside you." Ruppert reached out his hand to Ruth, but did not have the strength to utter another word. Trying to lift the older man's spirits, Ruth said, "Colonel, you are going to snap out of this and you and I are going to the opening game of the season." Ruppert smiled at the comment projecting more than three months into the future. Ruth had tears in his eyes.

Ruth began to leave, but Ruppert found the energy to request his return. When Ruth got back to the bed, Ruppert reached out and held Ruth's hand and said, "Babe."

After departing, Ruth told sportswriters, "It was the only time in his life he ever called me 'Babe' to my face. I couldn't help crying when I went out."[6]

In life the two men had feuded over money and Ruppert had disappointed Ruth mightily by not making him manager of the Yankees. But they both seemed to realize they had done great things together, had helped to make one another more famous and wealthier, and were linked for the better because of their Yankees relationship.

When Ruppert died, fans might have wondered what would become of the team, but he had provided carefully for it to be left in good hands — he thought. Ruppert's will left his fortune, which included the property of the Yankees, to a female ward and two nieces. But he established a four-man trust to run the team, one of whose members was Ed Barrow. Another was Ruppert's brother, George, who operated the Ruppert Brewery for the family. He also left $150,000 to the hospital where he died and gave the Metropolitan Museum of Art permission to take any of his paintings and artwork from his two homes that it wished to add to its collection.

If Ruppert's wealth was estimated at between $40 million and $45 million, the Yankees share of that was estimated at $10 million.

The trick to Ruppert's bequest of the Yankees was that the nieces were infants and that protected the trust for years until they were of age to make sound decisions about the team if they wished to sell it. "The last will and testament of the late Col. Jacob Ruppert, which provided for the perpetuation of the New York Yankees as long as legally possible, substantiated the belief that above all his other interests, he took most pride in his baseball club," one sports columnist wrote.[7] The author was probably correct. Ruppert did indeed seem to derive great joy from his association with the world championship Yankees.

Babe Ruth (left) and Yankees owner Jacob Ruppert rarely were so cheerful during contract negotiations. Ruth was one of the few top Yankees stars who got what he wanted in his paycheck. Despite tenseness during his playing days, when Ruth visited Ruppert on his death bed in a hospital, he shed tears and they displayed affection for one another.

Ruppert's funeral took place at St. Patrick's Cathedral in New York, and 15,000 people overflowed the church (and adjacent streets) as a requiem mass was conducted. The hearse carrying Ruppert's body from his home on Fifth Avenue to the church passed mourners who doffed their hats in respect.

Also in Ruppert's final days, Barrow, his right-hand man with the team, was a frequent visitor. At times Ruppert lapsed into a coma, but once he awoke and saw Barrow hovering over him and asked, "Do you think we will win the pennant again?" Barrow gave the right answer. "We'll win again, Colonel." He was not just saying that to make a dying man feel good.

10. Joe D. Gets Hitched

The Yankees did win the 1939 pennant after Ruppert passed away. And the World Series again, too.[8]

One of the first acts of the trustees was to elect Barrow president of the team. It was only fitting, though he was already 70 years old.

Despite Ruppert's complex plan to keep the Yankees intact and in his family, almost as soon as he was in the ground, offers to buy the team were floated. They poured in for months. The trustees kept repeating that they had no intention of selling the team, but authorized Barrow to do a formal evaluation to determine if the team was really worth what was muttered at the time of the reading of the will. Barrow returned with a figure of $7 million.

As months passed and closer inspection of the books and the values of items were scrutinized, Ruppert's estate took on an entirely different picture. Rather than $40 million-plus it was valued at $7 million, with the Yankees figured in at $2.4 million. There were tax issues galore if anyone wanted to buy, as well. The business end of things was more complicated than Ruppert expected them to be or wanted them to be.

But on the field, the team was the same old Yankees. The Yankees kept winning and they kept adding young players to the roster, cultivated in an extraordinary farm system. It became more and more apparent over the years that for all of Ruppert's and Barrow's acumen, and all of the wisdom of the scouts, the leadership had an additional secret weapon in-house.

George M. Weiss had rebuilt the moribund Baltimore Orioles franchise of the International League between 1929 and 1931, and his work caught Ruppert's attention. Born in New Haven in 1895, Weiss attended Yale. He also operated the New Haven Colonials before joining the Orioles.

Ruppert hired Weiss in 1932 with the marching orders to build New York's farm system and grow future Yankees, beginning his 29-year connection with the team. Weiss did a brilliant job sending top player after top player to the Yankees while shrewdly selling off other players whom he felt would never make it to the big leagues. In all, Weiss sold $2 million worth of players while feeding the major league club fresh talent. Before he became general manager in 1948, Weiss helped supply the players that won nine pennants and eight World Series crowns.

It could almost be said that Ruppert found a second Ed Barrow.

Reflecting on Weiss' accomplishments after his first 14 years with the Yankees, one sports columnist said Weiss' wisdom in recognizing young talent, developing it, and also making a profit on distributing players he didn't want to keep "calls for the protean skills of the trapeze artist who can play the fiddle while doing his flipflops."[9]

Weiss, who almost never gave extended interviews and was called "The Man of Silence" when he yielded his thoughts to *Sports Illustrated* months after being eased out of the Yankees' picture in 1960, said he learned a lot from Barrow. "Barrow was a great baseball man from whom I learned the art of constant application," Weiss said, "of attending to business 12 hours a day, 12 months a year."[10]

Weiss was not the most beloved man in baseball. Certainly there was jealousy over the Yankees' success, but he was not a gregarious man, and he was focused on the business of taking care of business whenever he was awake. He recognized the way he and his team were viewed within the sport — as making a pastime overly corporate.

"The Yankees have often been accused of being a hard-headed, hard-hearted organization of unsentimental businessmen with a bunch of talented, but mechanical ballplayers carrying out their functions in the field," he said. "This isn't so at all. We have simply always realized that modern-day baseball is a highly practical enterprise that has to be run systematically, and this includes everything from operating a good restaurant for members of the Stadium Club to two-platooning on the field when the circumstances demand it."[11]

He added that it wasn't just the Yankees that people misunderstood, but him, too. "I've sometimes been accused of being distant and aloof myself, but if I've given that impression it's because the job of overseeing all the round-the-clock chores that have mounted up through the years since those quiet days at Bryant Park hasn't given me much time to be a good-time Charlie. And unlike some of the more flamboyant executives in the game today, I haven't ever believed in operating on the executive side as if baseball were a game of musical chairs ... (or) playing with franchises as if they were circuses and making trades helter-skelter for the sake of glamour and change alone."[12]

There was no question that Weiss had a more reserved style than general managers like Frank "Trader" Lane with Chicago and Cleveland, or Bill Veeck, with Chicago, who used to knock ashes from the end of his cigarettes into the ashtray built into the wooden leg he got as souvenir of World War II service.

10. Joe D. Gets Hitched

What no one could argue with was Weiss' or the Yankees' success. The partnerships had shifted through the years in New York from Ruppert and Huston, to Ruppert, Huston, Barrow and McCarthy, to Ruppert, Barrow, McCarthy and Weiss, to Barrow, McCarthy and Weiss.

The Yankees did win the American League pennant and the World Series again in 1939, the season after Ruppert died. It was their fifth championship of the decade of the 1930s and fourth in a row. Ruppert had hired wisely.

11

Shut Up and Play Like King Kong

If on-field reliability was the main measuring stick of whether or not you were good enough to be a Yankee, it was still possible to talk your way out of a job. Or at least put a big "X" next to your name in the heads of the top administrators in the organization.

Jake Powell's big mouth got him into more trouble than his bat or glove ever did.

The 6-foot, 180-pound Powell was born in 1908 in Silver Spring, Maryland, made a brief debut with the nearby Washington Senators and returned to the majors to stay in 1934. He became a Yankee midway through the 1936 season, hitting .302 for New York, and had an 11-year big-league career.

Powell played the game about as recklessly as he lived off the diamond. Before being shipped to the Yankees he was described by a Washington newspaper columnist as "The Wild Man of the Base Paths in the American League," and as a player who could get his uniform dirty in one inning of play.[1]

In his first World Series for the Yankees against the Giants, the newly acquired left-fielder batted .455. He was completely unfazed about going against premier hurler Carl Hubbell. Before he had the chance, he said, "This guy Carl Hubbell is only an ordinary pitcher."[2]

Not to most people, but Powell hit Hubbell well enough that no complaints about his batting were uttered. The New York fans swooned at his performance. Powell did so well during that short series he decided he had earned a raise and rebuffed the Yankees' original contract offer. Powell made just $6,000 with the Senators and wanted more money.

108

11. Shut Up and Play Like King Kong 109

"I was the World Series hero," he said.[3] Powell did talk himself into a slight raise.

During the 1937 season, Powell started a fist-fight with one of his old Senators' teammates when the player tagged him out. When Washington fans showed their displeasure at his aggression by throwing soda pop bottles at him on the field, Powell picked them up and began smashing them against the outfield wall. This action did not prove popular with the local constabulary and they persuaded him to cease. There was also less enthusiasm about Powell's contributions when he batted .263 in 1937.

Powell's relationship with the public deteriorated further in 1938. He got into a fight with Red Sox player-manager Joe Cronin, who cut Powell off when he was charging the mound after being hit by a pitch, and he was suspended ten games for that.

On July 29, the Yankees were in Chicago for a set with the White Sox when Powell was interviewed by well-known radio announcer Bob Elson on WGN about what he did in the off-season for a job to supplement his baseball salary.

"I'm a policeman in Dayton, Ohio," Powell said. This was not true. Elson asked how he kept busy. "I crack niggers on the head," Powell said.[4]

This was not true, either, but the rash, insulting, imprudent comment instantly got Powell cut off from the airwaves. Listeners immediately lit up the switchboard with complaints. The station promptly issued an apology and Commissioner Kenesaw Mountain Landis stepped in the next morning, suspending Powell for ten more games.

There was considerable irony in Landis taking such a strong stand (most thought to placate African-American ticket buyers) when he enforced unwritten, but very real rules which banned men with dark skin from competing with whites.

Recognizing the depth of the trouble he was in and how large a furor he had created by telling what he said was intended as a joke, a few weeks later Powell linked up with the New York bureau of the *Chicago Defender*, a newspaper with a black audience, to apologize again and to explain himself.

"Honestly, you can believe me when I say I regret the slur," he said to a *Defender* reporter, "as I had no intention to hurt anyone, or their feelings. Members of the Negro race have helped to earn my bread and butter and no one knows that better than I do. I have two members of your race taking care of my home while myself and my wife are away and I think they are two of the finest people in the world. I do hundreds of favors for them daily."[5]

As apologies went, it was not exceptionally elegant and in some ways made Powell sound like a plantation owner.

The Yankees did their own apologizing after baseball administrators wrote a critical letter to the team. Ed Barrow did the composing on behalf of Colonel Ruppert, who was already sick, and the club. Barrow wrote in part, "There is hardly any need of my telling you that everybody connected with the Yankee Baseball Club, including Jake Powell himself, is sorry for the unfortunate remark from Comiskey Park in Chicago the other day. Mr. Powell has since apologized not only over the radio, but also through the newspapers for his regrettable blunder. Knowing Mr. Powell as I do, I am quite sure that he did not realize what he was saying, and certainly did not mean any harm. He was born in the South, and as you no doubt know, white men can say things in the South that sound different in the North."[6]

In the late 1930s, the clamor to allow African-American players to emerge from the shadows of the Negro Leagues and be given tryouts by major league clubs was in its infancy in the mainstream press, though a cause loudly led by the black press. Victory would not be achieved until after World War II when Jackie Robinson broke the color line for the Brooklyn Dodgers—three years after Commissioner Landis' death. However, the Powell incident prodded widely influential columnist Westbrook Pegler to take a stand.

Pegler took the tactic of saying that Landis was being hypocritical in suspending Powell for his comments while condoning a ban on blacks in the big leagues. Pegler referred to "the national game (that) has always treated the Negroes as Adolph Hitler treats the Jews. If all American employers did the same the entire Negro population of this country would starve, become public charges, or go back to slavery.... Thus no Negro ever has been permitted to play ball or even to try out for a job in the organized industry, and Babe Ruth, were he a colored man, would not have risen above the rank and pay of the leaky-roof leagues in which dark men operate as semi-pros."[7]

That was sizzling stuff and black newspapers embraced Pegler's voice as another demanding fairness in major league baseball.

11. Shut Up and Play Like King Kong 111

Between his suspensions, his diminished stature, and the Yankees finding other ways to buttress the outfield position, Powell played in just 45 games in 1938, and although he was kept around in 1939 appeared in only 31 games that year.

It was difficult to imagine things getting much worse for Powell with the Yankees, but they did. At the very end of spring training in 1940, Powell ran into an outfield wall during an exhibition game in Lynchburg, Virginia, and fractured his skull. Powell was knocked unconscious by the impact for an estimated two minutes, according to outfield partner Tommy Henrich, but awoke before an ambulance transported him to a local hospital.

Powell did not return to the Yankees lineup until June 15, but manager Joe McCarthy used him in just 12 games that season. During the off-season winter, the Yankees sold Powell to the San Francisco Seals of the Pacific Coast League, ending his controversy-filled career in New York.

Powell's final major league appearance was with the Philadelphia Phillies in 1945. In 1948 he attempted a baseball comeback with a Class D team, but could only muster a .220 batting average. In early November, Powell was arrested with a woman in Washington, D.C. for passing $300 worth of bad checks. They said they planned to marry later that day after taking a train to New York.

While in police custody, Powell asked to speak to his companion, and after she visited with him for a short while, Powell yelled, "Hell, I'm going to end it all!" He reached into a pocket, pulled out a .25-caliber handgun and shot himself first in the chest and then in the head. It later came out that Powell was still married to his first wife. The suicide ended Powell's life at age 39.[8]

The Yankees' trade of Powell for Ben Chapman was ironic. Chapman was a talented outfielder from Alabama who earned a place on the New York roster in 1930 and stayed until 1936. A cantankerous Southerner, Chapman was more bigoted than Powell.

In his home park of Yankee Stadium, Chapman insulted Jewish fans with Nazi salutes and made insulting ethnic comments. In 1933, in a game against the Washington Senators, Chapman instigated a confrontation with Buddy Myer, a Jewish infielder, which grew into a 20-minute brawl involving 300 fans. Chapman was suspended for five games.

Although a good enough outfielder and adept enough base stealer to be named to the first American League All-Star team in 1933, Chapman, who hit .302 during his career, was regarded as a bad-tempered player, though when McCarthy manipulated the trade of Chapman for Powell he blamed a series of leg problems and a dropping batting average for exiling Chapman from the world champions. In more candid conversations with those close to him, McCarthy said Chapman's personality was all wrong for the Yankees and his outbursts were bad for the chemistry of the team. "Chapman should be the best player in baseball," McCarthy said. "But his temperament is all wrong."[9]

Chapman had done good work for the Yankees at different times. In 1931, Chapman batted .315 and stole 61 bases. That figure led the league and he also topped the AL in steals in 1932 and 1933. Chapman's infield play was just good enough to keep him in the lineup — as an outfielder.

Later, Chapman incurred the wrath of millions and drew a reprimand from Commissioner A.B. "Happy" Chandler when as manager of the Phillies he orchestrated vicious taunting of Jackie Robinson. Chapman defended the racial content of the insults as routine riding of a rookie the way any other rookie would be tested.

In retirement, prior to his death in 1993 at age 84, Chapman told interviewers that his being labeled a bigot by "liberal" journalists such as a national TV personality Howard Cosell kept him out of the Hall of Fame.

A 1973 *Sporting News* story quoted Chapman as saying that players rode Robinson, for sure, just as he was verbally assaulted when he was a rookie. "The first thing I heard from the fans when I stepped on the field in a Yankee uniform," Chapman said, "was 'Go back where you belong, you Southern SOB,' and the first thing I heard from the opposing dugout was, 'Stick it in the Southern SOB's ear and see how he looks sitting down.'"[10]

Without being a mind reader, it was impossible to tell where the real Ben Chapman left off and someone trying to explain inexplicable behavior began, but pretty soon the Yankees had outfielders who made fans forget about the Chapman era pretty quickly. The Jake Powell era, too.

The Yankees had that guy Joe DiMaggio show up in 1936 and take over center field with his instant stardom. Tommy Henrich joined the team in 1937 and found a home in right field. In 1939 another new face arrived, promoted from Newark to a regular's role in New York. Slugging

11. Shut Up and Play Like King Kong   113

Charlie Keller may not have been a gazelle in left field, but he added another big-time bat to the lineup. Keller hit the ball so hard and sometimes so deep that he acquired the nickname "King Kong."

The Fay Wray version of the big gorilla movie came out in 1933, and Keller's power gained him comparisons when he was still in high school. However, he disliked being rated against a big ape and frowned at direct calls to him by his nickname. Knowing his distaste for the moniker, some New York sportswriters tried to come up with a better one, but never did better than "Killer Diller," something that did not catch on.

Keller was born in Middleton, Maryland, in 1916, grew up on a farm, and after high school enrolled at the University of Maryland where he played a minimal amount of college football before exiting. Originally, the Cleveland Indians spied him, but as a minor Keller needed his parents' consent to sign a contract. They refused on the grounds that they wanted their boy to be a college man.

During Keller's senior year, however, the Yankees talked him out of the rest of his college education. Scout Paul Krichell came to town and spent some time making a speech on the virtues of life as a Yankee. Keller signed the deal leaning against the side of his home. The Yankees assigned him to their AAA Newark team where Keller led the International League in batting at .353 as a 20-year-old.

A year later, the 5-foot-10, 185-pounder who looked larger than his frame and possessed the strength that belied it, hit .364 for Newark. Keller had a broad chest and well-muscled arms that he said he built up by doing chores on the family farm as a boy. The dark hair and curl in front that spilled over onto his forehead despite the use of combs and brushes, he came by naturally. By the spring of 1939, Keller was married, penciled into the Yankees' lineup and not finding major league pitching terribly difficult to hit either, since he batted .334 as a rookie.

Some had predicted that Keller would sit on the bench as a young newcomer barely 22, but he thought otherwise and proved it that first year. Keller played in 111 games in 1939, hit 11 home runs and drove in 83 runs. Keller's hitting caught fire when he switched from a 42-ounce to a 39-ounce bat upon McCarthy's urging. Even though the competition included Ted Williams, by mid-season McCarthy was touting Keller as the top candidate to be recognized as the best rookie to be found. "Keller is one newcomer who is living up to all the fine things they wrote about him in the lower company," McCarthy said. "Not that he is so polished that he has nothing more to learn. There isn't a more consistent freshman in the major leagues."[11]

But Keller truly shined in the 1939 World Series against the Cincinnati Reds, his first world championship competition, but the Yankees' fourth in a row.

In Game 1, Keller tripled in the ninth inning and scored the winning run on a Bill Dickey single. The Yanks beat Paul Derringer, 2–1, behind Red Ruffing.

In Game 2, Keller doubled in the midst of New York's game-winning, three-run rally.

In Game 3, Keller hit two home runs.

In Game 4, Keller homered and singled as the Yankees swept to their record-setting fourth consecutive World Series title.

Keller batted .438 for the Series, and the addition of a new star to the already star-laden Yankees prompted Reds fans to muster a phrase that would be declared frequently over the coming decades: "Break up the Yankees!" The only breaking up of the Yankees was done by Barrow when he decided a player had out lived his usefulness.

Keller was just starting out, but only near the very end of his career with the Detroit Tigers did Keller once again hit within 20 points of his rookie year .334. What he did do was settle into the role of a power hitter. The Yankees, with Babe Ruth and then Lou Gehrig, practically invented the home run as a key offensive weapon. Keller five times hit between 21 and 33 home runs and three times drove in more than 100 runs. He was a five-time All-Star.

Unlike Chapman and Powell, he never embarrassed the pinstripes with strident views. "Everybody knew Charlie Keller was a great ballplayer, but he was a lot more than that," Henrich said of his outfield partner in 1990. "He was a true-blue man. Charlie Keller personified what the Yankees used to stand for."[12]

One thing Keller was forced to do was play through a fair number of injuries, including a chipped bone in his ankle in 1941. At a time when home run hitters were in decline compared to the late 1920s and early 1930s, Keller quickly became someone pitchers sought to throw to very carefully. He walked more than 100 times five years and led the American League in bases on balls twice.

11. Shut Up and Play Like King Kong

When someone asked St. Louis Cardinals manager Billy Southworth if he thought Keller was a dangerous hitter, Southworth almost choked on his cough drop. "Dangerous?" Southworth said. "The man is positively frightening."[13]

Keller began breeding and training horses for harness racing on his 100-acre Frederick, Maryland, farm in 1957. He called it "Yankeeland." "I was proud of being a Yankee," Keller said. "It carried over into the business. I was a farm kid before. My family had dairy cows, but I knew I didn't want to milk cows."[14]

In a late-in-life interview, however, Keller made the rather surprising statement that "I detested baseball, especially after my back operation in 1947. I couldn't do anything after that. Night ball ruined it for me. It used to be a pleasure to play a ballgame at two o'clock in the afternoon. Nowadays, a ball player goes to work at five o'clock at night and doesn't get home until one or two o'clock in the morning."[15]

The commentary seemed oddly out of place, as if Keller needed to make a few clarifications. This was particularly so given his other talk about being proud to be a Yankee and also his habit of naming all of his horses with names that incorporated the word "Yankee" in them. He bred such harness horses as "Gay Yankee," "Fresh Yankee," and "Hoot Yankee."

The part about Keller detesting baseball seemed even weirder since he had two sons play ball in the Yankees' farm system. If someone speculated, it would seem that Keller liked baseball fine when he was ripping up the International League and holding sway in a World Series, but that he lost his passion for the game when injuries mounted up.

But in his first four seasons as a Yankee, at the tail end of the 1930s and the early part of the 1940s, Keller was a critical find, the missing piece in a sterling outfit that could lead New York to its fourth World Series title in a row and keep the team fighting for more pennants, even as it went through upheaval.

12

The Search for Fresh Arms

Lefty Gomez and Red Ruffing were the kings of the mound for the Yankees and it seemed as if they could pitch forever. But the search for more pitching was never ending. Not only because that duo could not go on indefinitely at the top of the rotation, but because the Yankees always seemed to need one more guy, a fifth starter who could spot the four arms that were sent out every fourth day by manager Joe McCarthy.

Even in the days before baseball shifted to five-man rotations, teams had difficulty coming up with four top-of-the-line throwers who stayed healthy and could win between 15 and 20 games every year. Finding a fifth to keep the manager's heartburn to a minimum was just that much harder.

The Yankees, even with their world championship club, their resources, and their scouting brilliance, could not assure McCarthy each spring that he had all the tools he needed for the 154-game season. Whenever a new pitcher surfaced, there was excitement.

New York's pitching newcomer of the year in 1937, lifting the hopes of McCarthy, was Ferdinand Spurgeon Chandler, born in 1907 in Commerce, Georgia. A right-handed thrower, Chandler turned into the real deal for the Yankees. When he made the roster in 1937 it was the beginning of an 11-year ride with New York that carried him through 1947. He truly cemented his stature in 1943 when he won the American League's Most Valuable Player Award.

Chandler grew up on a cotton farm in Royston, Georgia, about seven miles from Ty Cobb's home. Cobb, who made a habit of winning American League batting titles during Chandler's youth, became the boy's baseball idol. A multi-talented athlete, Chandler heard considerable badmouthing about the game of football from his father, who thought the sport was too dangerous.

"He objected strenuously to my playing football," Chandler said. "Told me he didn't want me to ruin my life getting all battered up. Dad didn't mind baseball, but he surely got no kick out of my baseball career. But I guess I was just a natural-born athlete. As long as I can remember, that's what I would rather have done more than anything, play baseball and football."[1]

Chandler enrolled at the University of Georgia and competed in football, baseball and track. He was a pretty good football player and threw a game-winning touchdown pass during his undergraduate days. He stuck around long enough to earn a degree in agriculture, but he took the slow boat to the majors even after that late professional start.

As good as Chandler was when he joined the Yankees, he had to spend five years in the minors before making the roster. That made him a 29-year-old rookie in 1937, and since he never had a losing season, compiled a lifetime 2.84 earned run average, and finished his pitching career 66 games over .500, one had to wonder if he hadn't been ignored too long. It was one thing to wait for the crop to ripen, but quite another to gather it when it was past due.

As it was, even in 1937, Chandler was used in only 12 games, though an injury played a role in that situation. He finished 7–4 in 82-plus innings, exactly matching his lifetime ERA of 2.84. Chandler earned his spot in the rotation coming out of spring training that year, but came down with bursitis later in the summer. After a layoff, he was exported to Newark to get back in shape and pitched again before the off-season beckoned.

Chandler once again gained a spot coming out of spring training in St. Petersburg and was back in the rotation for 1938. He threw 172 innings that year and finished 14–5, showing hints of what was to follow, but he inexplicably posted an earned run average over 4.00. That did not merit extra trust in him by manager McCarthy.

What it did reflect was the bone chips floating around in Chandler's elbow. By all rights he should have backed out on the season because he needed surgery, not repetitive throwing of a fastball, to improve his arm's health. But he took his turn and groaned in private. Chandler was surly on the days he pitched and he did not welcome the company of his teammates as he put on his game face and focused.

Chandler was in so much pain that when the games he pitched ended, he did not put on a neck tie because he couldn't raise his right arm high enough to button the top button of his shirt. Teammates notice that type of commitment and admire a player who hangs it out on the edge like that.

When sportswriters asked Chandler if there was anything wrong, he would not admit to the injury, only saying that his arm got stiff after he pitched. In mid-season, however, one New York paper reported the elbow problem and said that was why the Yankees brass was in search of another pitcher to complete the season.

Chandler enjoyed hunting in the off-season, and one time he hooked up with Chicago White Sox shortstop Luke Appling on a bird-hunting expedition in his native Georgia. It was a convivial occasion. The way Yankees teammate Tommy Henrich remembered the story, the hunting was good and so was the 80-proof stuff that they sipped. The shooters sat around quite some time waiting for the winged creatures to appear in the sky. At one point Chandler asked Appling a personal question because he thought he was just drunk enough to answer.

Chandler asked Appling how the White Sox signaled for the hit-and-run. Appling told him, spelling out the signals involving a few taps of the bat and some hand jive. Next season, in a game Chandler was pitching, the White Sox put one man on first and Appling strode into the batter's box. He promptly ran through all of the signs as he had described them to Chandler.

The hurler let catcher Bill Dickey know what was up and Dickey called for a pitch-out so he could have an easy throw to catch the runner heading into second base. Only the runner didn't run and Appling didn't swing. Chandler and Dickey played this game for three straight pitches while Appling comfortably stood at the plate. After it was 3–0, Chandler threw ball four.

When Chandler and Dickey returned to the New York dugout after the inning ended, Dickey looked at his battery mate and asked, "Which one of you guys did you say was drunk last fall?"[2]

In 1939, Chandler again ran into trouble. He finished 3–0 with his familiar 2.84 earned run average, but he suffered a broken leg. The 1940 campaign was not particularly kind to Chandler either. He went 8–7, but his ERA was 4.60, a number way too high to preserve a regular pitching turn.

At that point in his career, after investing time in college, several years in the minors, and holding together his body's health for only short stretches, Chandler was running out of time to put very much of major league note on his resume. By the start of the 1941 season, Chandler was 33 years old and had recorded double digits in victories exactly once. If he had retired then, practically no one would have remembered his Yankees' career. He had not even appeared in New York's World Series victories of 1937, 1938 or 1939.

Ivy Andrews, Kemp Wicker, and Steve Sundra, lesser-known Yankee pitchers, had at least made it to the mound in a Series game, something they could tell their grandchildren about some day.

Chandler had to wait to gather any first-person material for a World Series story with the exception of watching his teammates win them left and right. But things were looking better for him in 1941, when he stuck on the roster despite all of his woes, and he threw well on the mound, with a 10–4 record and a 3.19 earned run average. One more season of surrendering too many runs and Chandler might well have been cut or traded by Ed Barrow.

One thing that gained Chandler an advantage against batters that year was his development of a slider in his pitching arsenal. One sportswriter said he looked like Christy Mathewson, but he said he neither copied anyone nor learned from anyone.

"No," he said. "I worked it out by experimentation. I wasn't making enough progress ... I thought I had better learn a few new tricks."[3] It was some of the best experimentation seen since Madame Marie Curie hunkered down in a laboratory and came up with two Nobel Prizes.

When it came to finding other pitchers, Ed Barrow was hoping his touch would reach out and tap Wes Ferrell on the shoulder and make it as good as new.

For a stretch of time in the 1930s, Ferrell, the right-handed thrower from North Carolina, was one of the finest pitchers in the American League. He was temperamental and he had arm trouble, but when he was right he was something else. Ferrell won between 21 and 25 games for the Indians four times from 1929 to 1932. He won 25 for the Red Sox in 1935 and 20 in 1936.

By the time Barrow plucked Ferrell off the market in 1938 when he somehow had won 13 games for the Washington Senators with a 5.92 earned run average, Ferrell was near the end of his career, but fighting for a few more years. Despite his 13–8 record, the Senators released him.

"This is a new one," Ferrell said of his circumstances, "releasing a pitcher who has won more games than anybody else on the club."[4] Ferrell promised that he would be back in the majors, probably not that season, but the next year for sure. Two days later the Yankees called. Joe Vance, one of their peripheral pitchers, underwent an emergency appendectomy and Colonel Ruppert wanted to let his younger pitchers finish out the year in Newark.

"I'll admit my fast one isn't like it was six or seven years ago," Ferrell said. "But my control is good."[5] Ferrell appeared in five games for the Yankees that summer and went 2–2, but his ERA was a horrible 8.10.

One of the best hitting pitchers of all time, Ferrell also had a major league brother in catcher Rick, who was elected to the Hall of Fame and had a long career as a baseball administrator after he retired. It was Wes, though, who was trying to prolong his playing days when he joined the Yankees. He gave it another try in 1939, but only went 1–2 for the Yankees in three games. By 1942, having won just two more major league games for a total of 193, Ferrell was player-manager for Lynchburg in the Virginia League.

In the end, the signing of Ferrell was a gamble that didn't pan out for Barrow. Barrow had a little bit more luck with a fading veteran when he traded with the St. Louis Browns to obtain Oral Hildebrand, who during his best season of 16–11 with the Cleveland Indians in 1933 was chosen for baseball's first All-Star team.

Hildebrand, who attended Butler University and played on that school's national championship basketball team a decade before the NCAA conducted its first tournament, had one last good year in his right arm. Hildebrand gave the Yankees a 10–4 season in 1939 with a 3.06 earned run average.

Hildebrand pitched shutout ball in the first four innings against Cincinnati in the game-clinching fourth win in the '39 Series. But a year later he was finished, going 1–1 in 13 appearances to complete his ten-year career.

An incoming guy who was more of a blank slate, but who excited the Yankees on the mound, was the right-hander born in Morton, Mississippi, raised in Louisiana, and nicknamed "Swampy." After a two-game, 0–1 cup of coffee with New York in 1938 — at age 27 — Richard Atley Donald, who preferred Atley over Richard, made it to The Show in 1939 and stunned onlookers by going 12–0 to start his official rookie season.

12. The Search for Fresh Arms

Donald was given his first baseball glove at age eight by his father and supposedly responded, "I'm going to make you proud of me, paw, for some day I'll be pitching for the Yanks." Such syntax seems a long-shot for use by an elementary school student, and in 1918 it's hard to believe anyone in small-town Louisiana was enamored of a Yankees team playing about 1,200 miles away that was a perpetual second-division American League team.[6]

But for certain, Donald did live the rest of his life as if he had uttered those words and that the only thing that mattered was convincing the Yankees he was what they needed. He was not a hot prospect signed out of a college or after demonstrating his skill in a lower minor league. But he was known to scout Johnny Nee and in 1934 Nee brought Donald to meet Joe McCarthy, basically telling him he was from Louisiana and wanted to work out with the team. McCarthy authorized dressing Donald out in a uniform.

Reportedly, McCarthy made a little bit of fun of Nee, asking, "Is this another of those local wonders, or have you taken the trouble to find out if he has anything?"[7] Nee had seen Donald throw in college, but didn't like his stuff enough to offer a deal. Later, Nee's college coach wrote to Ed Barrow saying the kid deserved a chance, but no promises were made and the letter either disappeared into the round file or a very crowded file cabinet for as much good as it did Donald. Still, he did not give up.

In 1934, Donald believed in his ability so much that he took buses from Louisiana to St. Petersburg to gain his tryout, but arrived three months before spring training that March with little money. So he went to work in a grocery store until the Yankees pulled into town. That's how he supported his existence until he got to throw with New York. He worked out for three days, and on the fourth day McCarthy offered him a contract.

With three years at Louisiana Tech behind him, Donald had been working on a farm when he took the risk of his life trying to show he could fit in with the world champion baseball team. He pitched for Wheeling, Norfolk, Binghamton and Newark, battled arm injuries and at the wrong time the flu, as well, but always thought he would reach the majors.

Once, he said, he revisited the old grocery store and watched a replacement weigh out the sugar and thought, "Atley, no more of that for you."[8]

After finishing 17–7 at Newark in '38, Donald was in the Yankees' plans for 1939. He said he was working on an additional pitch, a fast curve, with the aid of Dickey. "Bill Dickey is coaching me every day and all of the other pitchers are giving me hints," Donald said. "It's a grand gang to be with. Everybody wants to help you. There isn't a mite of what you would call jealousy in the whole clubhouse."[9]

No matter the player's flair or talent, nobody ever foresees a rookie pitcher coming into the majors and setting a record. But Donald had won 12 in a row for the Binghamton Triplets and 14 in a row for Newark. So why was anybody surprised that he could win 12 in a row for the Yankees? Perhaps because no rookie had ever done it before, with the Yankees or any other major league club.

Donald did not lose a game until August of 1939 for the Yankees, when the kids were getting ready to go back to school. Donald gave up six of the runs in a 7–2 loss to the Detroit Tigers. Streak over. Donald finished 13–3 that season.

For the next six years, Donald put up winning records each season for the Yankees, once more, in 1944, winning as many as 13 games. His last season was 1945 and Donald's career record, all with New York, was 65–33.

One of the things that made Marius Russo so popular in New York was that he was local. Conflicting accounts have Russo born in Ozone Park, Queens or Brooklyn in 1914, but he spent his entire youth in New York's boroughs. Russo was playing first base in high school when his coach, Pinky Match, gave him a try on the mound. Russo struck out 16 hitters in his debut effort.

Signed by the Yankees out of Long Island University after two years at Brooklyn College, Russo was known as "The Kid From L.I." Russo said he learned a lot playing semi-pro baseball on Long Island while he was in college. Former Brooklyn Dodgers catcher Charles Hargreaves was the backstop for the Bushwicks in 1936 when Russo signed on.

"Working with Hargreaves was a great experience for me," Russo said. "He was smart, experienced in big-league ways, and he taught me a lot about pitching that I never learned in college ball. He taught me when to let go of the fast one and when to hold it back. An old catcher often knows what a pitcher can do and what he can't do. Hargreaves gave me a lot of pointers."[10]

A southpaw who excelled at Newark and made a good impression as a rookie in 1939, the Yankees hoped Russo might become the heir apparent

12. The Search for Fresh Arms

to Red Ruffing or Lefty Gomez in the rotation. The Yankees had also had good luck fielding several Italian players, though none had been pitchers. In his first season Russo showed considerable promise, going 8–3 with a 2.41 earned run average in 21 games. Scout Paul Krichell believed that the same fastball that attracted Russo's high school coach would pay off for the Yankees.

"Russo has one of the best fastballs of any young pitcher in the game," Krichell said. "He's not as fast as (Bob) Feller, nor as fast as was Gomez when Lefty first came to us, but Marius is plenty fast. Pitchers can't get anywhere with just a fastball, but no kid pitcher ever makes any real headway in the majors unless he has a real fastball to build his stock of trade on."[11]

Unlike some of the Yankees hurlers who made only cameo appearances on the big club's roster and had little impact on the team's ability to win, Russo became a regular in the New York rotation in 1940 and went 14–8. In 1941, when he made the All-Star team, he finished 14–10. His career interrupted by World War II, Russo pitched just one season for New York after coming back from the service and completed his career with a 45–34 record, all with the Yankees.

Ernie "Tiny" Bonham was playing for the Oakland Oaks in the Pacific Coast League when the Yankees signed him and assigned him to their new AAA team in Kansas City, a brain-child of George Weiss, who wanted to expand New York's minor-league farm system.

Joe McCarthy knew as well as anyone that Gomez was nearing the end of his star years and he lobbied the front office to find him more frontline starting pitchers following the conclusion of the four-year World Series run in 1939. Goofy finished 12–8 in 1940 and just 3–3 in nine appearances for New York in 1940.

"I had a bad arm and a bad side last season, but I'm OK now," Gomez said during the 1941 season. "I'd like to lay one bet, anyway. I'll bet nobody on this club works harder."[12] Gomez worked so hard that he acquired a knuckleball, a new weapon that he hoped would restore his A game.

"I'm fooling around with one," he said. "I beat the Browns with it. That and a slow curveball. I've had to go slow with it because my control hasn't been so good. The new stuff has helped. But the real reason I am doing better this year than I did last is that I feel better. I weigh 167 pounds and I never felt better."

One thing Gomez disliked in the off-season was hearing trade rumors that included his name. "Every time I picked up a paper last winter I read where I was going," he said. "I went to Boston ... to Brooklyn ... to St. Louis ... to Newark. I sure got around, didn't I?"[13] Sure enough, Gomez had not forgotten all he knew about pitching and went 15–5 for the Yankees in 1941.

Bonham, meanwhile, made a splash with the Yankees in 1940, going 9–3 with a 1.90 earned run average in 12 games. McCarthy had been worried about his pitching since spring training, but falling behind in the pennant race convinced him he had to make a late-season move. That's when he summoned Bonham from Kansas City.

"There's no doubt he was the best pitcher in the league the last six weeks," McCarthy said. "Too bad we didn't send for him before."[14] Bonham went 9–6 in 1941. But by 1942, he was the ace of the staff, with a 21–5 record, an ERA of 2.27 and six shutouts. He was 6-foot-2, 215 pounds and strong.

During his early minor-league days with Akron, in 1936, the one-time football lover was a one-pitch wonder. He threw just a fastball and hoped it was blinding enough to fool the hitters. That only works for so long and is less of a strategy than a death wish as a pitcher moves up the ladder.

Once Bonham learned how to throw a forkball, however, he was onto something special. "I picked up a forkball, but my control was nothing to brag about until 1940," Bonham said. "Guess that bum back of mine made me wild. When that was cured I found myself able to throw the ball just about where I wanted to pitch it."[15]

It was a break for the Yankees, who needed new talent on the mound, and in 1941 Bonham, whose nickname of "Tiny" contradicted his size, was just about the most dominant pitcher in the American League.

13

New Guys on the Block

The challenge was always to improve the club. Colonel Jacob Ruppert set a high standard and he didn't have to repeat his philosophy of winning being the goal at all times very often. Ed Barrow was on board, knew the ins and outs of the trading market and had tremendous confidence in his scouting staff.

Ruppert and the Yankees were not satisfied with one World Series title in 1936. As Roy Johnson so unceremoniously found out as he was given his exit papers, the owner did want to win every game. The last three seasons of Ruppert's life, the Yankees did win the American League pennant and the World Series, in 1936, 1937, and 1938.

He passed away in January of 1939 and the Yankees won it all that year, as well, making four world titles in a row.

No matter how many miles they put on their automobiles, no matter how much research they did, and no matter how many players they looked at, the scouts were not going to provide a Joe DiMaggio out of the minors every year. The mark of a good scout is how many of his players become major leaguers. That means they have helped the big club. They may not all be stars, but if they were good enough to make the roster at some point, it was the right decision to sign them.

The scouts looked for the raw talent that might develop into something special. Barrow looked for other teams' castoffs and considered whether they might shore up a weaker position on the Yankees or be worthwhile fill-ins for a year or so while the best young players at Newark or Kansas City honed their skills to be ready for a future call-up.

Sometimes you just couldn't tell if a player was going to become an All-Star or stall out as a back-up. It was a roll of the dice, but the tribute to the Yankees was that they could pretty much keep rolling at the top of the league with their formidable lineup and their just-strong-enough pitching while tossing in the occasional newcomer. Of course, the Yankees had more money than other teams to spend on players, too.

The financial muscle allowed New York to sign more prospects, and the Yankees' reputation was a psychological aid when approaching a young player. The player's eyes might light up at the mention of the Yankees. He was already envisioning himself patrolling Yankee Stadium and competing for a championship team. Rarely did a player picture being held down in the farm system for five years before he got his shot at the majors, because players had so much confidence they didn't think that way. Give them a year, maybe two, they believed, and they would be in the Yanks' lineup alongside DiMaggio or Gehrig.

But that was the other thing about the Yankees. They had so much depth they could afford to stock pile talented players at Newark (where that team won seven pennants in ten years at AAA) who might have been useful additions to other teams.

The cries of "Break Up The Yankees" were a trifle misguided. Ruppert, Barrow and McCarthy were more or less always breaking up the Yankees. There were always personnel changes, even if they were made around the edges of the roster rather than at its core.

DiMaggio wasn't going anywhere. The only way he wouldn't be in center field was if he pulled a muscle or broke a bone. As for Gehrig, he had been at first base forever. Heck, he predated McCarthy by years. Gehrig had been located at first base so long he had to pay taxes. Not to mention Bill Dickey, who spent more time in New York behind the plate than he did inside the walls of his Arkansas home.

There might be five or six All-Stars in the lineup, counting the starting pitcher on a given day, but the New York brass worked tirelessly to upgrade. You could build something special once and win it all, but you couldn't win year after year by resting on your laurels or taking any time off. The world never stopped spinning, players never reversed the aging process, and things like hangnails, pulled muscles, financial or family problems that could disturb the mind happened in the off-season. Baseball was not a static business. On paper a team might look the same from one year to the next, but that was the thing, no two years were alike.

Ruppert and Barrow were originally just employer and employee in their relationship. But the longer they worked together, the more suc-

13. New Guys on the Block

cess they engendered, the closer they became until they eventually took vacations together to French Lick, Indiana, where they could enjoy the spas and talk baseball. No one thought for a minute that the duo expressed more intense interest in steam baths, long walks in the shade, or dining on fine cuisine than trying to find ways to enhance the chances of winning.

Barrow was the heartbeat of the Yankees' operation and the conduit between Ruppert's money invested wisely and Ruppert's less-disciplined enthusiasm. Barrow's building of the Yankees, one sportswriter noted, was consistent with the pattern of his entire life. "He rolled up his sleeves and he went to work, surrounded himself with the best men he could find ... and saw to it they worked as hard as he did." He also took one look at the way money flowed from Ruppert into the franchise and shook his head at the imprudent spending. "If your brewery and your real estate business were conducted along the lines of your ball club, you would go broke in no time," he informed Ruppert.[1]

Not even Barrow or his sharp-eyed scouts could read what was inside of a man. Nor could they tell the future to determine if he would stay healthy. They hired the young players, sent them out for seasoning, or plucked them from another team's rejects, and gave them the best chance to succeed.

As is the case in every minor-league operation, most were never seen by a big-league audience. The small percentage kept moving up and got a crack at the Yankees. Some became famous. Some became items stashed in Joe McCarthy's tool box, to be brought out in times of need for special roles. If they were great, McCarthy embraced them. If they were good, he kept them, and tried to find a good excuse to justify their use on the 25-man (or in some years 23) roster.

Shortstop Bill Knickerbocker had better years for other teams, but between 1938 and 1940 he helped the Yankees win two World Series. Sort of. The 5-foot-11, 170-pound infielder didn't play in more than 46 games during his three seasons in New York and although his lifetime average over 10 years was .276 he never hit better than .250 for the Yankees.

Warren Vincent "Buddy" Rosar of Buffalo, New York, was a much different case from most of the spare parts the Yankees tried to mesh into their lineup. He recorded an extraordinary .387 season for the Newark Bears, winning the International League batting title, and was brought up to the Yankees in 1939. He was a member of that World Series title team, but didn't get into any of the games. In 1940, Rosar hit for the cycle in a game against the Indians.

In four years with the Yankees, Rosar never played in more than 73 games. He mostly backed up Bill Dickey, but in his first three Yankees years Rosar produced solid .276, .298 and .287 averages. What made Rosar extra special was his glove work. He was a terrific fielding catcher and although he only once again matched the type of average he compiled for the Yankees in those early years, Rosar became a five-time All-Star. All except one of those years were for other teams, however. Two of Rosar's most successful years came during World War II when he was able to play.

At one point during the war, Rosar asked McCarthy for permission to return to Buffalo to take the policeman's exam so he could perform an essential home-front service and be near his pregnant wife. Dickey had a shoulder injury so McCarthy said no. Rosar went anyway and when he rejoined the Yankees, rather than being tabbed as Dickey's long-term replacement, he was dropped to third-string. The next year, 1943, Rosar was playing for the Cleveland Indians, which at least was near Buffalo.

When Joe McCarthy said no, he meant it. And when Joe McCarthy wanted you punished for insubordination, he did the job, or collaborated with Ed Barrow.

The beneficiary of Rosar's decline in stature was Rollie Hemsley. Hemsley was nicknamed "Rollicking Rollie," and had played for the Pirates, Reds, Cubs, Browns, Indians and Reds again by the time the Yankees signed him. Hemsley was a five-time All-Star in a 19-year career, but although his ability was acknowledged, his dependence on alcohol spoiled his connections with several teams.

Behaving out of control when he was drunk, Hemsley picked fights with strangers and frequently got beat up. "I had so many black eyes," he said, "that some of my friends thought I was born with them."[2]

Most often, whether it was in formal boxing matches that he lost, losing his dignity, costing himself jobs and money, teammates and teams, Hemsley hurt himself most by his drinking. It was embarrassing to baseball teams that counted on Hemsley and explained why a man of his skills was no longer wanted in so many places where he stopped.

Early in his career, before the extent of his drinking was known, Hemsley was a highly touted player. Rogers Hornsby, the Hall of Fame second baseman, in 1935 gave Hemsley the greatest of compliments.

"Ralston Hemsley ought to be the greatest catcher in baseball," the Rajah said.[3]

If baseball writers and experts were puzzled by the up-and-down nature of Hemsley's contributions and why he got into trouble with the law in connection with a brouhaha, they weren't yet making mention of Hemsley's involvement with alcohol. His erratic temperament was talked about instead.

Hemsley began the 1942 season with the Reds, but after McCarthy's contretemps with Rosar he shopped around for an immediate replacement. Cincinnati had dumped Hemsley because he was hitting .113, and McCarthy found him in his apartment and telephoned.

The catcher didn't even believe it was really McCarthy on the line at first. McCarthy wanted to know if Hemsley could get to Yankee Stadium in time for the next day's game. "You'll have to catch a double-header," McCarthy said. "For you, I'll catch a triple-header and ask no questions," Hemsley said.[4]

So how did the peripatetic catcher do in that double-header? He went 5-for-8 at the plate. He started out 10-for-17, including a four-hit day against the Indians. "Don't wake me up," Hemsley said. "Let me dream."[5]

Hemsley played 31 games for New York and made critical contributions. By the time Hemsley was signed by the Yankees he realized he had a drinking problem and made moves to combat it and straighten out his life away from the ballpark.

It was once catalogued that Hemsley was the 77th member of Alcoholics Anonymous, which was founded in 1935. After his problems with the Indians, two men from the organization introduced themselves to Hemsley and persuaded him to attend an AA meeting in Akron. His connection with AA paid off and Helmsley learned how to stay sober.

"I wasn't the kind who could take a drink or two and go on my way," Hemsley said. "I just drank and drank. Many a time I'd have to take a cold shower before putting on my uniform. And a lot of times I was in terrible shape."[6]

One of the main premises of Alcoholics Anonymous is that meetings, counseling, and contacts remain anonymous. The belief is that many more people will take advantage of the program if their involvement remains secret. Hemsley chose to break the bonds of secrecy in 1940 because he felt he could help more people in dire straits by bringing attention to alcoholism and showing that even professional athletes could be afflicted by the disease.

Hemsley played part-time for the Yankees in 1943 and was the regular catcher in 1944 until called into the service. Drafted by the Army, Hemsley ended up being inducted into the Navy, after playing 81 games his last active year with New York.

The natural evolution of the roster, coupled with the start of World War II in 1941 and players enlisting or being drafted, gave eligible players a better shot at making the Yankees roster than at any time during the 1930s.

Johnny Lindell had been a knuckleball pitcher in the Yankees' organization and in 1941 he even compiled a 23–4 record in Newark. That was an attention-getter that seemed to announce he deserved a chance with the Yanks. Lindell got that opportunity to stick with New York in 1942 and in 23 games he finished 2–1 with a 3.74 earned run average.

However, Lindell looked worse than his record and more surprising as a pitcher with a good stick. Pondering the loss of players to the military and Lindell's iffy prospects on the mound, McCarthy converted Lindell into an outfielder. "I know he can hit," McCarthy said, "but I don't know if he can hit playing every day."[7]

Lindell, who had played some outfield in the minors, ended up in 122 games in '43 and batted .245 with 51 RBI. A year later he truly proved he could handle the switch, batting .300 in 149 games with 18 home runs and 103 RBI. Not bad for a pitcher.

Roy Cullenbine was born in Nashville, Tennessee, but grew up in Detroit where as a youngster he was the batboy for the Tigers. The switch-hitting outfielder and first baseman played ten years in the majors, but nothing matched his 1942 season for adventure.

In 1941, representing the St. Louis Browns, Cullenbine put together his finest all-around performance. He batted .317 with 98 RBI, had a .452 on-base-percentage and was chosen for the American League All-Star team. However, after playing 38 games in 1942 and slumping to a .193 average, Cullenbine was shipped to the Washington Senators. Despite hitting .286 in 64 games for the Senators, Cullenbine was released.

That's when the Yankees picked him up for the stretch run following Tommy Henrich's departure for the Coast Guard. Cullenbine batted .364 in 21 games for New York and earned the starting right field position in the 1942 World Series against the St. Louis Cardinals.

"Cullenbine is not the most graceful outfielder in the world," McCarthy said, "but he can run, and has done some fine hitting for us."[8] Cullenbine was just a stop-gap hire, but he helped the Yankees in the World Series. By the next year he had been traded to Cleveland.

Much like Cullenbine, the acquisition of Buddy Hassett, who was New York–raised and spent three years at Manhattan College, after he played six seasons with the Brooklyn Dodgers and the temporarily named Boston Bees (soon to revert to Braves), was a hire for need.

He was a known commodity, previously buried in the New York farm system so deeply—and with Gehrig rooted at first in the majors, too— that he asked to be traded to get a chance to play somewhere. The Yankees complied with the request, but not before Hassett ran into Gehrig at an event and the incumbent said, "They're talking about you taking my job." Hassett merely laughed at the suggestion. "Hey, don't worry about that. The way you play, I'll never take your job. All I want to do is get to the major leagues."[9]

The Yanks were trying to squeeze out those pennants and World Series championships in 1942. In his other major league stops, Hassett had been known for his yodeling and singing of "Home on the Range," but he rightly sensed that McCarthy was not a yodeling kind of guy and that he might well tick off the hard-nosed manager if he tried to entertain the troops with his tonsils.

John Aloysius Hassett was not a power hitter, but he was terribly difficult for twirlers to strike out. In 1936, Hassett struck out just 17 times in 635 at-bats. Many years later Hassett explained that when he was in the minors he trained himself to hit for average more than home runs because that's what teams were looking for at the time. So he made himself into a contact hitter.

"I decided then to try to meet the ball and I guess I cut down on the bat a little bit," Hassett said. "I had a little bit of the bat hanging out of the bottom of my hands, so I had better control of the barrel of the bat. It's a matter of eyes and muscle control, but I always tried to get a piece of the ball."[10]

Hassett's lifetime average was .292, including .284 for the Yankees in 132 games in 1942. In Brooklyn, in 1940, Hassett had stroked ten consecutive hits. At one point for New York, Hassett had a 20-game hitting streak, but it was shut down by the Tigers' Dizzy Trout. "I deserved to be stopped by the way I was going after bad balls," Hassett said. "I played the sucker up there twice when I might have gotten a hit."[11]

Hassett played three games in the 1942 World Series against the Cardinals, hitting .333, before a thumb injury benched him and left New York with no regular first baseman.

After waiting out the last chunk of Lou Gehrig's career in a kind of exile, Hassett got to play just one season at first base for the Yankees because of World War II. Just as he was about to be drafted into the Army, he enlisted in the Navy. Barrow said goodbye in his own way. "I thought we had a first baseman for a couple more years," the boss said as his player departed.[12]

When Hassett went off to war, the Yankees introduced Nick Etten as the new first baseman in 1943. He was the seventh to try the position since Gehrig relinquished the job in 1939, and he made some friends with timely hitting. Etten had made a tour of Philadelphia, with the Athletics and Phillies both, since making his major league debut in 1938. Playing in all 154 games, Etten, a one-time attendee of Villanova University, knocked in 107 runs, by far his most to date, and hit .271 for New York once given the starting job for 1943.

Etten brought smiles to faces with his bat and heartburn to chests with his fielding. He committed 17 errors in his first season with New York and never got much better. A wiseacre player once said Etten's glove fielded much better without him wearing it.

Etten was a better hitter than he ever had been before versus major league hurling. For one thing, he changed his stance, he said. For another, he got more and better advice with the Yankees. "It's being with the Yankees," he said of the fundamental reason for his hitting improvement. "The company you keep in baseball is important. Our team is not just a winning ball club. It's a family. I came in from another league, overawed. I wasn't sure of my reception. But (Joe) Gordon, (Charlie) Keller, Dickey, and the rest, took me in. I was a member, from the first day."[13]

For awhile, New York would try anyone at first base if he brought a glove and an eager attitude. Before Etten, there was also Jerry Priddy, though only for ten games. In his two years in New York, Priddy bounced around the other infield positions. The rest of his 11-year career he played second base with other teams.

The 5-foot-11, 180-pound transplant from Los Angeles broke in with the Yankees in 1941, hitting .213 in 56 games. He did a bit better the next year, hitting .280 in 59 games.

Priddy did not ingratiate himself with Yankees management very well, criticizing Joe McCarthy for not playing him more. Not a savvy approach for a 21-year-old.

"He was convinced the big leagues needed him," a sportswriter said of the young player's attitude upon reviewing Priddy's career years later.[14] McCarthy tested Priddy in various infield positions for two years, listening to him gripe for two summers, and wished him luck getting the chance to play more when he sent him to the Washington Senators for the 1943 season. No, Priddy was not going to be the next Lou Gehrig, Joe Gordon, Tony Lazzeri, or Red Rolfe.

Those types of players, as Jacob Ruppert, Ed Barrow and Joe McCarthy knew, did not become available — even to the Yankees — every day.

14

Gehrig and the Other Babe

The ordeal of Lou Gehrig, and one of the saddest chapters in the history of American sport, began late in the 1938 season. No one pinpointed the minute, or even the day, but the signs of physical deterioration in one of baseball's most prominent specimens became subtly apparent.

Gehrig joined the Yankees for limited action in 1923 and 1924. He hit .423 in 13 games at age 20 in 1923 and hit .500 in ten games in 1924. By 1925, he was New York's regular first baseman, replacing Wally Pipp, and on his way to one of the best careers of all time. Even more than 70 years after Gehrig's last game, most people consider him to be the best first baseman in history.

Starting in 1926, Gehrig hit between .300 and .379 every year through 1937. Gehrig hit as many as 49 home runs in a year—twice—and drove in as many as 184 runs. He and Babe Ruth formed the grandest one-two punch in a lineup ever in 1927. Ruth hit his record 60 home runs in 1927, but under rules of the time, he was ineligible to win the Most Valuable Player Award a second time. (He won it in 1923.) This year it was Gehrig's turn.

Gehrig amassed his famous 2,130-game playing streak between 1925 and 1939, a mark that was baseball's seemingly unbreakable record until Cal Ripken Jr. of the Baltimore Orioles eclipsed it in 1995 and set a new record of playing in 2,632 straight games. Gehrig's streak gave him the nickname "The Iron Horse." He was as reliable as any large hunk of machinery and seemingly as indestructible.

Even as he aged, Gehrig showed no signs of dropping off in performance until the latter portion of the 1938 season. The great Yankees of that time period were marching to a third straight pennant and World Series, and Gehrig was playing well enough and surrounded by great talent. So manager Joe McCarthy had no reason to worry when Gehrig's hitting slumped.

14. Gehrig and the Other Babe

In 1938, Gehrig hit 29 home runs, drove in 114 runs and batted .295. He also walked 107 times and had a .410 on-base percentage. Almost anyone in the game would have been happy with such a season. Of course Gehrig played in every game, as well.

Alarmingly, however, Gehrig began dropping things around the dugout and clubhouse. No one could offer a reason for that, but no one suspected there was anything major wrong with Gehrig. No hitter had ever maintained his peak years much beyond his mid- to late-30s, so some thought it might just be that time was catching up to Gehrig. He was 35 before the end of the 1938 season. Some players experienced gradual declines in their skills. Some fell apart all at once. You couldn't tell about these things.

Gehrig actually started the 1938 season poorly. He had a particular relish and fondness for opening day and loved it when the games started to count in the standings. But he went hitless in the opener, went 0-for-7 in a doubleheader, and those horse collar days weren't as rare as they used to be. The always determined, but usually quiet Gehrig burst out in anger after one of his oh-for days. "Every time up there, it's something else," he said.[1]

What Gehrig, and a few close observers, started to notice was that some of the long hits that used to result in homers were being caught in the outfield. A couple of weeks into the season, Gehrig's average bottomed out at .109, the lowest mark in the league. McCarthy moved him to sixth in the order while saying he expected Gehrig to regroup and come back hitting as well as ever, and then move right back into the clean-up spot.

After this worrisome stretch, Gehrig did start to hit with his old authority, building his average with a hot May, though still not hitting homers with the same frequency.

Gehrig still held onto his starting position, but he was lifted from games early when necessary. Another hard-to-explain problem kept surfacing. Gehrig began having regular painful twitches in his lower back that made it hard for him to breathe. "It's just a cold," Gehrig said. "The only difference is it doesn't come out on me. It settles in my back."[2]

Gehrig was fighting physical ills, but didn't believe they were serious. His frustration showed through, especially at home, and he seemed weary and achy. Wife Eleanor suggested that Gehrig take a day off, stop his streak at 1,999 straight. She told him it would be more memorable. Whether she concocted the plan of him staying home for a day and taking a break from baseball for this peculiar idea of notoriety, or really because she wanted him to use it as an excuse to rest, is not known for sure, although she was protective of her husband.

But no way was Gehrig skipping out on a day in the lineup. He was like a factory worker punching the clock, or a businessman opening his store. It was Gehrig's job to play baseball and as long as his body allowed it he was going to show up on time and be available if the manager wanted him. McCarthy was never going to say he didn't want Lou Gehrig, and Lou Gehrig was never going to sit around on his bum and fail to be available to help his teammates.

"I couldn't," he told his wife.[3]

At Yankee Stadium, photographers and teammates made a big deal of Gehrig's 2,000th consecutive game, on May 31, but the accomplishment wasn't even announced to the fans. Sportswriters were asked, in light of his slump, if it made sense to go on playing every day without rest. Later, when he was going through his own slump with minor, everyday injuries, Ripken was asked the same questions.

Gehrig said he couldn't imagine himself sitting in the dugout watching a game when he knew he should play. "The worrying and fretting would take too much out of me."[4]

So he stayed in the lineup and played every day — just not as well as before — as the Yankees, fewer and fewer of them left from the good old days of the 1920s, worked their way towards another pennant and what became a brushing aside of the Chicago Cubs in the World Series.

Gehrig was a player who had absorbed the aphorism "the legs go first." He believed it. He was a broad-shouldered man with powerful legs and he did not sense any weakness in his legs. He also could hear and see pretty well and listened closely to conversations where his name was dropped as a player just hanging on, or eyed those types of insinuations in newspapers. Gehrig protested that his legs were as strong as ever. "When they begin to fail, I will be the first to know about it, and I will be the first to know when the end of my playing days is near," he said.[5]

Unfortunately, that day was approaching faster than either Gehrig or anyone around him recognized. The first cry was for Gehrig to take a rest, not take out retirement papers. He was holding on to what he had and to the record he was adding to daily. Gehrig was not admitting that he was through. He was clinging to the streak as a motivating tool to stay in the lineup.

McCarthy was in a tricky position. He was Gehrig's boss and could bench him at any time. But this was a man who had been a mainstay for him during his entire career with the Yankees. Gehrig had never created trouble like that out-of-control Ruth. He had won so many games for New York that neither an abacus nor an adding machine could compute an accurate figure. And then there was the record. Every time Gehrig suited up for the starting lineup, he made history.

What McCarthy hoped to do was instill fresh confidence in Gehrig and hope that he rebounded. "I wouldn't take Lou out even if he asked me," McCarthy said during the summer of 1938. "Sure, he's not hitting the ball the way he should. But let the others take up the slack."[6]

They didn't really have to, given that Gehrig ended the season with an average near .300 after his terrible start, just shy of 30 homers, and with those 114 RBI. In Gehrig's mind his slump was over and he would be much better the next year.

Lord knows what types of bodily changes Gehrig felt during the off-season, or what he told his wife, but he did not seek expert medical care and reported to the Yankees as usual at St. Petersburg to prepare for the 1939 season.

The sunshine of a Florida spring is supposed to be invigorating, but for Gehrig spring training that February and March was just about the worst time of his life. The timing of his swing was off and he couldn't hit. He stumbled on the base paths running between bases. He did not hit a home run. And he was very tired all of the time.

Yet most of what takes place in spring training is discarded once the regular season begins. For Gehrig, spring training was a nightmare, a continuation, and a worsening of the problems he started having the season before. Sportswriters said the decline of his baseball skills was so extreme as to be shocking.

Few players witnessed the erosion of their talents so visibly and swiftly. During his streak Gehrig played through a broken toe, broken thumb, broken ribs, a twisted back, lumbago and a variety of basic illnesses like colds.

Gehrig's swing in spring training did not resemble that of a man with a lifetime average of .341. Teammates concerned about Gehrig's health were afraid he might not have the reflexes to get out of the way of a high, inside fastball, or might misjudge a line drive in the field. He'd had gall bladder problems over the winter and his coordination seemed off in the field, including poor throwing.

"He was the team captain," said outfielder George Selkirk, "our leader. We all looked up to Lou for leadership. We just took him for granted. But by 1939 we knew something was wrong with Lou. But nobody knew what it was."[7]

Still, Gehrig started the season at first base after the Yankees broke camp. After so long relying on his athletic build and smooth abilities, Gehrig had to hope that they would come through for him again, that he wasn't finished as a player.

He played throughout April and unlike the previous season when he corrected any hitting flaws and ended his slump ,Gehrig could not get hits to help the team. He was 4-for-28 by the end of the month with one RBI. Gehrig, as always, was on first on April 29, 1939, when the Yankees met the Washington Senators at Yankee Stadium.

Gehrig came into the batter's box in the fourth inning and stroked a single. There were only 11,473 people in the house on one of those unseasonably cool days that don't recognize that spring has arrived on the calendar, and the clouds made it seem likely to rain. Gehrig had already walked in the game, making it a rare occasion when he reached base twice safely in the same contest at that early stage of what was soon to be revealed as a life-threatening illness.

The next day Gehrig had an 0-for-4 game that got him thinking about removing himself from the starting lineup. After contemplating the situation for days, Gehrig knew it was time to give up his playing streak and take a break, leaving it to his own resurgence or McCarthy's judgment when to re-insert him in the lineup.

On May 2, 1939, Gehrig went to McCarthy and told him he should start someone else at first base. It marked the end of an era, for sure, the end of a streak that no one thought would be broken, for certain, and the beginning of the end of Gehrig's baseball career and, before too long, his life.

After the lineup for that day's game was revealed, Gehrig met with sportswriters to discuss the change. He said he long ago had decided that if he was hurting the team he would bench himself, and after his poor hitting month to start the season, it had come to that.

"I haven't been a bit of good to the team since the season started," Gehrig said. "It wouldn't be fair to the boys, to Joe, or to the baseball public for me to try going on," Gehrig said. "In fact, it would not be fair to myself and I'm the last consideration."[8]

Gehrig was unaware of why he couldn't perform well, the way he had as recently as parts of the last summer. He did not understand why he seemed to suffer minor ailments. He could not figure out why he was starting to feel like an old man at 35. Teammates, who did not know what was happening to him either, believed Gehrig had simply lost his skills, although rather abruptly, and didn't think he should be out on the field, if only for safety reasons. "It had to happen," outfielder Charlie Keller said of Gehrig's removal from the starting lineup. "Lou could hardly defend himself anymore."[9]

Imagine the blow to such a star's pride, a man of such will that he had ignored injuries and the normal wear-and-tear on the body to play every single day for years without interruption. He wasn't even permitted to age gracefully, to wind down slowly, as so many other stars had. With Gehrig it was a snap of the fingers and his talent had evaporated.

"It's tough to see your mates on base, have a chance to win a ball game, and not be able to do anything about it," Gehrig said. "McCarthy has been swell about it all the time. He'd let me go until the cows came home. He is that considerate of my feelings, but I knew in Sunday's game I should get out of there."[10]

Even with his powers reduced so suddenly, Gehrig is the fifth-leading RBI man in history with 1,995. Usually, when Gehrig strode to the plate with men on base, pitchers cowered. Instead, in the game he referred to he had four chances at the plate with runners on and didn't knock in any of them, and New York lost the game. "A hit would have won the ball game for the Yankees, but I missed, leaving five stranded as the Yankees lost," Gehrig said. "Maybe a rest will do me some good. Maybe it won't. Who knows? Who can tell? I'm just hoping."[11]

There was no reason why Gehrig should not have felt rested after the off-season. He was just reaching for any explanation, and the hopeless nature of his monologue was both poignant and illustrated how he did not have any knowledge that would help him regain his strength and top-notch hitting stroke.

The day that Lou Gehrig skipped a turn at first base, Joe McCarthy wrote the name of Ellsworth Tenney "Babe" Dahlgren into the lineup as a replacement and made him the answer to an enduring trivia question.

Born in 1912, Dahlgren broke into the majors in 1935 with the Boston Red Sox. The Yankees acquired him in 1937, when he played just one game for New York. In 1938, Dahlgren sneaked into the lineup for 27 games. Being the back-up first-baseman for the New York Yankees when Lou Gehrig held the job was not so different from being Babe Ruth's roommate in his hey-day. You almost never got in on the action.

That changed in 1939, of course. Dahlgren played in 144 games, hit 15 home runs and knocked in 89 runs, which was very respectable duty considering how much pressure he was under. However, his batting average was only .235. The next season Dahlgren played in 155 games, all of the regularly scheduled ones plus one re-scheduled game, hit 12 home runs with 73 runs batted in and an improved .264 average.

Although Dahlgren had a 12-year major league career, that was his swan song in New York. The Yankees shipped him to the Boston Bees (Braves) for the 1941 season and took some grief from fans that missed his magnificent glove. Dahlgren joined the Navy in 1943 in the U.S. war effort.

At one point in 1940, Dahlgren was in a deep enough slump that McCarthy mulled moving Tommy Henrich from the infield to first. But Dahlgren rallied with seven straight hits to save his job. Dahlgren had one thing going for him as a bonus, too. He was an exceptional fielder who could make plays on balls many first basemen couldn't reach. One sportswriter said Dahlgren was the finest fielding first baseman in New York since Hal Chase made the city his home in 1913.

Dahlgren was very careful not to say that he was Gehrig's replacement, even the next season when Gehrig wasn't around the team. The word successor suited him better. "I never expect to be a Gehrig, or anything close to him," Dahlgren said. "If I can make myself a good, strong member of the team that will be satisfaction enough for me." Dahlgren said he was nervous in 1939 when given the job and it was clear that Gehrig still hoped he could regain his old spot. "I tried so hard to make good that I made a botch of things generally."[12] The mess he made of things was his batting average, but McCarthy realized that Dahlgren had other skills and he hoped his average would increase the next season, which it did.

Dahlgren once said that he came across a baseball article commenting on his succession of Gehrig at first that called him "the little-known Babe Dahlgren." He said, "I'm just glad to be remembered at all. I hated to break his streak."[13]

As a baseball fan growing up in San Francisco, Dahlgren had a scrapbook full of pictures of Ruth and Gehrig. Dahlgren took over for Gehrig against the Detroit Tigers and New York won, 22–2, that day. Dahlgren hit a home run, a double and had two deep fly-outs, but that was not what he recalled most clearly about that day.

McCarthy had Gehrig carry the lineup card to the umpires at home plate, and when he returned to the dugout he went straight to the water cooler for the longest drink of water Dahlgren ever saw. "He started to cry," Dahlgren said. "Lou stood there with a towel on his head."[14]

Not even then did Gehrig's Yankees teammates want to believe that Gehrig was finished as a player, especially not his long-time roommate and friend Bill Dickey. "Certainly I am far from happy over Lou's going to the bench," the All-Star catcher said. "But the day comes to all of us, and besides, who's to say that he's finished? I never saw a big man lose his power the way Gehrig did. He hit the ball pretty well, but the ball didn't go anywhere. For himself and the club he did the best thing stepping out."[15]

Dahlgren said the team sensed Gehrig would cease playing soon. He had switched to using a Joe Gordon bat, one of the lightest anyone had in the rack, and sometimes it appeared Gehrig had difficulty straightening up to his full height.

Diplomacy and statements of loyalty to a man who had given so much to his teammates, to his team, and to the city that loved him for his play and his character, were the order of the day. Only Lefty Gomez, who had a quip for every occasion, dared to make a joke to Gehrig. "Well, Lou," said Gomez, "here you are starting your career all over again. You've got to learn to sit on the bench, just as you did until June 2, 1925. It took you 15 years to get out of the game and very often it takes me only 15 minutes."[16]

Although Dahlgren had one of the toughest acts to follow in baseball history, and his average was one of the worst of his career, his other skills did help the Yankees win an American League pennant and a World Series. On the train back to New York after the championship was recorded, McCarthy took the opportunity to give advice to Dahlgren about not chasing bad balls and building his image with sportswriters.

"Why don't you fellows give Babe some credit," McCarthy asked a couple of writers. "This fellow is entitled to a better break. Don't forget, he had a hard man to follow. He stepped in right behind Lou Gehrig, one of the greatest first basemen that ever lived, and played a whale of a game. Just as I said to him, he isn't the hitter he should be because he hits at too many bad balls. But he made plenty of hits just the same and drove in plenty of runs. What else does a fellow have to do to get a tumble from you?"[17]

15

Diagnosis and Death

By the time Lou Gehrig yanked himself out of the New York Yankees lineup he had been thinking over his demoralizing situation for two days.

Gehrig recorded his last hit on April 29, 1939. He distressingly flubbed his chances to drive in runs in the Yankees' April 30 game. Then the team had an off-day. Rather than spend the travel day to Detroit trying to take his mind off things with amusements like the World's Fair in New York and President Franklin D. Roosevelt's ceremonial opening of the grand party, Gehrig harshly reviewed his own circumstances.

It has been famously told that one of the incidents that stung Gehrig most greatly was his teammates applauding, cheering a play he made in the field in the April 30 game. What bothered Gehrig was that it had been a routine play and what they were really doing was indulging him. "They don't think I can do it anymore," Gehrig told his wife Eleanor. "Maybe I can, maybe I can't. But they're talking about it now, they're even writing about it."[1]

Gehrig came to a firm conclusion. He had to end his playing streak, which reached 2,130 straight games, on Sunday, because his presence in the lineup was hurting the ball club. Manager Joe McCarthy, who had traveled separately from New York to Detroit, with a stop-over in his home town of Buffalo, ran into Gehrig in the lobby of the Book Cadillac Hotel.

The player was lobby sitting, reading a newspaper to kill time, when he spotted McCarthy. He approached his manager, told him he had something important to discuss, and they went to McCarthy's room. After a bellhop left, Gehrig told the boss to take him out of the lineup.

McCarthy returned to the lobby, gathered the traveling sportswriters around, and made the announcement. "It's a black day for me, and the Yankees," McCarthy said.[2]

After the jolt of Gehrig sitting out a game took hold and Babe Dahlgren began starting, Gehrig stayed around the team, but more as a haunting presence. He did not regain his physical sharpness, so any attempt to hit was met with failure.

To a large extent, Gehrig had played the macho man role and mostly ignored his condition during the previous off-season. During the winter between the 1938 and 1939 season, he had gone to the doctor and had a physical examination. He was diagnosed with gall bladder problems. Gall bladder difficulties can cause fevers and sharp pain in the stomach, but would not make a strong man like Gehrig permanently weak or cause him to stumble as he walked or ran. Still, a prescription of a healthier diet focused on eating fruits and vegetables made Gehrig believe that's all it would take to cure his ills.

That all might have been good for Gehrig's gall bladder, but his gall bladder was not his main concern. No matter how many apples he ate, he wasn't going to keep the doctor at bay. The cause of Gehrig's fall from superb athlete to someone who might make a mis-step and bump into a wall at any time was completely alarming to the player, who had relied on his body his entire life for his favorite activities and to make a living. He told some players that he was just getting weaker and weaker.

Neither McCarthy nor Yankee teammates, neither sportswriters nor others around the team made any public proclamations about Gehrig being sick. They may have had suppositions, but not even Gehrig knew what was wrong with him, so no one suggested illness was at the root of his problems.

At the beginning of June, word leaked out that Gehrig was thinking of going to the Mayo Clinic in Rochester, Minnesota, for a thorough checkup to solve the mystery of what ailed him. From the beginning of May on, even after he stopped playing first base, Gehrig traveled with the Yankees. It was a symbol, as if he might be ready to go at a moment's notice, as if one day all his physical woes would disappear and he would jump right back into the lineup.

On June 12, the Yankees played an exhibition game against their AAA minor-league affiliate, the Kansas City Blues, and Gehrig was in the lineup. When introduced to the crowd Gehrig received a standing ovation. When introduced to the pitcher, he was over-matched, and tapped a weak grounder to second. In the field, he was sloppy, dropping balls, and would have been charged with two errors if more serious scorekeeping was involved.

15. Diagnosis and Death

By then, Gehrig knew his condition was serious. He couldn't do the simplest things on the diamond any more. The next day Gehrig headed to Minnesota and before the end of the day he was at the Mayo Clinic, where the answers he got would shock not only him, but an entire nation.

All along, Gehrig said he was not having any pain, but just felt he was losing his strength. At first this was manifested in his baseball power. Gehrig had hit nearly 500 home runs, so he knew when wood met ball how it felt when the ball was destined to fly farther than the plane that brought him to Rochester. But for almost a year he was putting the same effort into his swing, without getting the same pop out of it. It was as if the real Lou Gehrig was being swallowed up by an outer shell Lou Gehrig that was melting.

Broad, strong shoulders, powerful hands, and muscled legs were all characteristic of Lou Gehrig of the New York Yankees, but this substitute Lou Gehrig had been wasting away, losing muscle, strength, power, and definitely weight.

The doctor who first examined Gehrig at the clinic recognized almost immediately what Gehrig was suffering from, a neurological wasting disease called amyotrophic lateral sclerosis. Not only was the doctor knowledgeable enough to see tell-tale symptoms in muscle twitching, but his own mother had died from the disease.

The doctor did not tell Gehrig right away. After all, the diagnosis was a death sentence, and he did not want to move too quickly, or without additional testing to make completely sure. It would take a more conclusive diagnosis by a neurologist before the information would be given to Gehrig. After their initial impressions and assumptions, something the doctors would have been happy to disprove, by the process of elimination they ruled out illness after illness.

One of the reputations that the Mayo Clinic had was for thoroughness. Gehrig was tested for two days straight before he took a little break and prepared to resume his stay with additional doctor visits a day later. Gehrig was at the clinic for a week, in his free time being affable to local sportswriters, visiting a former Yankees teammate in his job as a butcher, watching a softball game, granting an interview to two ten-year-olds for their "neighborhood" newspaper, and going out to dinner and even on a cruise with the doctor assigned to provide him with information about ALS.

By the time Gehrig went home to New York, he knew that he had an incurable disease, that he would never play baseball again, and that his symptoms would grow progressively worse. Yet he told his wife and others that there was a 50–50 chance the advance of the disease could be checked. That was not true. ALS is always progressive and just as was the case in 1874 when first identified, even 70 years after Gehrig incurred it, there is no cure. Lou Gehrig was going to die from his affliction and it wasn't a maybe.

Amyotrophic lateral sclerosis is an insidious, cruel disease that affects every muscle in the body. There would come a time when Gehrig would not be able to make a closed fist, walk, or even swallow, though his brain stayed actively aware of all that was happening to him. Death was inevitable, though just how quickly it would come was unknown.

If Gehrig did not know this, then his doctors at the Mayo Clinic sugarcoated a nonetheless grim diagnosis, though there is no reason they should have. It was possible that Gehrig processed the information he received and decided not to share it with others. Or he might have been in denial, thinking he might be the one who could beat this dreaded disease. He surely had no forethought that one day the disease would become better known under his name because of his fame.

When Gehrig returned to the Yankees, he was bearing a letter from the doctors for Ed Barrow and Joe McCarthy. Then information was released to the press. There was no discussion of the incurable nature of ALS, and even more confusing, it was quickly interpreted that Gehrig had polio. Gehrig told people he thought the illness was no longer progressing.

Gehrig retained his uniform, stayed with the Yankees, and traveled with the team — the team had made a commitment to pay him for the entire season and he still wanted to feel part of things with the boys. Although he had ceased making the gesture, Gehrig was persuaded once more to deliver the lineup card to the umpire in Philadelphia because A's manager Connie Mack asked him to do it. The fans gave Gehrig an eight-minute ovation that made him cry.

Public knowledge of ALS was almost non-existent before Gehrig contracted it. He could get away with statements to reporters that he knew he could beat it without fear of contradiction. Anyone who did research, however, knew Gehrig was going to die from the illness. People like Eleanor, his closest friends, and Barrow. But no one wanted to have those gloomy conversations with Gehrig, who deserved to have his spirits boosted, not brought down.

15. Diagnosis and Death

Gehrig was a New York Yankees fixture, one of the greatest players of all time, a cornerstone of the Murderers Row teams along with Babe Ruth, and the holder of a consecutive games played record that was inconceivable to many baseball folks. Now with his forced removal from the lineup by illness, and his health prognosis terribly grim for a 35-year-old man, the Yankees agreed to hold a "Lou Gehrig Appreciation Day" at Yankee Stadium on July 4, 1939.

This was not the kind of hoopla that Gehrig relished, and he had to be wondering how he would hold up to the rigors of the day when there were days he could barely hold up. The Yankees invited many of Gehrig's teammates from the early glory days to attend, including Ruth and pitchers Waite Hoyt, Bob Shawkey and Herb Pennock and hitters like Tony Lazzeri, Bob Meusel, and yes, Wally Pipp, the man Gehrig took the first-base job from so long before.

The 40-minute Gehrig ceremony did not take place until after the Yankees lost the first game of a doubleheader, 3–2, to the Washington Senators. Microphones were set up at home plate and Gehrig thought they looked pretty far away from the dugout. It was a distance he would have to walk with 61,808 pairs of eyes on him. Other luminaries spoke first and then McCarthy and Ruth, too, who was happy to reconcile with Gehrig after their strained relationship while playing together. Gehrig received an assortment of gifts, from the practical like a fishing rod and tackle, to the comparatively offbeat like a fruit bowl and candlesticks. The latter batch of gifts made it seem more like a wedding party than a farewell party.

As he stood in this hallowed place in his life, as the sands of time in his life were rapidly diminishing, Gehrig repeatedly had to wipe tears from his eyes. Only a few years earlier he had sought to play a tough-guy Tarzan in the movies. Now wherever he went, he seemed to be shedding tears. Forget candlesticks, Gehrig needed towels.

He had not wanted to speak. He had not wanted either the adulation or the sympathy. But everyone else had his say and everyone else had given him presents. Gehrig knew he had to talk to the fans who loved him. This was long before anyone thought of conducting concerts in big-league ballparks, and the acoustics could not match Carnegie Hall. There was a breeze in the air to carry words to some people's ears and away from others,' and for anyone who has seen and heard the moment on tape, there was an unforgettable echo in the microphones.

As Gehrig approached the microphones, Barrow steadied him by holding his left arm. Standing so bare in public, at the last moment Gehrig did not think he could talk, and public relations man Sid Mercer actually informed the crowd Gehrig said he was too moved to speak. But McCarthy stepped up to him and whispered in his ear, urging him on.

Then the most elegant Yankee of them all delivered a speech that is sports' Gettysburg Address, simple, direct, forceful, from the heart. Standing slightly stooped, hands on hips, Gehrig kept his address short, but his words drew out tears from thousands. In part, he said, "Fans, for the past two weeks you have been reading about a bad break I got. Yet today I consider myself the luckiest man on the face of the earth. I have been in ballparks for 17 years and have never received anything but kindness and encouragement from you fans.

"Look at these grand men. Which of you wouldn't consider it the highlight of his career just to associate with them for even one day?"

"When you have a wife who has been a tower of strength and shown more courage than you dreamed existed, that's the finest I know."

"So I close in saying that I may have had a tough break, but I have an awful lot to live for."[3]

Lesser known is what was written on the engraved trophy given to Gehrig by Yankee teammates in the form of a poem. It reads:

> We've been to the wars together,
> We took our foes as they came;
> And always you were the leader,
> And ever you played the game.
>
> Idol of cheering millions;
> Records are yours by sheaves;
> Iron of frame they hailed you,
> Decked you with laurel leaves.
>
> But higher than that we hold you,
> We who have known you best;
> Knowing the way you came through
> Every human test.
>
> Let this be a silent token
> Of lasting friendship's gleam
> And all that we've left unspoken
> — YOUR PALS ON THE YANKEE TEAM[4]

It is barely remembered that the players gave the trophy to Gehrig, never mind added such a touching message to it.

15. Diagnosis and Death

Throughout the decades that have followed, Gehrig's heartfelt utterances into the microphones that day have become known as "The Luckiest Man" speech.

"I don't think the people knew how badly he was afflicted," said Tommy Henrich, the Yankees outfielder. "They didn't know he was going to die from it." Henrich, who lived into his 90s, said he never thought of that day again the rest of his life without choking up.[5]

The *New York Times* reporter at the park foreshadowed that in the next day's paper, calling the Gehrig ceremony "without a doubt one of the most touching scenes ever witnessed on a ball field and one that made even case hardened ball players and chroniclers of the game swallow hard."[6]

After retiring from baseball in the face of his devastating health worries, Gehrig accepted a job working for Mayor Fiorello La Guardia as a commissioner on the New York City parole board. Among other things, Gehrig visited young people in prison and counseled them about how they could fix their lives.

Also, the Yankees retired Gehrig's No. 4 uniform jersey, making it the first number to be retired in major league history. "We always want Lou to feel he is still one of us," Barrow said.[7]

The National Baseball Hall of Fame held a special election on December 7 and Gehrig was chosen for the Hall. The only other time such action has been taken is after Roberto Clemente died on New Year's Eve, 1972, while trying to bring food and medical supplies to earthquake-torn Nicaragua.

Gehrig kept up a long-distance correspondence with Dr. Paul O'Leary, the doctor who first counseled him at the Mayo Clinic, either writing his own letters or, when he grew weaker, through dictation. At times Eleanor helped guide Gehrig's hand when he had to sign official documents for work and likely did so on personal letters as well.

Gehrig volunteered as a participant in experimental drug trials that researchers thought might lead to a cure for ALS, one that involved vitamin E, and another that involved histamines. "I do not want to be a hero and I would hate like hell to be a cry baby," Gehrig wrote of his case at one point. "But I would also like to know the facts."[8]

Neither accepted treatments nor experimental ones proved to be the answer, and Gehrig continued his slide at an alarming rate. Eventually, he no longer left his home or his bedroom. Days before the end came, ex–Yankees teammates Henrich, Dickey and other players visited Gehrig at his Riverdale home and he put on a show of being upbeat for them. His once-muscular body had shrunk to 125 pounds.

When Gehrig said goodbye that day, he told the other guys, "Well, boys, thanks for coming out. The doctor told me that I have to go down to rock bottom and then my body's going to take over and I'm coming back."

Outside the home the emotional players concurred that Gehrig just had to be that way. "He didn't fool anyone," Henrich said. "But Lou just had to believe."[9]

Lou Gehrig stopped believing on June 2, 1941. He was only 37 when he died. The irony of the date was that it was 16 years to the day after he assumed the New York Yankees' first-base job from Wally Pipp.

The Yankees were on a road trip, just arriving in Detroit to play the Tigers, and unprepared for how quickly Gehrig died after his diagnosis. They, and most baseball fans, thought Gehrig had years to live. New York players learned of Gehrig's afternoon death when they reached their hotel. McCarthy and Bill Dickey, Gehrig's best friend on the team and his longtime roommate, left the Yankees in Detroit and returned to New York for Gehrig's funeral.

Ed Barrow, president of the Yankees franchise that had made Gehrig famous, and had benefited so greatly from his talents, said he "felt like he lost a son when Gehrig died."[10]

At Briggs Stadium in Detroit, where most of the Yankees were assembled for a game against the Tigers, the American flag flew at half-mast in honor of Gehrig. Fans were asked for a moment of silence in Gehrig's memory.

In New York, a much smaller crowd gathered for Gehrig's funeral at Christ Episcopal Church in Riverdale than had for Colonel Ruppert's funeral, or would for Babe Ruth's seven years later. It is certain that New Yorkers would have turned out by the thousands to say farewell to Gehrig. But a large funeral was not sought. Eleanor preferred a small group, and there were only an estimated 100 people in attendance. However, despite her original reluctance, Mrs. Gehrig bowed to a barrage of requests and the night before the funeral an estimated 5,000 people paid respects as they filed past Gehrig's casket. Babe Ruth broke down crying when he saw the coffin.

15. Diagnosis and Death

"It was not so much the fact that he was a successful ball player, nor that he was famous," Jean Horie, executive secretary of the New York Youth Congress commented about what made Gehrig special. "But it was rather that with all his prominence he maintained his modesty, courage and sincerity."[11]

At the funeral, McCarthy and Dickey were pallbearers after a brief ceremony of about eight minutes that included no eulogy. Other pallbearers included people from other parts of Gehrig's life, including representatives of Mayor La Guardia, the parole commission, and Andy Coakley, Gehrig's baseball coach at Columbia University.

"Everybody loved Lou," said Yankees shortstop Frank Crosetti. "You couldn't help it. He was in there with everything he had, every minute of the game."

It rained on the funeral and it also happened to rain out the game in Detroit. McCarthy and Dickey caught up to the rest of the Yankees for a series in St. Louis against the Browns. While McCarthy was not especially effusive in his praise of Gehrig other than to comment on what a great guy he was and how he never gave him any trouble as a manager, he kept a photograph of the player in his home for the rest of his life.

Gehrig's body was cremated and buried in Kensico Cemetery in Valhalla, New York. In 1942, the movie "Pride of the Yankees" was released starring Gary Cooper as Gehrig. Babe Ruth had billing as himself on the movie poster and Bill Dickey also played himself.

The film was nominated for 11 Academy Awards, including one for Cooper, but it won only for film editing. However, in later years, "Pride of the Yankees" earned recognition on numerous lists of the most inspirational and best sports movies.

In 1989, the U.S. Postal Service issued a stamp to commemorate Lou Gehrig's life.

Most likely because amyotrophic lateral sclerosis is difficult to pronounce and more difficult to remember, and because Gehrig was the most high-profile American to contract the illness — and at the height of his powers in a short life — the disease that killed one of the greatest baseball stars of all time gained a new name. It is called "Lou Gehrig's Disease."

Much more so, he would have preferred the antidote to the illness be called "Lou Gehrig's Cure."

16

The Yankees Lose a Pennant

A different aspect of the Yankees Dynasty began in the summer of 1939. An Alabama native who was born Melvin Allen Israel moved into the broadcasting booth and soon introduced a phrase, "How about that!" which would resonate with New York Yankees fans for decades.

The man who became famous as Mel Allen was a baseball voice extraordinaire, and between 1939 and 1964, when the Yankees imprudently dumped him, Allen was as closely identified with the winningest team in baseball as any of its stars.

By the time Allen was hired from the Washington Senators to handle Yankees games, Lou Gehrig was already sick, but in a story often told as Allen aged, it seems that Allen's broadcasts were a comfort to the slugger during his dying days.

In 1940, the year after Gehrig stopped traveling with the team and when he made only rare appearances at Yankee Stadium, Gehrig got into a discussion with Allen in the dugout while the Yankees were on the field warming up.

"Lou turned toward me after a long silence and patted me on the knee," Allen said. "His voice was sort of hoarse and subdued. 'You know,' Lou said to me, 'I never really got a chance to listen to your broadcasts because I was always playing every day. But I want you to know you're the only thing that keeps me going.'"

Allen said he got up and walked away because he didn't want Gehrig to see the tears in his eyes.[1]

Born in 1913 in Birmingham, Alabama, Allen, who was smart enough to finish high school at 15, was still a young man when he became the main voice of Yankees baseball. During his long career he also hosted "This Week in Baseball," broadcast 20 World Series and 24 All-Star Games, and handled many other sporting events. Those included regular broadcasts of the Rose Bowl and sporadic assignments on the Orange Bowl and Sugar Bowl.

Allen shared broadcast booths with Red Barber, Curt Gowdy, Russ Hodges and Phil Rizzuto, among others, but over time became completely identified with the Yankees and was beloved by their fans. Radio was a major medium by the 1940s and Allen delivered the Yankees games into homes throughout that war-torn period, through the rejuvenating 1950s and into the 1960s. When Allen was let loose, the same owners who made that judgment had to cope with the team's first sustained win-loss slump since before Babe Ruth came to town.

Allen's early broadcast training and experience took place at the University of Alabama, where he broadcast the Crimson Tide football games and after his undergraduate years attended the law school. He once taught Bear Bryant in a speech class. It is not clear if Allen's teachings aided Bryant in his talks with the press and public after he became the school's fabulously successful football coach.

In 1937, Allen scheduled a week's vacation in New York and between doing touristy things he auditioned for CBS Radio. When he informed his parents he got the job, they were less than thrilled. After all, he had studied to become a lawyer and they thought that was a much better vocation. Allen convinced them that a few months spent in New York never hurt anybody and that he would benefit from the experience. However, the broadcaster never left the New York area. The city became the base of his operations for 58 years in broadcasting and his home for the rest of his life.

During his first year on the job, when he was working for $45 a week, Allen announced the crash of the Hindenburg on the air as an emergency interruption to regularly scheduled programming. A huge baseball fan, Allen took the subway to Yankee Stadium to see the Yankees play on his days off, and he dreamed about becoming the play-by-play announcer for the team.

In an unusual twist during the early 1940s, Allen broadcast both Yankees and New York Giants baseball games. He was also in shape and the teams let him put on a uniform and work out with them before games.

Allen's World War II service involved broadcasting "The Army Hour" and he was heard regularly on Armed Forces Radio. After the war Allen was no longer involved with the Giants; the Yankees wanted home and away broadcasts.

The phrase "How about that!" became Allen's signature call. But it was not to be heard until sometime after he called the meeting to order when he came on the air prepping for the start of a Yankees game by saying, "Hello there, everybody!"

Also, fans knew when a home run was hit (the Yankees provided plenty of practice) because Allen called, "Going, going, gone!" If present-day sports fans think the trend to slapping a sponsor's name on every aspect of the games is a recent one, it should be noted that when a home run was hit, Allen was required to observe that it was a "Ballantine Blast," Ballantine being the chief beer sponsor of the Yankees during the 1950s and 1960s.

"The voice, laced with a lilting Alabama drawl, was once as recognizable as the president's and as familiar as a friend's," is the way Allen's broadcasting was described in the introduction to his biography. "It invited you to huddle by your radio and listen, assuring you it would do the rest."[2]

Whether it was Allen's inflections from growing up in the South, combined with his broadcast training and his move to New York, where English was spoken in a completely different fashion, Allen's style, delivery and intonations grabbed baseball fans and held them close to their radios for each new Yankees development.

"The mere sound of his voice puts you in a baseball frame of mind," said Bob Costas, a renowned broadcast figure of a later generation.[3] The admiration of Allen's listeners ran deep, not only among the legion of Yankees fans who tuned in every night, but among his peers, the other top broadcasters in the business. "I think he'll be remembered as one of the great voices of baseball," said Ernie Harwell, who is as well from his decades with the Detroit Tigers.[4]

Allen worked for the team in 1939 when the Yankees won their fourth straight pennant and World Series. But then a funny thing happened on the way to number five. They lost. Maybe Lou Gehrig's illness was a symbol, but the Yankees' longstanding good luck ran out in 1940. Detroit won the American League pennant with a 90–64 record. The Cleveland Indians finished a game behind. The Yankees finished third with an 88–66 record, one game behind Cleveland in the standings and two games behind the Tigers.

The Yankees were not horrible, by any means, but they were not the

16. The Yankees Lose a Pennant

same old Yankees juggernaut. Gehrig, one of the greatest sluggers in the history of the game, was gone. There was no pretense, even from him, that he would regain his health and regain his role as the first baseman. He hardly ever even came to games. Lefty Gomez had lost his stuff and went 3–3 with a 6.59 earned run average.

Consistent starting pitching was the main concern. The Yankees did get good starting work from Marius Russo (14–8), Tiny Bonham (9–3), and Atley Donald (8–3), but the big guns the Yanks were counting on seemed to be wearing down and others they hoped would step up didn't. Red Ruffing went 15–12, but he was done as a 20-game winner who could be relied on as the ace of the staff. Spud Chandler was 8–7 with his best years ahead of him. Monte Pearson was 7–5, in his last season as a Yankee, and his best years were behind him. Marv Breuer, a second-year man from Rollo, Missouri, was the fifth starter and he finished 8–9. In his portions of five seasons in New York, Breuer compiled a lifetime mark of 25–26. Also, at various times Russo, Ruffing, Pearson, and Breuer were injured.

With a lineup that still included Bill Dickey, Babe Dahlgren, Joe Gordon, Red Rolfe, Frank Crosetti, George Selkirk, Charlie Keller and Joe DiMaggio, there was no reason to worry about hitting. Oh yes, it was the pitching that made manager Joe McCarthy miss restful nights of sleep. His club was still going to score plenty of runs. It just had to stop the other guys and it couldn't do that in 1940.

On May 20, as the baseball world watched, astounded, the Yankees fell into last place in the eight-team American League. There had been criticism that McCarthy was not as good as his record, that he was really a "push-button" manager. Those comments came from outsiders who didn't understand the business well. Players always said that McCarthy saw and remembered everything. If people thought it looked easy, so what, he didn't care as long as his teams won, and win they did.

Not this time. The challenges meant that McCarthy had to manage his tail off, only in a more visible way, changing up his rotation, switching lineups, making tough calls to yank pitchers in the middle of innings, figuring right on pinch-hitters. Injuries contributed to the slow start, too. At one point, outfielder Tommy Henrich was playing first base, an unfamiliar slot.

The rest of the infielders knew that Henrich was new to the position, so they tried to help him with their throws. Realizing he didn't have the experience of other first basemen, they tried to guide their throws and keep them out of the dirt. But that only made them wilder and made things harder for Henrich.

"They tried to help me," Henrich said. "They began to aim at me and started making bad throws. I remember the last one hit the dirt eight feet in front of me." Several balls he could not scoop out of the dirt skirted past him and the Yankees lost a game to the Indians as a result. After the game, McCarthy approached Henrich and said, "I thought you were a first baseman." Henrich said, "Yes, but not a coal miner."[5]

Although the Yankees did improve on their poor start, they were streaky. During the heart of the summer, when many clubs make their move for the pennant, the Yankees had a 25-day stretch when they went 9–17. The Yankees had so many injuries that the list would have been longer than any composed for a grocery-store stop. One player hurt his back, another took a line drive in his knee, and another needed stitches. On and on it went and the Yankees never got hot enough to challenge for the pennant until the end of the reason.

It was somewhat remarkable that they made a run at all, slowly passing most of the teams in the standings after May and rising from their own lowly standing in the AL basement. But from August 9 to September 2, the Yankees threw a scare into the rest of the league by going 20–3. The move injected them into the race and on September 11 they pulled within a half-game of the Tigers and Indians, who were tied for first before losing the second game of a doubleheader.

The hovering specter of the big, bad Yankees, problems solved, put considerable pressure on teams not used to being in the hunt in September. Unlike other years, though, the Yankees didn't have the goods to finish. And to compound the miseries of the season, on the final day of the campaign, outfielder George Selkirk's appendix burst and he had to be hospitalized.

McCarthy, who was never warm to sportswriters anyway, showed the stress of the season when a reporter asked the silly question of why the Yankees weren't winning pennant number five in a row. "What's the matter?" he testily responded. "Has everyone forgotten the other years?"[6]

They hadn't. That was the point. It wasn't a form of disrespect affronting the Yankees because they weren't winning. It was a sense of awe, so difficult to believe that they were losing.

16. The Yankees Lose a Pennant

One guy McCarthy didn't have much time to worry about (although he probably worried on general principles that he would be able to play) was Joe DiMaggio. The Yankees centerfielder did have one of his usual spate of injuries or illnesses (he had his tonsils out after spring training in 1937 and wrenched his knee in 1940), so he was limited to 132 games. But while many of his teammates were falling apart, DiMaggio hit 31 home runs with 133 RBIs, and his .352 average led the American League. It was DiMaggio's second batting title in a row. DiMaggio was 25 years old and as good as any player in the sport.

By 1940, DiMaggio was known as "The Yankee Clipper." He had won two batting titles, led the American League in home runs, and driven in as many as 167 runs in a single season. He was already a legend in New York, the revered Yankees tradition carried on his shoulders.

DiMaggio liked to date beautiful women and he liked to take a drink. He just didn't like the attention that came with being a celebrity in New York trying to enjoy the nightlife. As fit his desire for privacy in general and his overall shyness, DiMaggio wanted to enjoy his off-field life, but he didn't want it to be gossiped about in the New York tabloids.

By that time, Toots Shor was part of Joe D's life. He operated Toots Shor's Restaurant, the establishment at 51 West 51st Street, a restaurant, saloon, exclusive hideaway for sports celebrities and show business people, and Shor's personal hunk of Manhattan nightlife that along with the 21 Club, Sardi's, the Stork Club and El Morocco, epitomized a period in the life of Broadway and New York glitz.

Shor protected his guys, and DiMaggio became perhaps his most important guy, although patrons included Frank Sinatra, Jackie Gleason and Ernest Hemingway. Shor and Gleason once engaged in a drinking contest that left the actor stretched out on the floor of the restaurant, where Shor left him for a time in order to prove that the owner had won the contest. When introduced to the Nobel Prize-winning author, Yankees Future Hall of Fame catcher Yogi Berra reportedly asked Hemingway, "Which paper are you with, Ernie?"

DiMaggio knew that when he came to Shor's he could eat in peace and not be interrupted by customers clamoring for autographs. Shor did not allow such effrontery. DiMaggio knew that he could hang out with other athletes or show business people who expected nothing of him other than being DiMaggio. Shor was a sarcastic, sharp-tongued man who loved the glitter by association, but was very aware of providing an atmosphere that would keep the famous coming back.

Some sportswriters were among those welcome, but it was understood that unless explicitly stated by a ball player, what was said at Toots Shor's stayed at Toots Shor's. Shor's goal was to offer a place to relax, and if someone violated the confidence of the philosophy he was on the outs and on the outside of the front door. Suddenly, there would be no table for him.

Shor was an imbiber of his own liquid products, often after hours with a select clientele after the doors were locked, and you had to drink if you went to Shor's to hang out, rather than merely eat and leave. "Any bum who can't get drunk by midnight, ain't tryin,'" he said.[7]

Although Shor's fame came from catering to the famous, he was as much of a character as anyone who was a regular at his place. It was odd that a man who, like Don Rickles, insulted his friends, albeit in jest, was consumed by what he saw as "class" in his customers. Someone had class or he didn't and class, by his definition, is what Shor admired. Even today, decades later, anyone asked about Joe DiMaggio is likely to say, "He had class." That may have been the root of Shor's devotion to DiMaggio and his reported willingness to grant him any favor.

Just like DiMaggio's closest Italian teammates, Shor referred to the player as "Dago." He could get away with it because they were so close. He provided food, drink and a haven for DiMaggio when he was young and new to New York and needed it.

One thing DiMaggio did not lack was a work ethic. He loved baseball and he knew people loved him because of baseball, so he did not slack off. One of New York's premier sports columnists, Jimmy Cannon, once asked DiMaggio why he played so hard. DiMaggio issued the immortal response that ideally would reflect an outlook adopted by all professional athletes: "Because there might be somebody out there who has never seen me play before."[8]

In 1940, a third DiMaggio brother became a major leaguer. Younger brother Dom broke in as a rookie with the Boston Red Sox. Of course, Vince and Dom were starting the season on time and DiMaggio was not because of his strained knee. "All I know is that I can't run and the doctor told me not to try until the leg felt perfectly OK," DiMaggio said.[9]

DiMaggio, who had been a holdout whenever Ed Barrow appeared too stingy for his tastes in sending out annual contracts, reportedly signed for $30,000 that season. He hardly ever thought the Yankees were generous enough in acknowledging his contributions, but he rarely engaged in salary battles in public after his early years. He had taken too much of a public relations hit when he tried.

Another public relations bruise was incurred when newspapers speculated that DiMaggio might be beholden to boxing promoter Joe Gould, a friend, as an agent. They suggested Gould might be getting a cut of DiMaggio's salary. The idea of an agent representing a ball player with his team lay many years in the future. Commissioner Kenesaw Mountain Landis did call DiMaggio to his office for a hearing, but then announced that the player had done nothing wrong.

DiMaggio went back to playing ball.

Joe McCarthy was not kidding when he said he expected to win every game. It was at least metaphorically true. He knew the Yankees were not going to finish 154-0. What he meant was that he expected the Yankees to win enough games to win the pennant every year. They didn't do that in 1940, so he, Ed Barrow and farm system director George Weiss conferred on what to do about it.

Clearly, the Yankees needed more pitching. But minor league teams at the top of the chain in Newark and Kansas City kept producing more talent, too, and it was time to give some younger players the chance to make the jump to the big club.

The 1941 revival of Lefty Gomez, who rebounded to go 15–5, was a big help. The difference in his record between 1940 and 1941 was enough on paper to make up the difference between the Yankees in third place and the Yankees in front of Detroit and Cleveland. But the number one addition to the roster in 1941 was not a pitcher.

Phil Rizzuto stood 5-foot-5 and weighed 150 pounds. He was a New Yorker, from Queens, and all he wanted to do was play for the Yankees. He worked his way through the minors between 1938 and 1941 and although he encountered many skeptics because of his size, McCarthy was not one of them by the end of spring training in '41. Rizzuto made the club and made his debut on April 14. No one would have imagined that Rizzuto's affiliation with the Yankees would continue for the rest of his life.

Although he had seasons when he wielded an extraordinary bat, including his rookie year when he hit .307, Rizzuto's strength was his fielding. He was a vacuum cleaner at shortstop, scooping up grounders, diving to his right or left, making the tough throws. The Yankees had plenty of men who could win games with their bats. Rizzuto won games with his glove.

Rizzuto was small by big-league standards and he told the story of showing up for his first spring training in St. Petersburg, only to be among the "kids" on the field that clubhouse man Fred Logan tried to shoo off. It took the intervention of Lefty Gomez for Rizzuto to be recognized as a player.

"He had a towel wrapped around his middle and on his face a grin that I came to appreciate more and more as the season went along," Rizzuto said. "'G'wan Fred,' he said. 'Don't you know who this cockroach is?' Then he turned to me and added, 'C'mon in, Phil, before the ducks start stepping all over you.' That was my initiation."[10]

Rizzuto said when he entered the clubhouse he found his locker between Red Ruffing's and Bill Dickey's and he was almost too scared to say hello. It was a magical moment for Rizzuto, who before winning the starting shortstop job for the Yankees, had been rejected elsewhere. When he tried out for his public school team, the coach made fun of him when he asked to be an outfielder. "I can see you have covered the outfield," the coach said. "You are a cricket." Not exactly playing cricket with a youngster's feelings.[11] It didn't matter much, however, because Rizzuto made the team and became a starter in the outfield, after all.

Al Kunitz, the coach at Richmond Hill High School, had a better bedside manner and sound advice for Rizzuto. He told the hopeful that while his size would work against him in the outfield he had good hands and a good arm and would make a very good middle infielder. That was Rizzuto's start at playing shortstop.

When he was 16, Rizzuto begged tryouts from the New York Giants and Brooklyn Dodgers, both of whom sent him home because they didn't see a prospect in his body. Rizzuto didn't have to plead with the Yankees. By chance, when he was playing in a summer league game, New York scout Paul Krichell happened by and liked the smoothness with which the young man fielded at short. He offered a tryout with the Yankees.

In a tryout with 57 players, Rizzuto was the smallest. Yet he was the only one signed. Rizzuto had not even graduated from high school, but he quit school and for $75 a month went off to start his professional odyssey in Class D in Bennett, Virginia, in something called the Bi-State League that no longer exists.

Rizzuto made it to AAA in Kansas City, where his nickname "Scooter" was bestowed upon him. An off-hand comment by teammate Billy Hitchcock started it when he said, "You ain't runnin', you're scootin.'" Another teammate, Buzz Boyle, started calling Rizzuto "Scooter" and so did everyone else.[12]

During his time in the minors, Rizzuto suffered a torn muscle from being spiked that was so severe that gangrene set in and he almost loss his leg, injured his arm, and just before heading for training camp the year he made the Yankees, learned that his fiancé had died. For all of that, in a laudatory and sympathetic article, the headline in the *New York Journal-American* about Rizzuto being kept with the Yankees at the end of spring training, read: "The Shrimp Made It."

Rizzuto overcame all of that and played in 133 games as the starting shortstop, cast in the precise role in life he had dreamed of for years. The ascension of Rizzuto to the Yankees was something that Ed Barrow took pleasure in. He relished the team's ability to ferret out talent where no one else saw it and also for making good deals for players who later turned out to be worth quite a bit more. "Rizzuto cost me 15 cents, 10 for postage and five for a cup of coffee we gave him the last day he worked out at the stadium," Barrow said.[13]

Barrow was also extremely confident about how the Yankees would fare during the 1941 season after missing out on the 1940 pennant. "I know of no reason why we shouldn't come right back and finish on top again," he said.

Joe DiMaggio was Rizzuto's favorite player and he repeatedly said the best player he ever saw in his life. As a rookie, however, Rizzuto, who later became famous for how much he talked, was reticent. He was shy around the Yankees veterans and that especially meant DiMaggio.

But DiMaggio, the Great DiMaggio, befriended him and asked him to join him for his frequent forays to the movies. Rizzuto couldn't believe it. "I guess it was because I knew when to be quiet," Rizzuto said. "Joe was an introvert. He spoke very little."[14]

As a rookie, Rizzuto learned to speak with his glove and bat.

17

The Streak

Joe DiMaggio was a New York baseball hero by 1941. After 1941, he was a major league baseball god.

The streak did it. Few serious baseball fans who hear the word "streak" mentioned think of anything else besides DiMaggio's 56-game hitting streak. And those few probably aren't taken seriously.

There are great baseball records, numbers that stick in fans' minds better than any football, basketball or hockey record. Practically no one can name the holder of the all-time National Football League record for yards rushing, and only come within an educated guess of whether it is owned by Emmitt Smith, Walter Payton, or Barry Sanders. One other sports record that people do know is Wilt Chamberlain's 100-point game in the National Basketball Association. After that, few could say with certainty if the all-time scoring record is held by Chamberlain, Michael Jordan, or Kareem Abdul-Jabbar.

Baseball records have always been more universal. Joe Public knew that Babe Ruth's 60 home runs was the record. Joe Public knew all about it when Hank Aaron cracked home run 715 to pass Ruth. Barry Bonds' final total? Not so much.

But DiMaggio's streak? People know it, some are still alive who experienced it, and most feel that it is the record least likely to be broken. That may or may not be true, especially held up against another classic record of baseball history, Cy Young's 511 victories.

DiMaggio's streak played out during the 1941 season, when the Yankees were trying to rebound from their 1940 off-season and trying to regain the American League pennant. It didn't hurt any that DiMaggio played for a team located in the heart of the media center of the United States and that New York newspapers competed to one-up one another with every scrap of news.

17. The Streak

Dimaggio made himself the man of the hour with his bat, made himself the headline machine with his hits. During the hottest of summer months, he was a cool breeze, refreshing everyone's attitude, a personal unifier of people who loved the game. One thing everyone had in common that summer was rooting for DiMaggio to get another hit, to extend the streak one game longer, to just keep it up.

It was the summer that DiMaggio elevated himself from All-Star player to mythical status. Being Joe DiMaggio that summer was crazy. Not the least because a song was written about him and everybody, at Yankee Stadium or on the streets, seemed to know the words. It was called "Joltin' Joe DiMaggio," and DiMaggio gave the game of baseball quite a jolt that year.

The song was written by Ben Homer and Alan Courtney, and recorded by the Les Brown Orchestra (or as he was better known, Les Brown and his Band of Renown) and sung by Betty Bonney. Some of the lyrics are:

> He started baseball's famous streak
> That's got us all aglow
> He's just a man and not a freak
> Joltin' Joe DiMaggio.[1]

The refrain always returned to "Joltin' Joe DiMaggio.

DiMaggio began his hitting streak on May 15, 1941, at Yankee Stadium during a very unglamorous 13–1 loss to the Chicago White Sox. He had one hit, a single, that day. He was actually in a slump at the time and there was nothing to indicate that a solo hit was going to set him in the right direction.

Most intriguing considering this was scant proof of anything, how at least one sportswriter seized upon DiMaggio's hit as a harbinger. Maybe he was guessing. Maybe he was just looking for something to write about, but *New York World-Telegram* sportswriter Dan Daniel wrote, "Slumps are overcome suddenly, and once the bellwether shows the way, a whole club often will follow him. It is possible that when Joe DiMaggio begins to hit again he will pull the other Yankees with him."[2]

Researcher Michael Seidel, who wrote a book documenting DiMaggio's streak, suggests that the first time a newspaper covering the team made note of DiMaggio having a hitting streak going occurred after the 12th game. That would have been May 27, in a 10–8 New York victory over the Washington Senators. There were many reasons to notice DiMaggio that day. He went 4-for-5, with a home run, and scored three runs.

By the time the DiMaggio streak hit 20 games, in a June 3, 4–2 loss to the Tigers, most newspapermen were paying attention. That day DiMaggio's only safe hit was a home run. But 20 was an eye-catching number and if the streak was going to continue growing, then it was going to become more newsworthy.

DiMaggio was a long way from setting any kind of record, so for the time being, as his streak mounted, it was more of a curiosity. Twenty-five came and went. DiMaggio hit safely in his 30th straight game, on June 17, though again in a game New York lost, this time to Chicago, 8–7. It was another pedestrian one-hit game, but by then sportswriters and fans were examining record books, just to see where Joe rated.

At that point 30-game hitting streaks in the twentieth century had been recorded by Tris Speaker in 1912; Charlie Grimm in 1922 continuing into 1923; Lance Richbourg, 1927–28; Sam Rice, 1929–30; and Goose Goslin, 1934. Three other players, beginning with Cal McVey in 1876, hit safely in exactly 30 games before the turn of the century.

DiMaggio didn't light it up in his 31st straight game with a hit, either. He had one hit, a single, and the Yankees lost, 3–2, to the White Sox. Sam Rice of the Senators had compiled a separate 31-game streak from his 30-game streak, in 1924. Nap Lajoie, the revered Cleveland second-sacker, had done the same in 1906, and so had two pre–1900 players, Jimmy Wolf in 1885–86 and the esteemed Hall of Famer Ed Delahanty in 1899.

Harry Heilman of the Tigers had a 32-game streak spilling from 1922 into 1923. That was a more satisfying game for DiMaggio and the Yankees in his streak. The team battered Chicago, 7–2, and DiMaggio stroked three hits, including a home run.

Hal Chase (1907), Rogers Hornsby (1922) and Heinie Manush (1933) all made hits in 33 straight games, and so did pre–1900 Hall of Famer George Davis, who performed the trick in 1893. Now DiMaggio and the Yankees were both warming up. New York trounced the Tigers, 14–4, and DiMaggio collected four hits in his 33rd straight hitting game.

At 34 straight, DiMaggio joined the company of George McQuinn, who had his hot streak in 1938. Coincidentally, brother Dom DiMaggio later put together a 34-game hitting streak in 1949. The Yankees of 1941 lost to Detroit, 7–2, and DiMaggio had only one hit, but he kept things going.

DiMaggio joined rarefied company at 35 straight. George Sisler, the great St. Louis Browns hitter, hit that mark with a streak ending the 1924

17. The Streak

season and continuing into 1925. Ty Cobb, whose lifetime average of .366 is the highest of all time, and who led the American League in batting 12 times, hit in 35 straight games in 1917. Fred Clarke, another pre-1900 Hall of Famer, hit that level in 1895. In his 35th consecutive safe hitting game, DiMaggio slugged a double and a home run in a 5–4 New York victory over the Tigers.

The only prior hitter with a 36-game streak was Gene DeMontreville, who did it in a period covering parts of 1896 and 1897. In DiMaggio's 36th in a row, he went 1-for-4, but the Yankees beat the Browns, 9–1. At the time DiMaggio was alone when he reached 37 straight. That day he had one hit and New York topped St. Louis, 7–5. Tommy Holmes of the Boston Braves hit in 37 straight games in 1945, the earliest challenge to DiMaggio's record.

DiMaggio was alone at 38 and 39, too. The 38th time DiMaggio hit safely in a game it was a single that kept him going, and New York bested the Browns, 4–1. This game was one of DiMaggio's closest calls to going hitless during the streak. New York led 3–1 going into the bottom of the eighth inning and DiMaggio didn't have a hit. Because the Yankees were at home and ahead they were not likely to come to bat in the ninth inning. DiMaggio was the fourth New York batter scheduled to hit in the eighth, so if St. Louis set the order down 1-2-3 he would not even get a chance to bat.

Elden Auker, a very good pitcher, was throwing for the Browns. Johnny Sturm was a 25-year-old rookie, who was the odd player out in the Yankees' dazzling lineup. He played in 124 games at first base, batted 524 times, hit just three home runs and averaged just .239. He was also out of the big leagues after that season. At that moment, Sturm flied out. One down. However, Red Rolfe coaxed a walk out of Auker's side arm delivery.

Tommy Henrich recognized the danger of hitting into a double play and all but snuffing DiMaggio's streak unless the Browns could tie or go ahead in the ninth. Henrich asked manager Joe McCarthy if he could bunt and told him it was because he wanted to avoid the double play prospect and let DiMaggio settle things on his own.

Henrich dropped down a bunt, Rolfe was safe at second, and Henrich was thrown out at first for the sacrifice. DiMaggio got his opportunity at the plate and smacked a double. The hitting streak went on.

The next day's game required no maneuvering on DiMaggio's behalf.

DiMaggio went 2-for-3 in his 39th consecutive game with a hit, but the Yankees lost, 7–6, to the Philadelphia Athletics.

Cobb, the great batsman, had not only hit in 35 straight games in 1917, he also hit in 40 straight games in 1911. He had held the American League record for 11 years before it slipped into other hands in 1922. The Yankees topped Philadelphia, 7–4, and DiMaggio gathered two hits in his 40th straight safe hitting performance to equal Cobb.

The entire baseball universe was riveted to Yankees games and reports on how DiMaggio fared each day.

Tommy Henrich, who played in right field, next to DiMaggio, throughout the streak, said the Yankees were in the dumps before the streak began and he marveled how DiMaggio kept getting better and better and made key hits that uplifted the team while keeping the streak alive. "We weren't playing well at all," Henrich said of the Yankees being 14–15. "The Yankees didn't usually occupy that neighborhood in those days. That was all right if you were used to finishing in the middle of the pack, but we were the Yankees. We knew we were better than that. After our third-place finish of the year before, we knew we had to get hot. We did, and Joe D., 'the Yankee Clipper,' was the one who ignited our fire. Joe kept on hitting and he hit everything hard, including outs."[3]

For day games, fans who couldn't listen to the radio at work would ask friends, "Did DiMaggio get a hit today?" For night games, everyone listened to Mel Allen's broadcast. Sometimes they sat out front on the stoop of the high-rises, getting a little bit of night air on steamy evenings. It wasn't very cool, but it was a little better than being inside where no one had air conditioning.

While DiMaggio was showing no mercy to American League pitching, his latest rival for designation as the best player in the game was achieving something that had not been done much in recent years, and, as it turned out, would not be matched in the next 70 years.

Ted Williams, aka "The Splendid Splinter," moved into left field for the Boston Red Sox in 1939 and wasn't dislodged (except for military service) until 1960. A left-handed batter, the ultimate student of hitting, with the added dimension of power, Williams has been labeled the greatest hitter of all time.

Like DiMaggio, the 6-foot-3, 205-pound Williams was a star from the moment he stepped into a big-league lineup. Williams cracked 521 home runs, drove in 1,839 runs, and batted .344 for his career while appearing in 19 All-Star games. His lifetime numbers, though ranking high on the career all-time lists, were diluted because of several years spent as a Marine pilot in World War II and the Korean War.

The 1941 season was Williams' third in the majors after his ascent through the minors from his hometown of San Diego. He hit .327 as a rookie and .344 as a second-year man. In 1941, Williams was even hotter. When the season was over he had batted .406, to date the last man to hit .400 in the majors. That marked the first of six batting titles Williams won.

Although they were portrayed as rivals, it was theoretical. Williams and DiMaggio were only ever teammates on American League All-Star teams. They didn't spend time together in the off-season, either. But they admired one another's skills, even if they were not identical.

Williams made a science out of hitting. He knew what he was talking about and he knew what he was doing. He once said, "No one could throw a fastball past me. God could come down from heaven and he couldn't throw it past me."[4] God was one thing, but even Bob Feller had that difficulty and he had the best fastball on earth.

Hank Greenberg, the Tigers slugger and a contemporary, said Williams might have been a better hitter than DiMaggio, but he didn't like the fact that Williams also worked pitchers for walks. He believed Williams, who led the American League in bases on balls eight times and walked more than 2,000 times, should have gone after more pitches. But Williams, who was known to possess superior eyesight, wouldn't swing at balls out of the strike zone.

"DiMaggio, he would hit that ball on the corner," Greenberg said, "take that short stride and hit a ball off the plate. He would get a double and knock in two runs instead of taking the walk to load the bases and putting it up to the next guy. There was something else about DiMaggio that made him great. The pitchers couldn't intimidate him."[5]

Pitcher Bob Feller of the Cleveland Indians, who came off an Iowa farm to break into the majors at 17, won 266 games in a career that was also interrupted by World War II service. His time spent at war almost surely cost him membership in the 300-victory club, but did not keep him out of the Hall of Fame. Feller, who joined the Indians in 1936, also had nice things to say about Williams and DiMaggio. He said Williams was probably the best hitter he ever faced and DiMaggio was the best right-handed hitter he threw against.

"He seemed able to always get that crucial hit in the late innings any time he wanted," Feller said. "He had such great strength. He could just overpower the best fastball I could throw to him."[6]

Both DiMaggio and Williams were trying to gain acceptance into exclusive fraternities that summer, and each hit the ball with continuing authority throughout the hottest months of the year. Baseball had fiddled with its rules over the years, so most of the best averages in the sport's history were recorded prior to 1900 when the rules were still evolving.

The three highest averages of all time were recorded in 1887 when walks counted as hits. Tip O'Neill of St. Louis hit .485. Pete Browning of Louisville, the man who jump-started the Hillerich & Bradsby (Louisville Slugger) company when the firm replaced his bat, hit .453. And Bob Caruthers, also of St. Louis, hit .456. All three played in the American Association, at the time a major league.

The so-called modern era of baseball is often designated as beginning in 1900. The American League started in 1901. The World Series was first played in 1903. Larry "Nap" Lajoie hit .426 in 1901 while playing for the Athletics, an extraordinary performance.

According to Baseball Almanac, 14 of the highest 20 batting averages of all time were recorded before 1900. The highest batting average compiled after the end of the Deadball era in 1920 was Rogers Hornsby's magnificent .424 season for the St. Louis Cardinals in 1924. Hornsby hit better than .400 three times during the 1920s. Ty Cobb, who hit .420 in 1911 and .409 in 1912, hit .401 in 1922, again after the end of the Deadball era.

When Williams hit .406 in 1941, no one had topped .400 since Bill Terry's .401 in 1931, and no one has done so since. The brilliant George Sisler, who hit .407 in 1920, equaled Cobb for second on the post Deadball era list with a .420 mark in 1922.

Born in 1893 in Manchester, Ohio, Sisler was the author of several phenomenal feats during his 15-year major league career, mostly as a first baseman with the Browns between 1915 and 1927, and then finishing up with the Senators and Braves by 1930. His lifetime average was .340 and in 1920 he recorded 257 hits, the major league mark that lasted until broken by Ichiro Suzuki of the Seattle Mariners with 262 in 2004.

Sisler won two batting championships, going head-to-head with

17. The Streak

Cobb for a good chunk of his career, and a Most Valuable Player Award. Sisler's sons Dave and Dick also had major league careers, but they were journeymen players, not in the Hall of Fame class of their father.

As game after game in DiMaggio's streak piled up and he passed Cobb, Hornsby and Delahanty, newspapermen told everyone that it was Sisler's record of 41 straight games that DiMaggio was after.

It was definitely a summer for history being written, but looming even larger than these dual statistical assaults on baseball's record book authored by DiMaggio and Williams, were the much more deadly assaults being perpetrated in Europe by a rampaging, warmongering dictator in Germany named Adolph Hitler.

Hitler, more than either DiMaggio or Williams, was dramatically shaping the world during the summer of 1941. Although isolationists wanted to keep the United States out of this foreign war at all costs, President Franklin D. Roosevelt tried to mastermind a build-up of American forces so that when the inevitable time (in his mind) came when the U.S. had to enter the war it would be ready.

Fanning a brushfire of nationalism into a conflagration, Hitler whipped Germany into a frenzy of belief in its own militaristic and human superiority. Internally, Hitler worked to eradicate his country's entire Jewish population—and anyone else who was different—as he propagandized the notion of a pure-blood Aryan race. Externally, he set out to conquer the world, beginning on September 1, 1939, with the invasion of Poland.

Hitler had forged peace agreements with countries that he had never meant to keep, and between 1939 and 1941 his regular troops and Nazi storm troopers overran France, most of Europe, and despite stubborn resistance from England, set about trying to reduce the British Commonwealth to rubble with continuous bombing raids. Hitler's primary ally in Europe was Italy, led by the megalomaniac Benito Mussolini.

In Asia, Japan had invaded China in 1937 and been at war ever since, marching through the smaller nations of Asia, and alternately making menacing and conciliatory statements to the United States regarding supremacy over the Pacific Ocean.

If sports were the funny pages of the newspaper, with entertainment and light-hearted events involving play being reported on, the front pages were filled with dark news. A United States that had been a late participant in World War I (though not too late to absorb the brutality of large numbers of casualties) relaxed during the Roaring Twenties, but had only recently emerged from the Great Depression, and was not in the mood to send young Americans across the Atlantic Ocean to help Europe.

There were strident political factions that wanted no part of another world war. Yet FDR realized the futility of ignoring worldwide developments and did his best to try to ready the country for war. Americans watched uneasily as violent images rolled across screens in movie-house newsreels and listened carefully as news bulletins were announced by stern-voiced broadcasters.

That was the backdrop for the baseball being played during the summer of 1941. Baseball was the good-news relief, offering a brief respite, taking minds off the bad-news reports of what seemed to be a world gone mad. England fought back with great courage, its damaged Royal Air Force flying mission after mission against the Germans. Yet Germans were on the move in North Africa and even as his SS followers established concentration camps to murder six million Jews and wipe out anyone else deemed to be inferior, Hitler massed his huge army for an invasion of the Soviet Union. It was apparent by June of 1941 when the Germans launched that offensive that Hitler was going after everyone in a quest for world domination.

It was not obvious what the triggering incident would be, but with the Germans over-running Europe to the east and the Japanese over-running Asia to the west, one day the United States and its military might would be drawn into the war. How long could the U.S. afford to wait? How long did FDR have to build up the nation's strength? And what would it take for Congress to agree to enter the war?

Anyone who believed that "it's not our war" was being naïve. The Germans and the Japanese were making it into everyone's war.

Author Robert W. Creamer, a former *Sports Illustrated* staff writer, wrote a memoir of the time and said, "In the summer of 1941 I rooted for DiMaggio, the Dodgers, and the Russians, and I played stickball on the beach."[7]

Lou Gehrig actually died in the middle of DiMaggio's streak. It was June 2. On that day, DiMaggio went 2-for-4 in a 7–4 decision over the Cleveland Indians. Gehrig's shocking death at 37, so soon after his retirement from the Yankees, focused anew on the fact that this was Joe DiMaggio's Yankees team. The Babe had been king, with Gehrig as a prince. Then, too briefly, Gehrig had been king, yielding both to terminal illness and DiMaggio's rise.

Although everyone understood that Gehrig's illness was not some

17. The Streak

transitory thing and he was never coming back as a player, his death highlighted just how much the late 1930s and early 1940s Yankees were DiMaggio's club to lead.

There was that brief period when Joe McCarthy and Bill Dickey traveled east to represent the Yankees at Gehrig's funeral, but they were back a day later and the relentless baseball season, with games scheduled almost every day, picked up and moved on. The Yankees went from town to town like the circus, packing and unpacking every few days. And the swirl of attention only grew around DiMaggio as he took control of the center ring in the big top, just by swinging his bat.

So DiMaggio matched Ty Cobb at 40 games and the only obstacle left to break the consecutive games hitting streak mark was George Sisler's 41. Or not. Just as DiMaggio closed in on Sisler's figure, it was pointed out that pre–1900 there had been a couple of other guys who had long hitting streaks, longer, in fact, than Sisler's.

Both had played in the National League, so Sisler's record was still the American League high point. Bill Dahlen of the temporarily named Chicago Colts was an infielder known as "Bad Bill" because of his nasty personality. Dahlen hit in 42 straight games during the 1894 season. Then there was "Wee" Willie Keeler, propagator of the phrase, "Hit 'em where they ain't." Keeler, an original Baltimore Orioles teammate of John McGraw, the legendary manager, hit in 44 straight games spanning 1896 and 1897 (though many years later researchers revised his streak upward to 45).

By coincidence of scheduling, the Yankees had a doubleheader against the Senators in Washington on June 29, 1941. In the opener, a 9–4 Yankees victory, DiMaggio got one hit to tie Sisler, a double in the sixth inning. A hitter who rarely touted his own capabilities and who rarely let his emotions run free, DiMaggio loosened up in the clubhouse between games when he met the press.

"I'm tickled," he said. "Who wouldn't be? It's a great thing. I've realized an ambition."[8]

Then The Yankee Clipper went out to play another ballgame at Griffith Stadium. In the second game, won by the Yankees, 7–5, DiMaggio also notched one hit, a single in the seventh inning off pitcher Arnold Anderson. Afterwards, DiMaggio indulged himself in one of his favorite post-game past times, drinking a cold beer at his locker as he smilingly and obligingly told sportswriters how he felt.

He had matched and surpassed Sisler on the same day. There was no indication that he knew anything about Dahlen's 42-game streak, but by then he knew of Keeler's 44-game streak. "I'm glad the strain is over," DiMaggio said of passing Sisler for the American League record. "Now I've got to go after that 44-game mark. I'll keep on hitting and swinging as long as I can."[9]

However, one thing was amiss. Somehow, DiMaggio's favorite active Louisville Slugger bat was stolen. He was irate, and his superstitious teammates were gloomy about the missing 36-ounce, 36-inch instrument. Tommy Henrich remembered that he had the same model bat, borrowed previously, and gave it to DiMaggio to use. It was the closest thing available. DiMaggio used it and it worked out. Before the end of the day, though, he went public about the stolen bat.

Soon after, an unidentified caller telephoned DiMaggio in the clubhouse to tell him that he knew where the bat was. He told DiMaggio that the person who swiped it from the rack near the stands was a huge fan who didn't mean any harm.

DiMaggio said he didn't pay much attention to the streak until it reached the low 30s, but he admitted that on the eve of this doubleheader he was nervous. If DiMaggio were a football player he would have to wait a week between games and the mental strain might have been magnified. Playing baseball, with games every day, didn't leave much time for rumination.

Once again, as DiMaggio pursued Keeler, he found his potential games 43 and 44 scheduled for the same day, a doubleheader against the Red Sox on July 1 at Yankee Stadium. DiMaggio went 2-for-four in a 7–2 win over Boston in the first game and then he equaled Keeler's record with a 1-for-3 outing in the 9–2 win in the second game.

It was 95 degrees that day and DiMaggio, who arrived early, passed the time joking around with his pal Lefty Gomez and giving a long interview to a reporter. "Doesn't pay to get excited in this game," DiMaggio told *New York Times* reporter Russell Owen. "Some guys naturally are more tense than others. They can't help it and today I can understand why. Whether I break that record or not, there will just be a lot of ball games. It's my job. I'll do the best I can."[10]

DiMaggio puffed on a cigarette during his post-game press conference after he tied Keeler's 44-game streak for the major league mark. "I don't

17. The Streak

know how far I can go, but I'm not going to think about it now," DiMaggio said. "I'm glad it's over. It was quite a strain the last ten days. Now I can go back to swinging at good pitches. I was swinging at some bad ones so I wouldn't be walked."[11]

DiMaggio was wrong, of course. It wasn't over. He was still going and the interest didn't wane. A 1-for-5 day in an 8–4 win over the Red Sox put DiMaggio at 45 straight on July 2. He hit in his 50th straight game on July 11, going 4-for-5, one hit being a home run, in a 6–2 road win at St. Louis.

Just how long could DiMaggio keep it up? He did have that 61-game Pacific Coast League streak in his background. On he went, through 51, 52, 53, 54, 55, and 56. DiMaggio's 3-for-4 day in a 10–3 thumping of the Cleveland Indians on July 16 increased the streak to 56 games.

The next night, July 17, the Yankees and Indians met in a night game before 67,463 fans at Cleveland Municipal Stadium. Pitching for the Yankees was Lefty Gomez. Pitching for the Indians was Al Smith, a 32-year-old left-hander in the middle of a 12–13 season when he got the start. Smith surrendered seven hits in 7⅓ innings, but none to DiMaggio. Smith was relieved by Jim Bagby Jr. (who went 9–15 that season) in the eighth inning, and he gave up no hits to anyone on the Yankees, including DiMaggio.

The two pitchers combined to hold DiMaggio to an 0-for-3 night with a walk. For the first time since May he had been shut down. A co-conspirator in making sure that happened was Indians third baseman Ken Keltner, who robbed DiMaggio of two hits on shots down the third base line that he was able to snare and still throw to first base to get the runner.

Close call number one occurred on DiMaggio's first at-bat. He caught a Smith pitch flush and ripped it down the third base line where Keltner, a seven-time All-Star, backhanded the shot. Much later, DiMaggio was asked how far back Keltner was playing him. "Deep?" DiMaggio said. "My God, he was standing in left field."[12]

The seventh inning provided close to an instant replay. DiMaggio got good wood on the ball, sent it whistling down the third base line and Keltner backhanded it again. Then he threw DiMaggio out at first again.

"The throws were more difficult than the stops," Keltner said later, "and the throws were identical. I had to put something on them and the plays at first were both very close."[13]

In his final at-bat of the night, DiMaggio hit into a double play, but New York won, 4–3.

The streak was dead, but it never died, living on in memories and record books without even a seriously close challenge in the years since. Cincinnati's Pete Rose hit in 44 straight games in 1978, and that is as close as any player has gotten to DiMaggio's 56 in all of these years.

"Well, I'm glad it's over," DiMaggio said after the Indians halted him.[14]

During the streak, DiMaggio batted .408 with 56 runs scored and 55 runs batted in. His play sparked the Yankees into first place after their slow start that had sunk them into fourth. At the end of the streak, the Yankees were leading the American League by seven games.

18

A Brooklyn-Bronx Subway Series

By finishing in third place in 1940, the Yankees lost the aura of invincibility that had accrued from 1936 to 1939 with four straight American League pennants and four straight World Series championships. Joe McCarthy, Ed Barrow and George Weiss moved immediately to make fixits and fill holes, and vowed to put the Yankees back on top in 1941.

The addition of rookie Phil Rizzuto was one big change. But Joe DiMaggio's 56-game hitting streak that riveted the nation's attention did more than anything else to restore that super-powerful Yankees image. And DiMaggio's streak did focus the country on him.

Some months before the 1941 season, American League President Will Harridge told a sportswriter that the only true drawing card in major league baseball since Babe Ruth had retired was Bob Feller. The Indians pitcher was the only player whose presence on the field brought in extra people. "Whenever he appears, the attendance goes up," Harridge said. "That isn't true of any other individual in the game."[1]

DiMaggio's streak changed that. It could be documented that when the Yankees came to town while he was working his way up to the 56-game mark, more fans came out to see him, if only just so they could say they were there.

DiMaggio had such a swagger during the streak, not so much in the way he walked, but in how he handled the attention, that some pitchers must have been psyched out before they threw. They must have come into games thinking, "Nobody can get this guy out."

By the time the last out was recorded in the regular season, the Yankees were so far ahead that they made 1940 seem like a definite aberration, or perhaps even a mirage that never had quite happened, but was only imagined by the Tigers and Indians. New York finished 101–53, and if there was a new competitor in the American League in the Boston Red Sox, the challenge turned out to be a minimal one. The Red Sox, despite the fabulous efforts of Ted Williams, finished 17 games in arrears at 84–70.

DiMaggio batted .357 with 30 home runs and 125 RBI. Outfielder Charlie Keller swatted 33 homers with 122 RBI and a .298 average. Rizzuto hit .307. Tommy Henrich hit 31 home runs with 87 RBI. Joe Gordon hit 24 home runs with 85 RBI. Catcher Bill Dickey hit .284. The Yankees did not lack for pop.

The distribution of wins and losses on the pitching staff was impressive. Not a single hurler besides George Washburn, who was 0–1, had a losing record. Lefty Gomez bounced back and went 15–5. Red Ruffing, aging but effective, was 15–6. Marius Russo was 14–10 and Spud Chandler 10–4.

Atley Donald contributed at 9–5, Marv Breuer was 9–7, and Ernie "Tiny" Bonham was 9–6. Top reliever Johnny Murphy went 8–3. Even lower-tier pitchers who were not long for the Yankees did fine, with Norm Branch at 5–1, Steve Peek at 4–2, and Charley Stanceau at 3–3.

There was no dominant ace, but with the backing of a high-scoring lineup, everyone performed well.

Ruffing kept persevering. He was one of the best-hitting pitchers of any age, with 36 lifetime homers and topping .300 nine times, though of course his arm kept him in the game. Ruffing tried to maintain consistency, even as he aged, and benefited from being long-time partners with Dickey. "Bill and I never had any signs," Ruffing said. "I just told him to watch out for the fastball. Even in the Series games I never used signs. Dickey used to flash them, but I never paid attention."[2]

Only a year earlier, Gomez looked to be at the end of his career, prematurely, but with little likelihood of helping the Yankees again. Yet he righted himself, used his savvy as much as his fastball and won 15 games again in 1941.

Gomez was such a funny man, and always had been, that his humor was sometimes mistaken for a lack of seriousness in working at the game. Gomez said there was no connection. "Maybe if I had been more serious I would be pitching now in Split Lip, Nebraska. I like to win. Nobody ever hated to lose worse than I do. But when I lose I can't see any reason for making everybody else feel miserable just because I do. I never could holler at the other fellows, or tear up my uniform, or throw my stuff across the clubhouse. And I if I see something funny on the field, or in the clubhouse, I can laugh. Why shouldn't I? If a thing is funny, you laugh, don't you?"[3]

Having Gomez around laughing, and making others laugh, was good medicine in a clubhouse, and with him winning big, that was pretty good for everyone, too.

During spring training Phil Rizzuto was nervous, and one day when Gomez was pitching against the Brooklyn Dodgers, he sensed it. The Dodgers had two men on base and a ground ball could produce a double play. But when Gomez looked around at Rizzuto he thought he was so shaky he could easily make an error if the ball was grounded his way.

Gomez called time out and waved Rizzuto in for a visit to the mound. Gomez put his arm around the young player and said, "What's new, kid?" Rizzuto couldn't believe it. He thought Gomez wanted to talk strategy or positioning for the next hitter. "Whaddaya mean, 'What's new?' Is that what you called me over for?" he said.

The easy-going Gomez replied, "Naw. But I hear your folks are in the stands. I want to make them proud of you. Can't you see your mother saying to her friends now, 'See! When the great Lefty Gomez is in trouble, he turns to my boy Phil for advice.'"[4]

It was a strategy session, after all, one to ease Rizzuto's nerves, and since Gomez left him laughing, the little chat was deemed a success.

Like Ruffing, Gomez worked with Dickey behind the plate for years. Either for a rest or an injury, Dickey had to take days off. Squatting behind the dish is hard on a catcher's knees and that's why many of them shift to first base or the outfield late in their careers. Dickey was a catcher all of the way, but periodically back-ups got a chance to stretch their legs somewhere beyond the clubhouse and dugout.

One day, back-up catcher Joe Glenn was in the lineup and Gomez seemed to be shaking off all the signs, whether he put down one finger or two. Glenn was apparently a speed signer, because Gomez couldn't make out what he was doing. Glenn called time out, trotted out to the mound and greeted Gomez with the comment, "What's the matter? Don't you know the signs?" Not exactly a statement of respect for the veteran.

But nobody got into a bantering contest with Gomez and walked away unscathed. "Are those signals," Gomez asked, "or are you trying to hypnotize me?"[5]

Yes, it was good to have Lefty back in top form. Well, almost top form. During the 1941 season he pitched a 9–0 shutout against the St. Louis Browns — that was the good news. However, he walked 11 in the game, so calling it a masterpiece might have been a stretch.

Similarly, labeling the 1941 World Series against the Brooklyn Dodgers a masterpiece would be an exaggeration. An adventure, more like it, and memorable for all for sure.

The Dodgers of 1941 had nearly as marvelous a record as the Yankees. They finished 100–54, but they had a much tougher time beating back the opposition. The St. Louis Cardinals made it a pennant race all the way, before falling 2½ games short with a 97–56 record.

The teams stayed close all season and one reason was future Hall of Famer Joe Medwick being traded from the Cardinals to the Dodgers. Medwick, nicknamed "Ducky," was the St. Louis left-fielder and he wielded a powerful bat. Between 1932, when he made his major league debut, and 1940 when 37 games into the season he was transferred to Brooklyn, Medwick won one National League batting title, three RBI crowns, and led the league in hits twice, with a high of 237. In 1937, he won the Triple Crown and was the NL Most Valuable Player.

Only six days after being traded to the Dodgers, Medwick was beaned by a fastball that caused a concussion and threatened his life. Although he had several more fine seasons, Medwick never again led the league in any hitting category.

The reason for the trade was fundamental. Medwick kept asking the Cardinals for more money based on his continued success, and the Cardinals did not want to give him more than the $18,000 salary he had. When Medwick shifted to Brooklyn, he was paid $25,000 a year, and his playing for the Dodgers was probably the difference in Brooklyn's pennant triumph of 1941.

After World War II, the Yankees and Dodgers would become frequent foes in the World Series, but this was their first confrontation. The Yankees were used to seeing the New York Giants represent the National League, but Brooklyn had not won a pennant since 1920, before the Yankees' first dynasty emerged. It was definitely a subway Series and the New York–Brooklyn intensity was apparent at every step.

18. A Brooklyn-Bronx Subway Series

The "Boys of Summer" of Jackie Robinson, Gil Hodges, Duke Snider, Roy Campanella, and Carl Furillo came later. The Brooklyn leaders in 1941 were outfielders Medwick and Dixie Walker (.311), future Hall of Fame second baseman Billy Herman (.291), first baseman Dolph Camilli (.285 and 120 RBI)and catcher Mickey Owen. A potential superstar, Pete Reiser, the second-year player who had the reckless habit of running into outfield walls trying to make catches and instead gave himself concussions, hit .343. And 22-year-old shortstop Pee Wee Reese was the starter, but a year shy of making the first of ten All-Star teams on his way to the Hall of Fame.

Kirby Higbe and Whitlow Wyatt each won 22 games and Curt Davis won 13. Hugh Casey was the Dodgers' relief specialist and won 14 games out of the bullpen.

The local rooters had been calling them bums in Brooklyn during the 21-year gap between pennants, but these Dodgers felt they could take out the Yankees and win a world title. The Yankees were the big, bad bullies with history on their side and were favored. The Dodgers had nothing to be scared of for there was no pressure on them. As President Franklin D. Roosevelt said during that time period, though in a much more serious context, "The only thing we have to fear is fear itself." Everyone except the players, perhaps, expected the Yankees to win.

What were Brooklyn fans going to do to them if they didn't win? Run them over with a trolley? Beat them with the Dodgers Sym-phony's brass instruments?

Given that 70 years have passed, a fan must be pretty old to remember what happened in the 1941 World Series from any source beyond word of mouth or research. But it was painful for Dodgers fans and long-recalled as a would-have-been, could-have-been circumstance.

The Series opened on October 1 at Yankee Stadium and attendance was 68,540. If a facility had existed large enough, the game might well have attracted a million New Yorkers. Red Ruffing, the old war-horse, started for the Yankees and Curt Davis started for Brooklyn. It was a close game all of the way, but Ruffing threw a complete game. Davis was relieved first by Hugh Casey, and then Johnny Allen finished up in the 3–2 loss.

The Yankees took a 1–0 lead in the second inning on a Joe Gordon home run and kept it, also leading 2–0 and 3–1. The triumph gave the Yankees a 1–0 lead in games, too, in the best-four-out-of-seven Series.

In another well-pitched game, the Dodgers captured the second game at Yankee Stadium, also 3–2, overcoming a 2–0 lead with two runs in the fifth inning and one in the sixth. Wyatt bested Spud Chandler, who needed relief help from Johnny Murphy.

The entire scene transferred (some by subway) to Ebbets Field for the third game. Marius Russo earned the start for New York and Freddie Fitzsimmons was the starter for the Dodgers, a choice that surprised some since he was only 6–1 during the regular season. Nicknamed "Fat Freddie" for his physique, Fitzsimmons was already 40 when his World Series assignment rolled around. Although he won 217 regular-season games, Fitzsimmons had never won a World Series game and this was his big opportunity.

Russo and Fitzsimmons pitched a double shutout for seven innings in a juicy pitcher's duel. However, Russo smashed a line drive back to the mound at the end of the seventh inning that caromed off of Fitzsimmons' knee. Although he picked up the ball and made the throw that ended the inning, he had to leave the game because of the injury. Casey relieved, followed by Larry French and Allen in the ninth, but New York scored two runs in the eighth to win, 2–1.

Every game seemed to be like that for the Dodgers. They looked as if they might take a Series lead, and then some little thing would go wrong and the Yankees would win by one run. It was getting old. The Yankees may have had a 2–1 games advantage heading into the fourth game of the Series, but there was no reason to feel terribly secure. Each game was tight and the Dodgers were playing just about as well as they were.

There were 33,813 fans crammed into the Ebbets Field crackerjack box of a ball field for the October 5 game that would become one of the most infamous in baseball history. The Yankees took a 1–0 lead off of Higbe in the top of the first while Atley Donald held Brooklyn scoreless until the fourth inning. But that came after New York added two runs in the top half of the inning, and they retained a 3–2 lead.

Marv Breuer came in for Donald in the fifth when the Dodgers scored two runs for a 4–3 lead. The big blow was a Pete Reiser two-run home run. Dodgers manager Leo Durocher, the former Yankees shortstop, had a very short leash on this day and yanked Higbe for Larry French in the fourth. Johnny Allen came on in the fifth and Casey replaced him, holding the Yankees down until the ninth inning.

But it is the ninth inning that goes down in lore, an inning that changed baseball history and impacted men's lives for decades longer.

18. A Brooklyn-Bronx Subway Series

Casey was nicknamed "The Fireman" for his superb role as a relief pitcher. He had handled the Yankees fairly well from the time he appeared in the game until the ninth. But he quickly got two outs before the Yankees could mount a threat. When Casey got two strikes on Tommy Henrich, he was one pitch away from finishing off New York and knotting the Series at 2–2.

What followed was one of the most infamous gaffes in baseball history. Casey threw a pitch that broke and fooled Henrich. He swung and missed and the umpire, Larry Goetz, called the Yankees outfielder out on strikes. The only problem was that catcher Mickey Owen missed the ball and it bounced away. As Owen chased the ball, Henrich ran to first base and was safe. The official ruling was an error on Owen.

Instead of the game being over, Casey had to face the heart of the revived Yankees' order. Joe DiMaggio cracked a single to left, Charlie Keller hit a two-run double, Bill Dickey walked, and Joe Gordon doubled in two more runs. Before Casey checked another hitter, the Yankees led, 7–4, the final score. The stunning turn-around gave the Yankees a 3–1 lead in games instead of being knotted at 2–2.

In a most peculiar way, Henrich had lived up to his nickname of "Old Reliable." Owen later denied others' speculation that the pitch might have been an illegal spitball. Casey always insisted it was a curve. All Henrich knew was that the ball changed direction on him.

"I was fooled by the pitch," Henrich said. "The curveball started breaking and it never stopped. It was a high pitch and it was coming down in the strike zone. When I started to swing the darn thing didn't stop. It wasn't a surprise that he (Owen) dropped it because it fooled him just as much as it fooled me. And he had a glove on it. That was remarkable. A lot of guys say it was a spitter. But I say, 'You've never faced a guy like that.' It wasn't a spitter. I've faced spitters. They hop around. A curveball curves."[6]

That was the pivotal play in that World Series and gave New York a commanding 3–1 lead in games. Joe McCarthy started Ernie "Tiny" Bonham in the fifth game and he was superb. The Yankees scored two runs in the second inning, Brooklyn came back with a run in the third, and Henrich hit a home run in the fifth. The Yankees beat Whitlow Wyatt and won 3–1 to clinch their fifth World Series title in six years.

Henrich recalled Bonham and Dickey going over the Dodgers hitters before the game, looking for weaknesses. Dickey was the wise old head and Bonham had just completed his second season with the team, but had only appeared in 35 games in the majors. Teammates wondered if he might be nervous. Henrich overheard Bonham at the end of the study session. "Bill," he said to Dickey, "I'll never remember any of this stuff. Just put your glove where you want me to throw it and I'll throw it there."[7]

And that was exactly what Bonham did.

It was easy to see that the Dodgers were still smarting from the Game 3 loss and Henrich said pitcher Wyatt was particularly feisty, throwing a couple of high and inside fastballs to DiMaggio. After DiMaggio field out and was jogging back to the dugout, they had an exchange of words. Henrich attributed the comment "This Series isn't over yet" to Wyatt.[8]

Other sources attribute a similar phrase to DiMaggio. However, Wyatt charged at DiMaggio, players rushed at one another, but no punches were traded. "You couldn't call that a fight," DiMaggio said. "Whit and I never came within 20 feet of each other. He was shaving me pretty close with his pitches."[9]

The Yankees pinned the Series-deciding loss on Wyatt and their fans took the subway home to celebrate.

Owen spent 13 years in the majors and between 1941 and 1944 he was chosen for four National League All-Star teams. A .255 hitter known for his glove work, including the 1941 season when his fielding percentage was .995, it was always ironic that Owen was best-known for a fielding mistake. When founders were throwing around wads of cash in 1946, Owen jumped to the Mexican League.

After retiring in 1954 he opened the Mickey Owen Baseball School in Missouri. As an owner, and continuing as an instructor after selling the business, Owen attracted some famous clientele. When Michael Jordan, who had won three NBA championships with the Chicago Bulls, switched from basketball to give baseball a try, he attended the Mickey Owen Baseball School. So did Charlie Sheen, who played a relief pitcher in the movie "Major League" and the Yankees' current manager, Joe Girardi. Owen remained an instructor into the 1980s.

Knowledgeable baseball fans with good memories, however, always asked Owen about missing the third strike that allowed the Yankees to make a comeback. Affable by nature, Owen carried his burden well, often making jokes with fans about his miscue and never being gruff with his answers.

18. A Brooklyn-Bronx Subway Series 183

"Those are good memories now," Owen said in 1989. "I've gotten over it. It's part of baseball history. The ball hit my mitt pretty good, but it just got by me. It looked like a rabbit hopping away. That big curveball was the last thing I was expecting. He hadn't thrown it since about his first inning. I should have been ready for any type of curveball, but I wasn't."[10]

There were reasons — Henrich's swing, Owen expecting another kind of pitch — for him to miss catching Casey's pitch, but no excuses, and Owen played it that way the rest of his life when interviewed by sportswriters who wanted him to relive what he accurately said was a piece of baseball history.

"I was lousy that day, I admit it, but I sure ain't gonna worry about it the rest of my life," Owen said.[11] Owen maintained that attitude, even in his later years when he continued to get mail regularly from fans who invariably brought up the passed ball.

"It's ironic," Owen said in 1984. "That year I set a record for most consecutive chances (476) accepted without an error which still stands. Nobody knows that. I made a boo-boo after setting a record. Now they'll never forget me."[12]

Meanwhile, after serving in the Navy, Casey continued to be a sound relief pitcher for the Dodgers, pitching in another World Series in 1947. His career record was 75–42. Away from the field, Casey kept busy running a restaurant and sparring with Ernest Hemingway in the writer's living room. But in 1951 he turned a shotgun on himself and committed suicide, ending his life at 37.

The 1941 baseball season had begun with uncertainty for the Yankees, wondering if they could regain their pre–1940 luster. In the middle of it, Lou Gehrig died from a dreaded disease and was laid to rest, and Joe DiMaggio compiled his magnificent 56-game hitting streak. At the end, they returned to glory with another World Series championship, vindicating the greatness of the team and the cool judgment and leadership of Joe McCarthy, Ed Barrow and George Weiss.

Baseball was over for the year, but 1941 was not over yet. Events still to come were among the most momentous of the twentieth century for the United States. The war had been raging in Europe for two years, England was hanging on against the Nazi threat, and Japan had become more belligerent. Americans nervously read newspaper reports and listened to the radio for updates from President Franklin D. Roosevelt. They worried about being drawn into a war that no one wanted, but that more and more people recognized would probably be necessary to halt the advancement of conscienceless dictatorships.

As the Yankees recorded their title in the baseball record books, the dramatic shift, the triggering event, that everyone awaited, was etched into the history books. On December 7, 1941, the Japanese air force bombed Pearl Harbor in Hawaii. There was no more ignoring the war consuming much of the planet. The United States was officially a combatant.

19

War Changes Everything

Once the Japanese bombed Pearl Harbor and the United States was in the war on all fronts, no one knew if there would be another baseball season any time soon. Yet only weeks after the December 7, 1941, attack, Commissioner Kenesaw Mountain Landis received the so-called "Green Light Letter" from President Franklin D. Roosevelt that the sport should go ahead with its plans for a 1942 season.

In a letter dated January 15, FDR wrote to the commissioner, who only the day before had asked for advice in the face of the country's grim new task of fighting a war. Although Roosevelt couched his response to Landis' inquiry in what he called personal rather than official terms, it was the president speaking, so his words were going to be taken as the point of view of the nation's leader.

In part, Roosevelt wrote, "I honestly feel that it would be best for the country to keep baseball going. There will be fewer people unemployed and everybody will work longer hours and harder than ever before. And that means that they ought to have a chance for recreation and for taking their minds off their work even more than before."

Roosevelt specifically did not exempt ball players from military service and urged "without question" that players serve. As an aside, he put in a pitch for more night games "because it gives an opportunity to the day shift to see a game occasionally."[1]

So there would be baseball. But healthy, athletic young baseball players would be exchanging uniforms. As the world was falling apart, the Yankees were coming together again on top of the world in their sport. However, not even Ed Barrow could completely keep up with the changes on the roster with the first Yankees players joining the Armed Services. In 1942, pitchers Steve Peek and Charley Stanceau, catcher Ken Silvestri, and infielder Johnny Sturm went off to war, and not against the American League.

Most players on most teams completed the 1942 season before joining up to fight. But Hank Greenberg, the Tigers basher, was already signed up. So was Bob Feller of the Indians. They were the earliest military volunteers among the big stars in the American League. Feller enlisted in the Navy two days after Pearl Harbor and won eight Navy battle stars. Red Sox outfielder Ted Williams, also decorated as a Marine Corps pilot, entered the service in 1943.

Before the end of December of 1941, Congress enacted a new draft law that made all able-bodied American men between the ages of 20 and 45 eligible to be summoned into the service. Those who were 18 or 19 years old were required to register, but could not be drafted. Similarly, men older than 45 through 64 also had to register, but were not draft eligible.

During the war, that changed. The draft age was lowered to 18 and many men older than 45 volunteered. One of those was Hank Gowdy, the esteemed catcher who batted .270 in 17 major league seasons. Gowdy, then with the Braves, fought in the trenches in France during World War I and toured speaking about his military experiences after he returned. In early 1943, when he was 53, Gowdy, then a coach for the Cincinnati Reds, enlisted again. He was given the rank of captain and finished the war as a major. Then he resumed coaching with Cincinnati.

The nation's and baseball's environments were completely different in 1942.

Advertisements that mixed baseball and the war effort began appearing in print. One ad pumped up the availability of Al Schacht "The Clown Prince of Baseball," for appearances and tied his humor act to saving gasoline and rubber for military use.

The Sheldon-Claire Company, a Chicago-based advertising agency, produced a series of magazine-page-sized ads with the theme of "This is America" to inspire people. One such ad pictured a rural hometown scene of ball players in uniform with farmers in overalls hanging out at a gas station. The copy read "This is America ... where a fellow can start on the home team and wind up in the big leagues. Where there is always room at the top for the fellow who has it on the ball. This is YOUR America ... Keep it Free!"

19. War Changes Everything

It was against this backdrop that the Yankees set out to defend their American League pennant. One of the big reasons they were able to do so was another slick player acquisition. The Yankees used 13 pitchers during the summer of 1942, many of them big names, but some of them were winding down their careers.

This time Lefty Gomez really was done. He only managed a 6–4 season. This was the year of Tiny Bonham's emergence when he was a dominant 21–5. Red Ruffing was still good for a 14–7 season and Spud Chandler had one of his best years at 16–5. But the difference-maker, the pitcher who filled out the rotation, gave the Yankees depth, and enabled them to zoom away from AL competition with a 103–51 record, was a late comer.

The Yankees finished nine games ahead of the Red Sox, but were not threatened in the standings after May. The promotion of right-hander Hank Borowy, who had attended Fordham University, was the latest in sharp personnel moves the Yankees always seemed to have up their sleeves when they needed fresh blood. Borowy made his major league debut on April 18 and fit right in, taking his turn in the rotation all summer and finishing 15–4 with a 2.82 earned run average as a rookie.

Yes, this was another case of the Yankees reloading. The phrase was not in vogue in sports at the time, but became a cliché from overuse later about a team never having to rebuild, only reload, and that was certainly an accurate way of looking at McCarthy's Yankees. The one thing that bugged him, however, was sportswriters' jibes referring to him as a "push-button manager." The implication was that he didn't have to do anything except throw the players out on the field and they would win, and that any old manager could do that.

That feeling, from some people (since it surely was not the pervasive outlook, only a minority one) that he viewed as nincompoops, got under his skin nonetheless and represented one of the rare ways he could be truly bothered, as opposed to transitorily angry, by criticism. This was his life's work and it was belittled, not because of lack of success, but because of too much success. Not even the rankled McCarthy had a ready answer to combat a perception that seemed to make little sense.

"Yankee haters called him a push-button manager, implying that the bat boy could have won with those players," one sports columnist observed.[2] Jimmy Dykes, the long-time manager of other American League teams who was regarded as a smart leader, yet never won a pennant, was one who employed the derogatory phrase, although another writer noted, "(Dykes) used to wish that he could push the same buttons."[3]

Many statements of admiration for McCarthy's success came later, but sportswriter Red Smith, who did not fall for the junk about him being a push-button manager, said that the opposite was proven after the Yankees missed out on the 1940 pennant, but then quickly reversed their fortunes. "Joe McCarthy is the best manager in baseball and one of the best that the game has ever known," he wrote.[4]

It was Joe DiMaggio, who possessed a fair amount of knowledge about the game, who paid McCarthy the ultimate compliment. "Never a day went by when you didn't learn something from Joe McCarthy," he said.[5]

McCarthy had sharp vision and a calculating mind, like a chess player. He always absorbed every detail of what went on in the clubhouse, the dugout, and on the field, and he reached into his memory bank to retrieve information when he needed to make decisions. Usually, he made the right call, and usually the Yankees won.

After the 1940 interlude, the Yankees won their second straight pennant in 1942 and sixth in seven years. It was not one of DiMaggio's best hitting seasons, but it was still of All-Star caliber. His key statistics were 21 home runs, 114 runs batted in and a .305 average. DiMaggio was also surrounded by batsmen who could carry a team almost as well as he could. Joe Gordon stroked 18 home runs, drove in 103 runs and batted .322. Charlie Keller hit 26 home runs, knocked in 108 runs and batted .292. Any Yankee pitcher walking to the mound could be confident that his team was going to score a lot of runs for him.

For more than a decade, the Yankees had been blitzing National League opponents in the World Series. New York had not only ousted their foes to capture championships, most years the Series wasn't even close. This time would be different.

St. Louis finished 106–48, a record even better than the Yankees.' But the Cardinals had to be that good to survive. After August 15, the Cardinals trailed the Brooklyn Dodgers by 9½ games in the standings, and it took a monumental closing run to seize the pennant. The Dodgers finished 104–50. St. Louis was beyond-belief sharp down the stretch, going 43–8. The Cards set a team record for wins and almost all of the players were homegrown, coming up through the farm system that general manager Branch Rickey had established.

19. War Changes Everything

These successors to the Gas House Gang were managed by Billy Southworth. Pitcher Mort Cooper won the Most Valuable Award with a 22–7 record and a 1.78 earned run average, and rookie Johnny Beazley was 21–6. Enos Slaughter hit .318, young Stan Musial hit .315, and Harry "The Hat" Walker hit .314 in half a season. Marty Marion (who also hit .276) was brilliant at shortstop. Still, there was a feeling that the Yankees had enough pitching to control the Cardinals hitters.

This feeling was reinforced in the first game when New York's old veteran, Red Ruffing, outpitched St. Louis ace Cooper in a 7–4 Yankee win. The game was played in Sportsman's Park and there were 34,769 fans in the small park to witness the opening-game disappointment. Ruffing took a no-hitter into the eighth inning, but his bid for the first no-hit game in a Series was denied when St. Louis centerfielder Terry Moore singled.

The Cardinals made the home fans feel a little bit better the next day when they topped the Yankees, 4–3. Beazley beat Bonham, despite a game-tying home run from Charlie Keller in the eighth inning.

That moved the Series to New York, where the Yankees attracted 69,123 to the Stadium. Yet amidst the red, white and blue blunting and other World Series hoopla even during wartime, the Cardinals regained the momentum with a 2–0 victory on a six-hit shutout by Ernie White over Chandler.

With St. Louis leading the Series, 2–1, in games, Game 4 was pivotal. Surprisingly, it was the Cardinals not only prevailing, but doing so by outscoring New York, 9–6. Max Lanier got the win and Atley Donald took the loss, after surrendering a pair of seventh-inning runs that broke a 6–6 tie.

As powerful as the Yankees were, as rich as their history was in championship games, trailing 3–1, it was only a long-shot that New York could come back. The first task was merely extending the Series. But the Yankees couldn't even do that. The 1942 Series ended in their backyard before 69,052 subdued fans. Southworth threw Beazley, not Cooper, against Ruffing this time and St. Louis won, 4–2. It was the first time the Yankees had been on the losing side in a World Series since 1926, when they also lost to the Cardinals.

Winning the pennant was part of the goal every season, but losing the World Series was unacceptable if you were a Yankee. When you got there, you were supposed to win it all.

It was more difficult to plan for the 1943 season than any season before, or at least since the end of World War I. Forces much greater than the Yankees brass were at work that would affect the men's lives who wore the pinstripes.

Adolph Hitler, the maniac in Germany, marched on in pursuit of world domination, his seemingly inexhaustibly armed and manned war machine overrunning all of Western Europe except Great Britain, spilling into Africa, and now unleashing its might on Russia. Japan had conquered China and wished to hopscotch through all countries bordering the Pacific.

FDR was right in believing that the nation could use the respite from tragic and terrifying world reports by following its favorite pastime. But no one had his head deep enough in the sand to ignore the rest of worldwide happenings occurring beyond the left-field wall. You could root, root, root for the home team, but chances were that the home team was going to be missing some guys you were used to seeing because they were slipping on other uniforms. And even if your team continued to do well in the standings, there was too much death and destruction to believe that the story of the moment was guaranteed a happy ending.

Yankees roster changes because of the war had been minimal in 1942. They were far more substantive in 1943.

Red Ruffing, the rock of the pitching staff since 1930, was gone until 1945 and didn't pitch for New York again until he was 40. Lesser known hurler Norm Branch, who had been 5–1 in 1941, showing some promise, but had just one decision in 1942, was gone, too, and never pitched again in the majors. Randy Gumpert, formerly a Philadelphia Athletic, didn't play in the majors between 1938 and 1946 when he won 11 games for the Yankees after the war.

Buddy Hassett, who was just settling in at first base in 1942 when he hit .284, never played big-league ball again. Infielder Hank Majeski never played a minute for New York until 1946 after losing four years to the war.

The biggest loss in the infield was young Phil Rizzuto. Rizzuto played two seasons at shortstop, and then was drafted, missing the 1943 and 1944 seasons. His was a much larger hole to fill than those others. Except for the outfielders. In 1943, George Selkirk, Tommy Henrich and Joe DiMaggio all left for military service. Charlie Keller was still around, but the others were replaced by Johnny Lindell, Bud Metheny, Tuck Stainback, and Roy Weatherly. It was not the same.

Rizzuto batted .381 in the 1942 World Series that the Yankees lost to the Cardinals and reported for induction as a seaman first class immediately after the Series ended in five games. He said later that if the Series had extended to a sixth and seventh game he would have had to miss them. "The only ones who knew that were Cora (his soon-to-be-wife), (manager Joe) McCarthy and myself," Rizzuto said.[6]

Henrich was called to serve before the end of the 1942 regular season, playing his final game on August 30 against the Tigers. When he dug into the batter's box, the public address announcer informed the fans, "Ladies and Gentlemen, Tommy Henrich has been ordered to report for active duty with the Coast Guard. This is his last appearance in a Yankee uniform until the war is over."

The ovation that followed was memorable and touching for Henrich. "I wasn't sure I deserved all of it," he said. "I was just going into the service like everyone else."[7]

Of course, that was the point. He was doing what everyone else's sons and husbands were doing, putting his life at risk for the honor of his country. At various times, with various teams, in various cities during World War II there was a public backlash against individual players. In certain quarters the thinking was that these baseball players were athletes, so they must be physically capable of serving in the Army. But players had many physical ailments that would make them unfit, whether it was bad knees, poor eyesight, bad backs, or poor hearing. Manager Leo Durocher was exempt because he had a perforated ear drum.

While it became more difficult to field teams with major league–caliber players and some owners wanted to shut the doors of their parks until after the war, Barrow was one of the stalwarts who insisted the majors keep on playing even if rosters had to be reduced to 16 players. But there were changes.

Commissioner Landis did not relish the image of players at spring training being photographed lounging around in bathing suits in Florida, and there were wartime restrictions on gasoline and travel, so he ordered teams to run their camps close to their home cities. The Yankees held spring training in Asbury Park, New Jersey, a summer destination, but one of those places that understood the meaning of spring coming in like a lion in March and going out like a lamb in April.

The Pittsburgh Pirates trained in Muncie, Indiana, that year and the Brooklyn Dodgers near West Point, New York. By the end of spring the teams training so far north were more familiar with snow than sand. Teenagers too young to sign up for the Army tried to sign up with professional baseball teams. It was estimated that 200 hopefuls tried out with the Dodgers. Harold Parrott, the Dodgers' traveling secretary, said, "I was used to players coming to me for advances on their salaries. But I think Duke Snider was the first player who ever asked me for candy money."[8]

The late Duke, who died in 2011, did not turn 18 until 1944, but later blossomed into a Hall of Fame outfielder.

As the war years dragged on and the United States plumbed deeper and deeper into the male population to replenish the branches of the service, being adjudged 4-F became more difficult. By 1944, in a symbol of the times, the St. Louis Browns lined up Pete Gray, a one-armed outfielder, for 77 games. Given his disability, Gray was a marvel, hitting .333 with 63 stolen bases in the Southern Association, but still probably wouldn't have been given a big-league chance without the majors' manpower shortage. Gray batted .217 for St. Louis in 1945 and earned the admiration of baseball followers forever.

In a controversial vote, DiMaggio had won the Most Valuable Player award ahead of Ted Williams in 1941. DiMaggio hit .408 during his streak, but Williams hit .406 for the entire season. DiMaggio was the Most Valuable Player and author of the most electrifying new baseball record, and still the cornerstone of a championship team. Yet Barrow sent him a contract without offering any raise. DiMaggio was frustrated and Barrow uttered his famous comment, "Doesn't he know there's a war on?"[9] DiMaggio ended up with a $2,000 raise to $42,000.

By 1942, the United States had banned alien residents from participating in the Fisherman's Wharf crab fishing fleet, and that included Giuseppe DiMaggio, then 67, Joe's father. The U.S. was at war with Italy, Germany's chief partner in Europe. Joe D's brother also informed him that his restaurant was struggling because there was no tourism in San Francisco from other parts of the country, also because of the war.

On February 17, 1943, DiMaggio enlisted in the Army at the San Francisco Armed Services induction center. Unlike many other major leaguers, however, DiMaggio did not go to the front. He was assigned the rank of sergeant and assigned to play baseball in California at first. He was in the midst of his divorce case with Dorothy Arnold when he was sent to Hawaii. In Hawaii he again played ball for the morale of U.S. men in uni-

19. War Changes Everything

form rather than for civilian fans buying tickets. His salary in the Army was $50 a month, considerably less than Barrow offered on his chintziest days.

So many Yankees were deployed in so many parts of the world that Barrow could have mounted a map on his office wall and placed pins in it to remind him of where his guys were. The one attachment to normality was trying to win another pennant. If they were going to play out the season, then the Yankees were in it to win.

Every team was depleted, and every team would continue to lose players, so there was no telling who would pose the greatest competition or how this most unusual of seasons would play out. Yet McCarthy's Yankees did claim another pennant, finishing 98–56, 13½ games ahead of the Washington Senators. For once the cynical comment, "Washington, first in war, first in peace, and last in the American League," did not apply. The Yankees broke open a close race with 20 wins in 25 games during July.

This was Spud Chandler's epic year on the mound, his 20–4 season with a 1.64 ERA. Tiny Bonham won 15 games with an excellent 2.27 ERA and Hank Borowy came through again with a 14–9 mark. After an off-season the year before, Johnny Murphy was 12–4. Butch Wensloff went 13–11 as a 28-year-old rookie before going into the service, and that season represented his main baseball glory.

At 36, Bill Dickey hit .351 in 85 games. Charlie Keller crushed 31 home runs. First baseman Nick Etten hit 14 home runs with 107 RBI while batting .271, and rookie third baseman Billy Johnson drove in 94 runs. Johnson promptly went into the service, too, after the year, not to return to the Yankees until 1946. Another rookie that year was George "Snuffy" Stirnweiss, who batted .219 in half a season at shortstop, but who improved greatly the next year when he hit 100 points higher and in 1945 when he led the American League with a .309 average. Stirnweiss was 4F because of stomach ulcers.

In the National League the Cardinals, who had so easily disposed of the Yankees in the 1943 World Series, were again kings of the hill with a stunning 105–49 record, although Enos Slaughter, Johnny Beazley and Terry Moore were serving their country. St. Louis finished 18 games ahead of the Reds. Billy Southworth had the goods to work with and he used the talent well. The Cardinals batted .279 as a team with 22-year-old Stan Musial tops at .357. Catcher Walker Cooper hit .318. Marion was still performing magic with his glove at short and hit .280.

It might be argued that despite the heavy hitters, the Cardinals had their way with the league because of their pitching. Howie Pollett (8–4) led the NL with a 1.75 earned run average. Max Lanier (15–7) was second at 1.90 and Mort Cooper (21–8) was third at 2.30. They figured to make it tough for a Yankees lineup missing DiMaggio, Henrich, Rizzuto, Selkirk and others to be able to string together big innings.

War-time travel restrictions led Commissioner Landis to decree that the seven-game Series be broken up in an unusual format. The first three games were scheduled for Yankee Stadium and the last four games, if necessary, were scheduled for Sportsman's Park.

The Series opened on October 5 before 68,676 fans at Yankee Stadium with Spud Chandler, the best pitcher in the American League that year, going against Max Lanier. Any prophecy that the Yankees would find it challenging to score heavily turned out to be true, but it also turned out not to matter because the Yankees out-pitched the Cardinals.

It started with Chandler, who hurled a complete game in New York's 4–2 victory, allowing seven hits. The only home run came off the bat of the Yankees' Joe Gordon.

Mort Cooper and Tiny Bonham faced off in a good match-up in the second game, also in the Bronx, and the Cardinals evened the Series with a 4–3 win. Marty Marion, who rarely hit the ball much farther than the shortstop base-path that he covered on defense, and Ray Sanders hit homers for St. Louis.

If home-field advantage meant anything, it was important for New York to win the final Series game at Yankee Stadium, and the Yanks came through with a 6–2 win. Hank Borowy held the Cards down with relief help from Johnny Murphy. The Cardinals had used their top two starters already and turned to Al Brazle, who had gone 8–2 with a 1.53 ERA during the regular season.

That sent the World Series to St. Louis with the Yankees leading 2–1 in games and feeling pretty good about their chances. Joe McCarthy relied on Marius Russo in the fourth game, and Russo came through with a solid outing, beating reliever Harry Brecheen, 2–1. St. Louis' only run was unearned and came home because of two New York errors.

Now the Yankees were in position to wrap it up and reverse the results from the year before when the Cardinals swamped them, 4–1.

The fifth game, before 33,872 fans at Sportsman's Park, was a battle of aces. McCarthy sent Chandler out again and Southworth sent Mort Cooper out. Although he allowed ten hits, Chandler won his second game of the Series with a 2–0 triumph. Bill Dickey, the old warhorse, hit a two-run home run for the game's only scoring.

The Yankees were world champions again, winners of their seventh pennant and sixth World Series crown in eight years.

"Beating any other National League club would never have given us the same amount of satisfaction," McCarthy said. "They made us look bad last year. This time I think we repaid the compliment."[10]

After the 1943 season, baseball's player shortage became more acute. The complications of the times, the loss of players to military service, the difficulties in securing replacements, all caught up to the Yankees. Bill Dickey had been the one great constant from the late 1920s era with Babe Ruth, through the ascendancy and death of Lou Gehrig, through the rise of Joe DiMaggio. But he was one of the aging Yankees still on the roster. DiMaggio was in the service. So were Phil Rizzuto, Tommy Henrich, and Red Ruffing. The Yankees lost the American League pennant to the St. Louis Browns in 1944. New York didn't win the pennant in 1945 or 1946, either. Joe McCarthy was out as manager and the front office was under new management.

The Second Yankees Dynasty, spanning one of the single winningest periods by any professional team in any sport, was over. As life in the United States returned to normalcy after World War II in the 1940s and 1950s, it was hard to imagine the Yankees would be able to again find stars of the caliber of Joe DiMaggio, a manager the equal of Joe McCarthy, and a team capable of doing such great things again.

Who would have believed that a Third Yankees Dynasty lay just around the corner?

Epilogue

They have all passed on now, all of the players from the Second Yankees Dynasty, even Yankee Stadium, the version that Ruth built. That was replaced in 2009 with a new $2.3 billion house that George Steinbrenner built.

Most of the Yankee players of the 1930s and 1940s died many years ago. Some never returned to the majors after World War II. Some returned to the Yankees and thrived.

Joe DiMaggio, who retired in 1951 because of an Achilles heel problem, became the greatest legend of them all. The Yankee Clipper's fame only increased in retirement and in legendary status when he married blonde bombshell actress Marilyn Monroe. Although his statistics do not match many of the statistics compiled by other Hall of Fame greats that his reputation keeps company with, some fans consider DiMaggio the greatest player of all time.

DiMaggio died in 1999 at the age of 84, after he had been reinvented for modern audiences as an advertising pitchman, notably as Mr. Coffee. Somehow he retained a general standing as someone with class and dignity.

Phil Rizzuto won a Most Valuable Player award in 1950, was a five-time All-Star and seven-time World Series champion in a Hall of Fame career before becoming a decades-long broadcaster known for shouting "Holy cow!" into the microphone. He was 89 when he died in 2007.

Lefty Gomez won nearly twice as many games as he lost, hanging on with his weakening arm into 1943 and eventually being elected to the Hall of Fame. For years he told stories about his days with the Yankees on the banquet circuit and was 80 when he died in 1989.

Manager Joe McCarthy left the Yankees in 1946, sat out one season, and then signed to manage the Red Sox. He could never capture another

American League flag with Boston, whose intense rivalry with the Yankees that continues today was initiated by those confrontations. Elected to the Hall of Fame in 1957, McCarthy was 90 when he died in 1978.

Ed Barrow's tenure ended with the Yankees in 1945. Between 1921 and that year, while he served in executive capacities, the Yankees won 14 pennants and ten World Series. He obtained Babe Ruth from the Red Sox and supervised the signing of Lou Gehrig and Joe DiMaggio. Barrow died at 85 in 1953.

Lou Gehrig is still regarded by many as the greatest first baseman of all-time, 70 years after his death. Few of his accomplishments have been approached by specialists at the position, and when all time All-Star rosters are chosen Gehrig is always on them. He would no doubt be grievously disappointed to learn that there is still no cure for amyotrophic lateral sclerosis, the disease that killed him. It is impossible to know what Gehrig would feel if he realized that the illness has come to be named after him and that is how most Americans know it.

Soon after World War II, under the ownership of Dan Topping and Del Webb, the general manager guidance of holdover George Weiss, and manager Casey Stengel, the Yankees answered the question of what team might become the next great dynasty. The answer was ... the Yankees.

With Hall of Famers like Mickey Mantle, Yogi Berra and Whitey Ford, home run record-setter Roger Maris, Bobby Richardson, Elston Howard, Clete Boyer, Bill Skowron, Tony Kubek, Hank Bauer, Johnny Mize, Billy Martin, Gil McDougald, Allie Reynolds, Vic Raschi and Ed Lopat, the Yankees won ten pennants in 12 years under Stengel. They also kept rolling and between 1947 and 1964 the Yankees won 15 pennants in 18 years. Twice during that stretch the Yankees won five pennants in a row, and under Stengel between 1949 and 1953, they won five straight World Series titles.

That was the Third Yankees Dynasty.

In a different kind of competitive baseball world, with more teams and player free agency permitting stars to jump from team to team when their contracts ran out, George Steinbrenner's Yankees teams won 11 pennants and seven World Series during his 37-year ownership from 1973 to his death in 2010. He changed general managers 11 times and managers 20 times, so Steinbrenner was essentially the only common denominator during his tenure.

Steinbrenner teams won three pennants in a row between 1976 and

1978, and four in a row between 1998 and 2001. Although it would be difficult to classify Steinbrenner's Yankees teams as a dynasty, he certainly worked hard and spent heavily to keep the winning tradition going.

From the days of Jacob Ruppert to the present-day ownership of Steinbrenner's heirs, the New York Yankees have won 40 pennants and 27 World Series. No franchise in baseball, or any other sport, has come close.

Chapter Notes

Introduction

1. Leigh Montville, *The Big Bam: The Life and Times of Babe Ruth* (New York: Doubleday, 2006), p. 109.
2. Ibid., p. 110.
3. BaseballAlmanac.com.
4. Montville, *The Big Bam*, p. 303.

Chapter 1

1. George DeGregorio, *Joe DiMaggio, An Informal Biography* (Princeton, NJ Townhouse, 1981), p. 23.
2. Ibid., p. 23.
3. Daniel R. Levitt, *Ed Barrow: The Bulldog Who Built the Yankees' First Dynasty* (Lincoln: The University of Nebraska Press, 2008), p. 7.
4. Alan H. Levy, Joe McCarthy: Architect of the Yankee Dynasty (Jefferson, NC: McFarland, 2005), p. 150.
5. Ibid., p. 151.
6. DeGregorio, *Joe DiMaggio*, p. 83.
7. Ibid., p. 83.
8. Richard Ben Cramer, *Joe DiMaggio: The Hero's Life* (New York: Simon & Schuster, 2000), p. 69.
9. Joseph Durso, *The Last American Knight* (Boston: Little, Brown, 1995), p. 77.

Chapter 2

1. Lou Gehrig Official Web Site, www.lougehrig.com.
2. Ibid.
3. Ibid.
4. "Kid Who Retrieved Babe's 700th Home Run Ball Still Has $20 Bill, *New York Daily News*, July 15, 1973 (National Baseball Hall of Fame Library Archives).
5. Ibid.
6. Bill Furlong, "The Day Ruth Called It Quits," *Chicago Daily Times*, May 21, 1960.
7. Henry P. Edwards, American League Service Bureau press release, Dec. 13, 1936.
8. Leo Trachtenberg, *The Answer To: Who Replaced Babe Ruth in Right Field* for the Yankees, *Yankees Magazine*, Oct. 13, 1983.

9. Edwards, American League Service Bureau press release.
10. Ibid.

Chapter 3

1. Richard Ben Cramer, *Joe DiMaggio: The Hero's Life* (New York: Simon & Schuster, 2000), p. 74.
2. Ibid., p. 108.
3. Ibid.
4. Maury Allen, *Where Have You Gone, Joe DiMaggio?* (New York: New American Library, 1976), p. 30.
5. Ibid.
6. Ibid., p. 31.
7. Ibid.
8. Leo Trachtenberg, "Lefty Gomez, Fastballer and Funnyman," *Yankees Magazine*, n.d. (National Baseball Hall of Fame Library archives).
9. Lefty Gomez, "I learned about Baseball," Home Newspapers, March 15, 1935.
10. Trachtenberg, "Lefty Gomez."
11. "Gomez called time in Series to watch plane," *St. Louis Post-Dispatch*, May 22, 1967.
12. Gene Schoor, *The World Series: The Complete Chronology of America's Greatest Sports Tradition* (New York: William Morrow, 1990), p. 163.
13. Rud Rennie, "Yankees, 8 Clubs Split Players' Pool Of $460,002," *New York Herald-Tribune*, Oct. 23, 1936.
14. Ibid.

Chapter 4

1. Douglas G. Simpson, "Red Ruffing," *Biographical Dictionary of American Sport* (National Baseball Hall of Fame Library Archives).
2. Leo Trachtenberg, "Red," *Yankees Magazine*, March 2002.
3. Will Wedge, "Red Ruffing Comes of Fighting Clan," *New York Sun*, Oct. 1, 1942.
4. Trachtenberg, "Red."
5. Ted Shane, "Big Red," *American Magazine*, August 1939.
6. Dan Daniel, "Broaca in Great Form," *New York World-Telegram*, March 20, 1935.
7. Ibid.
8. United Press International, "Broaca Testifies Wife Was Very Temperamental," *New York World-Telegram*, Dec. 16, 1937.
9. Ibid.
10. "Playboy Pitcher Admits He Spent $28,000 on Parties," *New York Journal-American*, Dec. 15, 1937.
11. "Broaca Balks At Alimony," *New York Daily News*, Feb. 23, 1938.
12. Sid Mercer, "Broaca in Training For Career in Ring," *New York Journal-American*, Jan. 26, 1938.
13. "Broaca Pitches Plea for Son At Ex-Wife," *New York Journal-American*, Aug. 4, 1939.
14. Radio transcript, "Out of the Past," with Jacob Ruppert, Aug. 5, 1938.

15. Dan Daniel, "Cousin Ed Tough on Surface, But Softie on Inside," *The Sporting News*, Dec. 23, 1953.
16. Edward G. Barrow, "My Baseball Story," *Collier's Magazine*, May 20, 1950.

Chapter 5

1. Obituaries, Monte Pearson, *The Sporting News*, Feb. 18, 1978.
2. Ibid.
3. Ibid.
4. Alan H. Levy, *Joe McCarthy, Architect of the Yankee Dynasty* (Jefferson, NC: McFarland, 2005), p. 214.
5. Leo Trachtenberg, "No-Hitter Author," *Yankees Magazine*, n.d. (National Baseball Hall of Fame Library Archives).
6. Ibid.
7. Paul Votano, *Tony Lazzeri: A Baseball Biography* (Jefferson, NC: McFarland, 2005), p. 160.
8. John J. Ward, *Blubber Malone, Boss Pitcher of the Bull-Pen* source unknown, February 1937 (National Baseball Hall of Fame Library Archives).
9. Ibid.
10. "Yanks Buy Malone From Cards To Bolster Doubtful Mound Staff," *New York Herald-Tribune*, March 27, 1935.
11. Ward, "Blubber Malone."
12. Ibid.
13. Frank Graham, "Setting the Pace," *New York Sun*, Aug. 7, 1936.
14. "Ex-Twirler Hadley Dead," source unknown, March 2, 1963 (National Baseball Hall of Fame Library Archives).
15. Dan Daniel, "The Rise of Bump Hadley," *New York World-Telegram*, Sept. 15, 1937.
16. "Ex-Twirler Hadley Dead."
17. Sid Mercer, "Hadley Downcast Over Injury to Cochrane," *New York Journal-American*, May 27, 1937.
18. Leo Trachtenberg, "Grandma Johnny," *Yankees Magazine*, n.d.
19. Ibid.

Chapter 6

1. Unknown source, Jan. 25, 1954 (National Baseball Hall of Fame Library Archives).
2. Paul Votano, *Tony Lazzeri: A Baseball Biography* (Jefferson, NC: McFarland, 2005), p. 13.
3. Ibid., p. 71.
4. Ibid., p. 133.
5. Harry T. Brundidge, "Believe It Or Not, Tony Lazzeri Got His Greatest Thrill When He Fanned with Bases Loaded in World Series," *St. Louis Star-Chronicle*, Dec. 11, 1930.
6. Bob Considine, "Fans Remember Bad Points, But Not Good Ones, Lazzeri Says," *Pittsburgh Sun-Telegraph*, Sept. 10, 1945.
7. Ibid.
8. Harry Jupiter, "Lazzeri The Great," *Image Magazine*, Feb. 19, 1989.
9. Ibid.

10. Frank Graham, "Setting the Pace," *New York Sun*, Sept. 10, 1937.
11. Votano, *Tony Lazzeri*, p. 154.
12. Ibid., p. 163.
13. Shirley Povich, "This Morning," *Washington Post*, Aug. 9, 1946.
14. Joe Gergen, "Poosh 'Em Up," *Newsday*, July 16, 1991.

Chapter 7

1. Henry P. Edwards, American League Service Bureau press release, March 2, 1930.
2. Thomas Rogers, "Bill Dickey, the Yankee Catcher And Hall of Famer, Dies at 86," *New York Times*, Nov. 13, 1993.
3. Edwards, American League Service Bureau press release.
4. Bob Broeg, "A Yankee of Distinction," *The Sporting News*, June 13, 1970.
5. Bill Madden, "Dickey Maybe Greatest of All," *New York Daily News*, Nov. 14, 1993.
6. Rogers, "Bill Dickey."
7. Broeg, "A Yankee of Distinction."
8. Ibid.
9. J.G. Taylor Spink, "Looping the Loops," *The Sporting News*, Feb. 18, 1948.
10. John P. Carmichael, *My Greatest Day in Baseball* (New York: Grosset & Dunlap, 1951), p. 46.
11. Richard Ben Cramer, *Joe DiMaggio: The Hero's Life* (New York: Simon & Schuster, 2000), p. 93.
12. Broeg, "A Yankee of Distinction."

Chapter 8

1. Leo Trachtenberg, "A Great Teacher and Coach," *Yankees Magazine*, n.d. (National Baseball Hall of Fame Library Archives).
2. Joseph Sheehan, "A Proper Yankee," *New York Times*, Aug. 12, 1957.
3. Ibid.
4. Joseph Durso, *The Last American Knight* (Boston: Little, Brown, 1995), p. 95.
5. Ibid., p. 97.
6. Dan Daniel, "Yanks Rooting for Hoag," *New York World-Telegram*, April 23, 1937.
7. International News Service, "Must Strengthen National League, Declares Frick," *Chicago American*, Oct. 12, 1937.
8. Ibid.
9. Trachtenberg, "A Great Teacher and Coach."

Chapter 9

1. Joe Gordon, "Joe Gordon, New Yankee, Tells All About Career," *New York World-Telegram*, Nov. 16, 1937.
2. Alan H. Levy, *Joe McCarthy: Architect of the Yankee Dynasty* (Jefferson, NC: McFarland, 2005), p. 233.
3. Dan Daniel, "Daniel's Dope," *New York World-Telegram*, Sept. 20, 1938.
4. Ibid.

5. Levy, *Joe McCarthy*, p. 234.
6. Dan Daniel, "Fortune Flashes June Smile on Serious Joe Gordon; Yank Rookie Wins Bride — and Second Base Job Back," *New York World-Telegram*, June 30, 1938.
7. Harold C. Burr, "Joe Gordon Regrets Frosh Hazing Days Have Gone For Good," *New York Post*, March 6, 1939.
8. Ibid.
9. Joe Williams, "Cronin calls Gordon greatest second baseman he ever looked at," *New York World Telegram*, July 13, 1939.
10. Henry P. Edwards, American League Service Bureau press release, Jan. 26, 1936.
11. Ibid.
12. Jimmy Powers, "The Powerhouse," *New York Daily News*, April 4, 1940.
13. Will Wedge, "Rolfe Goes Into .400 Class," *New York Sun*, n.d. (National Baseball Hall of Fame Library Archives).
14. Arthur Daley, "The Rediscovery of Tommy Henrich," *New York Times*, Nov. 3, 1971.
15. Tommy Henrich, "I don't believe in defeat," *Guidepost Magazine* (1950).

Chapter 10

1. *Sport Magazine*, Sept. 1949 (Baseball Hall of Fame Library Archives).
2. Richard Ben Cramer, *Joe DiMaggio: The Hero's Life* (New York: Simon & Schuster, 2000), p. 52.
3. Joseph Durso, *The Last American Knight* (Boston: Little, Brown, 1995), p. 58.
4. Ibid., p. 59.
5. Ibid., p. 75.
6. Leo Trachtenberg, "Jake Ruppert Built Dynasties," *Yankees Magazine*, June 20, 1985.
7. Richard Vidmir, "Down In Front," *New York Tribune*, Jan. 19, 1939.
8. Daniel R. Levitt, *Ed Barrow: The Bulldog Who Built The Yankees' First Dynasty* (Lincoln: University of Nebraska Press, 2008), p. 317.
9. Dan Daniel, "Weiss Sold $550,000 in Players Before Yankees Beckoned," *New York World-Telegram*, n.d. (National Baseball Hall of Fame Library archives).
10. George M. Weiss told to Robert Shaplen, "The Man of Silence Speaks," *Sports Illustrated*, March 6, 1961.
11. Ibid.
12. Ibid.

Chapter 11

1. Shirley Povich, "This Morning," *Washington Post*, June 4, 1936.
2. "Jake Powell, Bad Boy of Big Leagues, Kills Self," source unknown Nov. 10, 1948 (National Baseball Hall of Fame Library Archives).
3. Shirley Povich, "This Morning," *Washington Post*, Sept. 29, 1937.
4. David Hinchley, "Regretting The Slur," *New York Daily News*, June 4, 2003.
5. Ibid.
6. "N.Y. Yankee Club Apologizes for Powell Act," source unknown Aug. 13, 1938 (National Baseball Hall of Fame Library Archives).
7. Westbrook Pegler, "Fair Enough," *Washington Post*, "Aug. 6, 1938.
8. "Powell, Ex-Yankee, Kills Self Following Arrest," *Philadelphia Daily News*, Nov. 4, 1948.

9. Alan H. Levy, *Joe McCarthy, Architect of the Yankee Dynasty* (Jefferson, NC: McFarland, 2005), p. 209.
10. Wayne Martin, "Sure We Rode, Jackie, Says Chapman," *The Sporting News*, March 24, 1973.
11. Dan Daniel, "McCarthy Rates Keller Outstanding Recruit of Year," *New York World-Telegram*, June 6, 1939.
12. Associated Press, "Charlie Keller, 73, baseball player, breeder of race horses," *Philadelphia Inquirer*, May 25, 1990.
13. Arthur Daley, "His Majesty, King Kong," *New York Times*, September (date unknown), 1948.
14. William Tanton, "I Detested Baseball," *Baltimore Sun Magazine*, July 17, 1960.
15. Rick Snider, "Only Keller's career as a Yankee rivals success as a horse breeder," *Washington Times*, June 22, 1986.

Chapter 12

1. Fred Lieb, "Spurgeon Chandler Gliding High On His Slider, Wins 26 Out of 31 Games for Yanks in Season and Half," *The Sporting News*, Sept. 24, 1942.
2. Tommy Henrich and Bill Gilbert, *Five O'Clock Lightning* (New York: Birch Lane Press, 1992), p. 49.
3. Lieb, "Spurgeon Chandler Gliding High on His Slider."
4. Dick Thompson, *The Ferrell Brothers of Baseball* (Jefferson, NC: McFarland, 2005), p. 235.
5. Ibid.
6. Ed Bang, "Between You and Me," *Cleveland News*, Aug. 11, 1939.
7. Dan Daniel, "Donald, Prize Freshman Pitcher, Wished Self on Yanks While Clerking in Grocery, So He Could Eat," *New York World-Telegram*, July 27, 1939.
8. Ibid.
9. Ibid.
10. Fred Lieb, "Viva Russo! Southpaw Poosh 'Em Downer of Yanks Promises to Give Italians Their First Major Hill Star," *New York Post*, Sept. 28, 1939.
11. Ibid.
12. Grantland Rice, "The Sportlight," North American Newspaper Alliance, June 29, 1941.
13. Frank Graham, "Setting the Pace," *New York Sun*, June 22, 1941.
14. Chet Smith, "Ernie's Best Game Victory Over Feller," *Pittsburgh Press*, October (unknown date) 1940.
15. Henry P. Edwards, American League Service Bureau press release, Jan. 16, 1941.

Chapter 13

1. Frank Graham, "Graham's Corner," *New York Journal-American*, June 17, 1953.
2. Obituaries, *The Sporting News*, Aug. 19, 1972.
3. John J. Ward, "A Bright but Vulnerable Star," source unknown, March 1935 (National Baseball Hall of Fame Library Archives).
4. Ed McAuley, "Rolling Stone Receiver, Cast Away by Cincy, Lands Right in Series Moss with Yankees," *Cleveland News*, July 29, 1942.
5. Tim Cohane, "Hemsley's Four Hits Help Yankees Again Trim Tribe," *New York World-Telegram*, July 23, 1942.

6. Ibid.
7. Bud Rennie, "Lindell Experiment in Outfield, Earning Spot as Yankee Slugger," *New York Herald-Tribune*, July 8, 1943.
8. Dan Daniel, "Cullenbine to Play Whole Series in Henrich's Spot," *New York World-Telegram*, Sept. 29, 1942.
9. Brent Kelley, "Buddy Hassett: One of a Vanishing Breed," *Sports Collector's Digest*, Nov. 1, 1991.
10. Ibid.
11. Red Smith, "Hassett Streak Ended By Trout At 20," *Philadelphia Record*, June 10, 1942.
12. Kelley, "Buddy Hassett."
13. Ibid.
14. Furman Bisher, "Priddy Was Always Out of Step," *The Sporting News*, Aug. 9, 1980.

Chapter 14

1. Jonathan Eig, *Luckiest Man: The Life and Death of Lou Gehrig* (New York: Simon & Schuster, 2005), p. 245.
2. Ibid., p. 250.
3. Ibid., p. 252.
4. Ibid., p. 253.
5. Ibid.
6. Ibid., p. 254.
7. Randy Schultz, "Gehrig Wasn't Defined by Streak," *The Sporting News*, June 19, 1989.
8. Ibid.
9. Ibid.
10. Ibid.
11. Ibid.
12. Joe Williams, "About Dahlgren Slugging Yankee With .235 Average," *New York World-Telegram*, March 23, 1940.
13. Richard Goldstein, "Babe Dahlgren, 84, Successor to Gehrig When Streak Ended," *New York Times*, Sept. 6, 1996.
14. Ibid.
15. Dan Daniel, "Dickey Misses Gehrig, But Carries On," *New York World-Telegram*, May 4, 1939.
16. Ibid.
17. Frank Graham, "Setting the Pace," *New York Sun*, Jan. 16, 1940.
18. Bill Madden, "Dahlgren Still Carrying Lou Gehrig's Glove," *The Sporting News*, June 16, 1975.
19. Bill Madden, "Collector Makes A Catch — Lou Gehrig's Glove," *The Sporting News*, Jan. 5, 1980.

Chapter 15

1. Jonathan *Eig, Luckiest Man: The Life And Death of Lou Gehrig* (New York: Simon & Schuster, 2005), p. 286.
2. Ibid., p. 288.

3. "Gehrig's Farewell Speech," *New York Post*, April 26, 1991.
4. John Drebinger, "61,808 Fans Roar Tribute to Gehrig," *New York Times*, July 5, 1939.
5. T.J. Quinn, "Luckiest Man on the Face of the Earth," *New York Daily News*, April 15, 2003.
6. Drebinger, "61,808 Fans Roar Tribute to Gehrig."
7. Eig, *Luckiest Man*, p. 335.
8. "Desperate Gehrig Revealed in Letters to Doc," *Philadelphia Daily News*, March 30, 2005.
9. Quinn, "Luckiest Man on the Face of the Earth."
10. Daniel R. Levitt, *Ed Barrow: The Bulldog Who Built the Yankees' First Dynasty* (Lincoln: University of Nebraska Press, 2008), p. 346.
11. Harold Friend, "It's Been 68 Years Since Lou Gehrig Passed Away," *Bleacher Report*, June 2, 2009.
12. Ibid.

Chapter 16

1. Ray Robinson, "Lou Gehrig: After The Ball Game Was Over," *COLUMBIA Magazine*, April/May 1989.
2. Stephen Borelli, "How About That!" (Champaign, IL: Sports Publishing, 2005), p. X.
3. Insiders Sportsletter, American Association of Broadcasters, August 1996.
4. Ibid.
5. Alan H. Levy, *Joe McCarthy, Architect of the Yankee Dynasty* (Jefferson, NC: McFarland, 2005), p. 259.
6. Ibid., p. 261.
7. Richard Ben Cramer, *The Hero's Life* (New York: Simon & Schuster, 2000), p. 154.
8. Joseph Durso, *DiMaggio: The Last American Knight* (Boston: Little, Brown, 1995), p. 108.
9. George DeGregorio, *Jo DiMaggio, An Informal Biography*, p. 87.
10. Phil Rizzuto and Milton Gross, "They Made Me A Big Leaguer," *Baseball Digest*, n.d. (Baseball Hall of Fame Library Archives).
11. Dan Daniel, "The Shrimp Made It," *New York Journal-American*, April 12, 1941.
12. Carlos DeVito, *Scooter: The Biography of Phil Rizzuto* (Chicago: Triumph Books, 2010), p. 29.
13. Ibid., p. 48.
14. Ibid., p. 72.

Chapter 17

1. "Joltin' Joe DiMaggio song," www.baseball-almanac.com
2. Michael Seidel, *Streak: Joe DiMaggio and the Summer of '41* (New York: Penguin Books, 1989), p. 30.
3. Tommy Henrich and Bill Gilbert, *Five O'Clock Lightning* (New York: Birch Lane Press, 1992), p. 99.
4. Sean J. O'Rourke, "Ted Williams Memorabilia Buying Guide," n.d. sports memorabilia.com.

5. Maury Allen, *Where have you gone, Joe DiMaggio?* (New York: New American Library, 1976), p. 51.
6. Ibid., p. 56.
7. Robert W. Creamer, *Baseball in '41* (New York: Penguin Books, 1991), p. 230.
8. George DeGregorio, *Joe DiMaggio: An Informal Biography* (Princeton, NJ: Townhouse, 1981), p. 98.
9. Ibid., p. 99.
10. Ibid., p. 99–100.
11. Ibid., p. 105.
12. Seidel, *Streak*, p. 202.
13. Ibid., p. 203–04.
14. Joseph Durso, *DiMaggio: The Last American Knight* (Boston: Little, Brown, 1995), p. 137.

Chapter 18

1. Joe Williams, "DiMaggio Goes Ahead of Feller As Turnstile Lure," *New York World-Telegram*, July 2, 1941.
2. John Cimko, "A Man and His Game — Ruffing Muses About Baseball," *Oneonta Star*, July 24, 1967.
3. Frank Graham, "Setting The Pace," *New York Sun*, June 27, 1941.
4. Carlos DeVito, *Scooter: The Biography of Phil Rizzuto* (Chicago: Triumph Books, 2010), p. 75.
5. Jimmy Powers, "Powerhouse," *New York Daily News*, June 28, 1940.
6. Paul Post, "Old Reliable Always Came Through in Clutch," *Sports Collector's Digest*, Jan. 10, 1997.
7. Tommy Henrich and Bill Gilbert, *Five O'Clock Lightning* (New York: Birch Lane Press, 1992), p. 126.
8. Ibid., p. 127.
9. George DeGregorio, *Joe DiMaggio: An Informal Biography* (Princeton, New Jersey, Townhouse, 1981), p. 163.
10. Associated Press, "Owen Not Letting Life Get Away From Him," *Washington Post*, May 16, 1989.
11. "1941 Series Recalled By Owen," source unknown, Aug. 2, 1950 (National Baseball Hall of Fame Library Archives).
12. Steve Calhoun, "Where Are They Now — Mickey Owen," *Dodger Blue*, February 1984.

Chapter 19

1. Baseball Almanac, "Green Light Letter," www.baseball-almanac.com.
2. Red Smith, "Joe McCarthy," *New York Times*, Jan. 22, 1978.
3. Joseph Durso, "Joe McCarthy Remembers," *New York Times*, Aug. 29, 1976.
4. Frank Graham, "Setting The Pace," *New York Sun*, Aug. 4, 1941.
5. Leo Trachtenberg, "Loved And Hated, McCarthy Was A Champion," *Yankees Magazine*, Aug. 7, 1986.
6. Carlos DeVito, *Scooter* (Chicago: Triumph Books, 2010), p. 103.
7. Tommy Henrich and Bill Gilbert, *Five O'Clock Lightning* (New York: Birch Lane Press, 1992), p. 136.

8. Frank Graham, Jr., "When Baseball Went to War," *Sports Illustrated*, April 17, 1967.

9. Richard Ben Cramer, *Joe DiMaggio: A Hero's Life* (New York: Simon & Schuster, 2000), p. 198.

10. Alan H. Levy, *Joe McCarthy: Architect of the Yankee Dynasty* (Jefferson, NC: McFarland, 2005), p. 293.

Bibliography

Books

Allen, Maury. *Where Have You Gone, Joe DiMaggio?* New York: New American Library, 1976.
Borelli, Stephen. "How About That!" Champaign, IL: Sports Publishing, 2005.
Carmichael, John P. *My Greatest Day in Baseball* New York: Grosset & Dunlap, 1951.
Cramer, Richard Ben. *Joe DiMaggio: The Hero's Life.* New York: Simon & Schuster, 2000.
Creamer, Robert W. *Baseball in '41.* New York: Penguin Books, 1991.
DeGregorio, George. *Joe DiMaggio, An Informal Biography.* Princeton, NJ: Townhouse, 1981.
DeVito, Carlos. *Scooter: The Biography of Phil Rizzuto.* Chicago: Triumph Books, 2010.
Durso, Joseph. *The Last American Knight.* Boston: Little, Brown, 1995.
Eig, Jonathan. *Luckiest Man: The Life and Death of Lou Gehrig.* New York: Simon & Schuster, 2005.
Henrich, Tommy, and Bill Gilbert. *Five O'Clock Lightning.* New York: Birch Lane Press, 1992.
Levitt, Daniel R. *Ed Barrow: The Bulldog Who Built the Yankees' First Dynasty."* Lincoln: University of Nebraska Press, 2008.
Levy, Alan H. *Joe McCarthy: Architect of the Yankee Dynasty.* Jefferson, NC: McFarland, 2005.
Montville, Leigh. *The Big Bam: The Life and Times of Babe Ruth.* New York: Doubleday, 2006.
Schoor, Gene. *The World Series: The Complete Chronology of America's Greatest Sports Tradition.* New York: William Morrow, 1990.
Seidel, Michael. *Streak: Joe DiMaggio and the Summer of '41.* New York: Penguin Books, 1989.
Simpson, Douglas G. *Biographical Dictionary of American Sport.* National Baseball Hall of Fame Library Archives.
Thompson, Dick. *The Ferrell Brothers of Baseball.* Jefferson, NC: McFarland, 2005.
Votano, Paul. *Tony Lazzeri: A Baseball Biography.* Jefferson, NC: McFarland, 2005.

Magazines

American Magazine
Baseball Digest
Collier's
COLUMBIA Magazine
Dodger Blue
Guidepost
Image
Sport
The Sporting News
Sports Collector's Digest
Sports Illustrated
Yankees Magazine

Newspapers

Chicago American
Chicago Daily Times
Cleveland News
Newsday
New York Daily News
New York Herald–Tribune
New York Journal–American
New York Post
New York Sun
New York Times
New York World–Telegram
Oneonta Star
Philadelphia Daily News
Philadelphia Inquirer
Pittsburgh Press
Philadelphia Record
Pittsburgh Sun–Telegraph
St. Louis Post–Dispatch
St. Louis Star–Chronicle
Washington Post
Washington Times

Other

American League Service Bureau
Associated Press
Home Newspapers
Insiders Sportsletter — American Association of Broadcasters
International News Service
National Baseball Hall of Fame Archives
North American Newspaper Alliance
Radio Transcript
Ted Williams Memorabilia Buying Guide
United Press International

Web Sites

Baseball Almanac, www.BaseballAlmanac.org
Bleacher Report, www.bleacherreport.com
Lou Gehrig Official Web Site, www.lougehrig.com

Index

Aaron, Hank 162
Abdul-Jabbar, Kareem 162
Academy Awards 151
Africa 190
African-Americans 109, 110
Akron 129
Akron (team) 124
Alabama 96, 111, 152, 154
Alcoholics Anonymous 129
Alexander, Grover Cleveland 62, 63
All Star Game/All Star Team 20, 31, 48, 56, 60, 71, 74, 78, 82, 84, 86, 91, 92, 93, 98, 112, 114, 120, 123, 125, 126, 130, 141, 152, 163, 167, 173, 182, 188
Allen, Johnny 47, 48, 49, 50, 179, 180
Allen, Mel 96, 152, 153, 154, 166
Altoona, Pennsylvania 52
American Association 168
American League 1, 3, 4, 8, 9, 10, 21, 31, 34, 36, 37, 49, 50, 57, 65, 67, 75, 78, 79, 80, 81, 85, 91, 92, 99, 100, 107, 112, 114, 121, 124, 125, 141, 154, 155, 156, 157, 162, 166, 167, 168, 171, 172, 174, 175, 176, 186, 187, 193, 194, 195, 197
amytrophic lateral sclerosis (ALS, Lou Gehrig's Disease) 145, 146, 151
Anderson, Arnold 171
Andrews, Ivy 119
Appling, Luke 118
Arkansas 71, 126
Armed Forces Radio 153
The Army Hour 153
Arnold, Dorothy (Olson, Dorothy) 97, 98, 192
Asbury Park, New Jersey 191
Asia 169
Atlanta 93
Atlantic Ocean 170
Auker, Elden 165

Bagby, Jim, Jr. 173
Ballantine 154
Baltimore Orioles 11, 105, 134, 171
Barber, Red 153
Barnes, Donald 99
Barnstable, Massachusetts 41
Barrow, Ed 3, 8, 9, 11, 17, 25, 26, 27, 33, 40, 43, 45, 46, 47, 48, 52, 74, 75, 81, 87, 95, 100, 102, 104, 105, 107, 110, 114, 119, 120, 121, 125, 126, 127, 128, 133, 146, 148, 149, 150, 158, 159, 161, 175, 183, 191, 193, 197
Baseball Almanac 168
Bauer, Hank 197
Bay Area Sports Hall of Fame 64
Beazley, Johnny 189, 193
Bennett, Virginia 160
Berra, Yogi 157, 197
Bielski, Lennie 22, 23
Binghamton Triplets 74, 121, 122
Birmingham, Alabama 152
Bi-State League 160
Bodie, Ping 1
Bonds, Barry 162
Bonham, Ernie "Tiny" 70, 123, 124, 155, 176, 181, 182, 187, 189, 193, 194
Bonney, Betty 163
Book Cadillac Hotel 143
Borowy, Hank 21, 187, 193, 194
Boston 43, 44, 124
Boston Bees 131, 140
Boston Braves 4, 23, 24, 41, 165, 168, 186
Boston Park League 44
Boston Red Sox 4, 8, 9, 14, 17, 21, 37, 39, 40, 57, 72, 74, 80, 84, 91, 100, 109, 119, 140, 158, 166, 172, 173, 176, 187, 196, 197
Bottomley, Jim 40
Boyer, Clete 197
Boyle, Buzz 161

211

Boys of Summer 179
Branch, Norm 176, 190
Braves Field 41
Brazle, Al 194
Brecheen, Harry 194
Breuer, Marv 155, 180
Briggs Stadium 150
British Commonwealth 169
Broaca, Cordelia (wife of Johnny) 41, 42, 43, 44
Broaca, Johnny 40, 41, 42, 43, 44, 46, 84
The Bronx Bombers 59, 78
Brooklyn 122, 124
Brooklyn College 122
Brooklyn Dodgers 65, 110, 131, 160, 170, 177, 178, 179, 180, 181, 183, 188, 191, 192
Brooklyn Dodgers Sym-phony 179
Brown University 55
Browning, Pete 168
Bryant, Bear 153
Bryant Park 106
Buffalo, New York 74, 128, 143
Burroughs, Edgar Rice 36
Bushwicks 122
Butler University 120

Cabrera, Melky 82
California 65, 192
Camilli, Dolph 179
Campanella, Roy 179
Cannon, Jimmy 158
Canton, Ohio 24
Carnegie Hall 147
Caruthers, Bob 168
Casey, Hugh 179, 180, 181, 183
Catalina Island 12
CBS Radio 153
Chamberlain, Wilt 162
Chandler, A.B. "Happy" 112
Chandler, Spud 46, 116, 117, 118, 119, 155, 176, 180, 187, 189, 193, 194, 195
Chapman, Ben 84, 111, 112, 114
Chase, Hal 140, 164
Chase Hotel 73
Chicago, Illinois 110
Chicago Bears 24
Chicago Bulls 182
Chicago Colts 171
Chicago Cubs 12, 13, 47, 52, 53, 65, 66, 79, 85, 90, 102, 128, 136
Chicago Defender 109
Chicago White Sox 4, 16, 55, 84, 100, 106, 109, 118, 163, 164
China 169, 181
Christ Episcopal Church 150

Cincinnati 96, 120
Cincinnati Reds 14, 100, 114, 128, 129, 174, 186, 193
Clarke, Fred 165
Clemente, Roberto 149
Cleveland 30, 41
Cleveland Indians 43, 48, 49, 50, 64, 71, 91, 92, 95, 100, 106, 113, 128, 131, 154, 156, 159, 164, 167, 170, 173, 174, 176, 186
Cleveland Municipal Stadium 173
Clown Prince of Baseball 186
Coakley, Andy 151
Cobb, Ty 21, 22, 116, 165, 166, 169, 171
Cochrane, Mickey 4, 27, 56, 73
Coffman, Dick 63
Columbia University 10, 20, 21, 151
Combs, Earle 2
Comiskey Park 110
Commerce, GA 116
Cooper, Gary 151
Cooper, Mort 189, 194
Cooper, Walker 193
Cooperstown, New York 64
Cosell, Howard 112
Costas, Bob 154
Cotton States League 69
Courtney, Alan 163
Creamer, Robert W. 170
Crimson Tide 153
Cronin, Joe 56, 80, 91, 109
Crosetti, Frank 7, 17, 28, 40, 63, 67, 78, 79, 80, 85, 86, 91, 102, 151, 155
Cuba 10
Cullenbine, Roy 130, 131
Curie, Marie 119

Dahlen, Bill 171, 172
Dahlgren, Ellsworth Tenney "Babe" 139, 140, 141, 144, 155
Daniel, Dan 163
Darrow, Clarence 55
Dartmouth College 92
Davis, Curt 179
Davis, George 164
Dayton, Ohio 109
Dean, Dizzy 85, 86
Dean, Paul "Daffy" 42
Decatur Staleys 24
Delahanty, Ed 164, 169
DeMontreville, Gene 165
Dempsey, Jack 97
Depression 4, 8, 12, 17, 26, 170
Derringer, Paul 114
Detroit 22, 23, 143, 150, 151

Detroit Tigers 4, 8, 21, 26, 27, 56, 79, 80, 83, 85, 89, 114, 122, 130, 131, 141, 150, 154, 156, 159, 164, 167, 176, 186, 191
Dickey, Bill 27, 35, 40, 68, 69, 70, 71, 72, 73, 74, 75, 76, 77, 91, 102, 114, 118, 122, 126, 128, 132, 141, 150, 151, 155, 160, 171, 176, 177, 181, 182, 193, 195
DiMaggio, Dom (brother of Joe) 14, 158, 164
DiMaggio, Giuseppe (father of Joe) 14, 15, 192
DiMaggio, Joe 5, 7, 8, 14, 15, 16, 17, 18, 26, 27, 28, 29, 30, 31, 34, 35, 40, 50, 57, 60, 63, 64, 65, 66, 73, 75, 79, 81, 82, 83, 84, 88, 91, 95, 97, 98, 99, 100, 101, 112, 125, 126, 155, 157, 158, 159, 161, 162, 163, 164, 165, 166, 167, 168, 169, 170, 171, 172, 173, 174, 175, 176, 181, 182, 183, 188, 192, 194, 195, 196, 197
DiMaggio, Joe, Jr. (son of Joe) 98
DiMaggio, Rosalie (mother of Joe) 14
DiMaggio, Tom (brother of Joe) 15, 81
DiMaggio, Vince (brother of Joe) 14, 15
Donald, Richard Atley 120, 121, 122, 155, 176, 180, 189
Doubleday, Abner 93
Duluth, Minnesota 97
Durocher, Leo 21, 23, 180, 191
Dykes, Jimmy 187, 188

Eastern League 8, 66
Ebbets Field 180
El Morocco Club 157
Elson, Bob 109
England 169, 170
Essick, Bill 16, 17, 27, 52, 87
Etten, Nick 132, 192

Face, Roy 49
Feller, Bob 71, 91, 123, 167, 168, 175, 186
Fenway Park 25, 37
Ferrell, Rick 120
Ferrell, Wes 119, 120
Fisherman's Wharf 59, 81, 192
Fitzsimmons, Freddie 180
Fletcher, Art 3
Flintstone, Fred 36
Ford, Whitey 197
Fordham University 21, 187
Four Horsemen of Notre Dame 73
Foxx, Jimmie 4, 80
France 169, 186
Frazee, Harry 9
Frederick, Maryland 115
Freedman, Andrew 10

French, Larry 180
French Lick, Indiana 127
Fresno, California 48
Frick, Ford 85
Fuchs, Judge 41
Furillo, Carl 179

Gashouse Gang 189
Gehrig, Christina (mother of Lou) 20
Gehrig, Eleanor (wife of Lou) 22, 35, 36, 135, 143, 146, 149, 150
Gehrig, Lou 2, 3, 19, 20, 21, 22, 23, 24, 25, 26, 27, 35, 36, 51, 59, 62, 71, 73, 81, 82, 91, 99, 102, 114, 126, 131, 132, 133, 134, 135, 136, 137, 138, 139, 140, 141, 142, 143, 144, 145, 146, 147, 148, 149, 150, 152, 154, 155, 170, 183, 195, 197
Gehringer, Charlie 26, 66, 89
George Halas Trophy 24
Germany 169, 170, 190, 192
Girardi, Joe 182
Gleason, Jackie 157
Glenn, Joe 74, 177
Goetz, Larry 181
Gomez, Lefty 17, 27, 28, 29, 30, 31, 33, 34, 35, 37, 40, 54, 55, 57, 58, 64, 76, 77, 80, 85, 98, 102, 116, 123, 124, 141, 155, 159, 160, 172, 173, 176, 177, 178, 187, 196
Gordon, Joe 17, 64, 65, 66, 87, 88, 89, 90, 91, 132, 133, 141, 155, 176, 179, 181, 188, 194
Goslin, Goose 83, 164
Gould, Joe 159
Gowdy, Curt 153
Gowdy, Hank 186
Graham, Frank 54, 64
Gray, Pete 192
Great Britain 190
Green Light Letter 185
Greenberg, Hank 26, 27, 80, 98, 167, 186
Griffith Stadium 171
Grimes, Burleigh 71
Grimm, Charlie 65, 164
Grove, Lefty 4, 49
Guideposts magazine 96
Guinness Book of World Records 75
Gumpert, Randy 190

Hadley, Bump 46, 54, 55, 56, 100
Halas, George 24
Hall of Fame 4, 7, 26, 27, 34, 40, 46, 56, 57, 58, 62, 64, 67, 71, 76, 91, 120, 128, 149, 164, 167, 196

Hargreaves, Charles 122
Harlow, Jean 98
Harridge, Will 175
Harris, Bucky 55
Hartnett, Gabby 65
Harwell, Ernie 154
Hassett, John Aloysius "Buddy" 131, 132, 190
Haverhill, Massachusetts 43
Hawaii 184, 192
Heffner, Don 93
Heilman, Harry 164
Heinrich, Tommy 50, 84, 95, 96, 102, 111, 112, 114, 118, 140, 149, 150, 156, 165, 166, 172, 176, 181, 182, 183, 190, 191, 194, 195
Hemingway, Ernest 157, 183
Hemsley, Rollie 128, 129, 130
Herman, Billy 179
Higbe, Kirby 179, 180
Hildebrand, Oral 100, 120
Hindenburg 153
Hitchcock, Billy 161
Hitler, Adolf 110, 169, 170, 190
Hoag, Myril 82, 83, 84, 95
Hodges, Gil 179
Hodges, Russ 153
Hollywood 47, 98
Hollywood Stars 15
Holmes, Tommy 21, 165
Homer, Ben 163
Hoover, Herbert 2
Horie, Jean 151
Hornsby, Rogers 128, 129, 164, 168, 169
Hotel New Yorker 95
Houk, Ralph 17
Howard, Elston 197
Hoyt, Waite 3, 4, 147
Hubbell, Carl 34, 35, 50, 56, 108
Huggins, Miller 3, 11, 12, 21, 39, 40, 64
Hughes, Howard 44
Humphries, Johnny 50
Huskies cereal 66
Huston, Tillinghast L'Hommedieu 3, 10, 11, 45, 102, 107

International League 9, 66, 105, 113, 115, 127
Israel, Melvin Allen *see* Allen, Mel
Italy 14, 28, 29, 59, 60, 62, 63, 78, 123, 158, 169, 192

Jackson, Mississippi (team) 68
Jacksonville, Florida 93
Japan 170, 183, 184, 185, 190
Jersey City 24

Johnson, Ban 10, 11
Johnson, Billy 193
Johnson, Roy 95, 125
Johnson, Walter 49, 55, 72
Joltin' Joe DiMaggio 163
Jordan, Michael 162, 182
Jorgens, Art 74
Juniata College 52

Kansas City Blues 123, 125, 144, 159, 161
Keeler, Wee Willie 1, 98, 171, 172
Keller, Charlie 21, 102, 113, 114, 132, 139, 155, 176, 181, 188, 189, 190, 193
Keltner, Ken 173
Kensico Cemetery 151
Kentucky Derby 80
King Kong 113
Knickerbocker, Bill 127
Koenig, Mark 21
Korean War 167
Krichell, Paul 21, 27, 47, 52, 57, 60, 113, 123, 160
Kubek, Tony 197
Kunitz, Al 160

La Guardia, Fiorello 149, 151
Lajoie, Larry "Nap" 164, 168
LaLanne, Jack 13
Landis, Kenesaw Mountain 95, 100, 109, 110, 159, 185, 191, 194
Lane, Frank "Trader" 106
Lanier, Max 189, 194
Lawrence, Massachusetts 41, 43, 44
Lawrence Eagle Tribune 44
Lazzeri, Tony 2, 7, 15, 21, 27, 28, 31, 40, 59, 60, 62, 63, 64, 65, 67, 79, 88, 91, 102, 133, 147
Leiber, Hank 34
Lenoir, North Carolina 47
Lenox Hill Hospital 102
Les Brown Orchestra (Les Brown and His Band of Renown) 163
Lindbergh, Charles 35
Lindell, Johnny 17, 130, 190
Little Rock, Arkansas 68
Little Rock (team) 68, 69
Logan, Fred 160
Lombardi, Vince 12
Lopat, Ed 197
Los Angeles 87, 132
Los Angeles Angels 15
Lou Gehrig Appreciation Day 147
Lou Gehrig Luckiest Man speech 149
Louisiana 68, 120, 121
Louisiana Tech 121

Louisville (team) 12
Louisville Slugger 168, 172
Lowell, Massachusetts 43
Lynchberg, Virginia 111
Lynchberg (team) 120
Lynn, Massachusetts 54

Mack, Connie 3, 4, 31, 146
Majeski, Hank 190
Major League 182
Malone, Perce Leigh (Pat) 46, 52, 53, 54
Manchester, Ohio 168
Manhattan College 131
Mantle, Mickey 5, 197
Manush, Heinie 164
Marion, Marty 189, 193, 194
Maris, Roger 197
Martin, Billy 197
Maryland 89
Match, Pinky 122
Mathewson, Christy 119
Mayflower 92
Mayo Clinic 144, 145, 146, 149
McCann, Gene 92
McCarthy, Joe 3, 12, 13, 14, 18, 21, 24, 25, 27, 31, 35, 47, 48, 49, 50, 51, 52, 54, 55, 56, 57, 62, 63, 64, 70, 71, 74, 75, 76, 81, 83, 84, 88, 89, 90, 92, 93, 95, 99, 107, 111, 112, 113, 114, 116, 117, 121, 123, 124, 126, 127, 128, 129, 130, 133, 134, 135, 136, 137, 138, 139, 140, 141, 143, 144, 146, 147, 148, 150, 151, 155, 156, 157, 159, 165, 171, 175, 181, 183, 187, 188, 191, 193, 194, 195, 196, 197
McDonald, Arch 99
McDougald, Gil 197
McGraw, John 10, 11, 20, 34, 85, 171
McKechnie, Bill 41
McVey, Cal 164
Medwick, Joe 91, 178, 179
Mercer, Sid 148
Metheny, Bud 190
Metropolitan Museum of Art 103
Meusel, Bob 2, 17, 147
Mexican League 182
Mickey Owen Baseball School 182
Middleton, Maryland 113
Millbrae, California 66
Minneapolis (team) 68
Missouri 182
Mize, Johnny 197
Monroe, Marilyn 196
Moore, Terry 189, 193
Morris, Glenn 36
Morton, Mississippi 120

Muncie, Indiana 191
Murderer's Row 2, 24, 50, 59, 67, 147
Murphy, Johnny 21, 46, 51, 52, 57, 58, 59, 91, 100, 102, 176, 180, 193, 194
Musial, Stan 189, 193
Muskogee, Oklahoma (team) 68
Mussolini, Benito 169
Myer, Buddy 111

Nashville, Tennessee 130
National Basketball Association 162
National Enquirer 42
National Football League 33, 162
National Italian American Sports Hall of Fame 64
National League 23, 34, 41, 50, 53, 85, 100, 178, 182, 188, 193, 194, 195
Navin Field 22
Nazi (SS) 169, 170, 183
Nazi salute 111
NCAA 120
Nee, Johnny 69, 70, 121
New Brunswick, New Jersey 21
New Haven 105
New Haven Colonials 105
New York 66, 68, 104, 111, 112, 131; sportswriters 8, 48, 50, 82, 113, 136, 141, 158
New York City Parole Board 149
New York Daily News 23, 66
New York Giants 10, 11, 14, 21, 34, 35, 45, 50, 51, 54, 56, 58, 63, 65, 85, 94, 108, 153, 154, 160, 178
New York Highlanders 1, 4, 10
New York Journal 33
New York Journal-American 161
New York Mets 57
New York–Penn League 74
New York Times 149, 172
New York University 21
New York World Telegram 163
New York Youth Congress 151
Newark Bears 4, 74, 87, 88, 95, 112, 113, 120, 121, 122, 124, 125, 127, 130, 144, 159
Newsday 67
Nicaragua 149
Nokomis, Illinois 38
Norfolk (team) 74, 121
North Africa 170
North Carolina 119

Oakland 31, 48, 88
Oakland Oaks 87, 123
O'Dea, James 53
O'Dea, June 33, 34, 98
Ohio 95

O'Leary, Dr. Paul 149
O'Neill, Steve 64
O'Neill, Tip 168
Orange Bowl 153
Oregon 65
Orleans, Massachusetts 42
Ott, Mel 34, 91
Owen, Mickey 179, 181, 183
Owen, Russell 172
Ozone Park 122

Pacific Coast League 8, 15, 28, 59, 80, 83, 111, 123, 173
Pacific Ocean 169, 190
Painter, Doc 55
Pan American 99
Parrott, Harold 192
Payton, Walter 162
Pearl Harbor 184, 185
Pearson, Monte 46, 47, 48, 49, 50, 51, 85, 100, 102, 155
Peek, Steve 176, 185
Pegler, Westbrook 110
Penacook, New Hampshire 92
Pennock, Herb 3, 31, 147
Philadelphia Athletics 3, 4, 8, 56, 63, 73, 79, 85, 132, 146, 166, 168, 190
Philadelphia Phillies 14, 111, 112, 132
Phillips Andover Academy 41
Phillips Exeter Academy 92
Piedmont League 66
Pipp, Wally 21, 134, 147, 150
Pittsburgh Pirates 4, 14, 23, 49, 128, 191
Pocahontas 92
Pollett, Howie 194
Polo Grounds 34, 35, 51, 63
Portland, Oregon 87c
Portsmouth (team) 66
Powell, Jake 84, 95, 108, 109, 110, 111, 112
Priddy, Jerry 132, 133
Pride of the Yankees 151
Pro Football Hall of Fame 24
Prohibition 11, 72
Providence, Rhode Island 55

Queens 122, 159

Raschi, Vic 197
Reese, Pee Wee 179
Reiser, Pete 179, 180
Reliance Coal Company 38
Reno, Nevada 34
Reynolds, Allie 197
Reynolds, Carl 70
Rice, Grantland 73

Rice, Sam 164
Richardson, Bobby 197
Richbourg, Lance 164
Richmond Hill High School 160
Rickey, Branch 53, 188
Rickles, Don 158
Ripken, Cal, Jr. 20, 134
Riverdale, NY 150
Rizzuto, Cora (wife of Phil) 191
Rizzuto, Phil 21, 153, 159, 161, 175, 176, 177, 190, 191, 194, 195, 196
Roaring Twenties 2, 8, 34, 170
Robinson, Jackie 35, 110, 112
Robinson, Wilbert 11
Rochester, Minnesota 144, 145
Rodeo, California 31
Rolfe, John 92
Rolfe, Red 21, 91, 92, 93, 94, 95, 102, 133, 155, 165
Rollo, Missouri 155
Roosevelt, Franklin Delano 34, 99, 143, 169, 170, 179, 183, 185, 190
Root, Charlie 13
Rosar, Buddy 74, 75, 127, 128, 129
Rose, Pete 174
Rose Bowl 153
Royal Air Force 170
Royston, Georgia 116
Ruffing, John (father of Red) 38
Ruffing, John, Jr. (brother of Red) 38
Ruffing, Red 26, 27, 34, 37, 38, 39, 40, 54, 55, 70, 80, 85, 86, 91, 100, 102, 114, 116, 123, 155, 176, 177, 179, 187, 190, 195
Runyon, Damon 40
Ruppert, George (brother of Jacob) 103
Ruppert, Jacob 3, 10, 11, 12, 13, 17, 23, 25, 26, 45, 46, 80, 81, 84, 99, 102, 103, 104, 105, 110, 120, 125, 126, 127, 133, 150, 198
Ruppert Brewery 103
Russia 190
Russo, Marius 21, 122, 123, 155, 176, 180, 194
Rutgers University 21
Ruth, Babe 1, 3, 4, 5, 8, 9, 10, 11, 13, 14, 17, 19, 20, 22, 23, 24, 25, 27, 28, 30, 38, 40, 45, 47, 55, 60, 62, 64, 70, 71, 72, 73, 80, 91, 92, 99, 101, 102, 103, 110, 114, 134, 137, 140, 147, 150, 153, 162, 170, 175, 195

Sacramento (team) 83
St. Louis 15, 124
St. Louis Browns 21, 28, 55, 74, 99, 100, 120, 123, 130, 151, 164, 165, 168, 173, 178, 192, 195

Index

St. Louis Cardinals 11, 42, 53, 62, 85, 115, 130, 132, 168, 178, 188, 189, 191, 193, 194
St. Patrick's Cathedral 104
St. Petersburg, Florida 7, 12, 82, 87, 117, 121, 137
Salt Lake City 60
Salt Lake City Bees 15, 59
Sanders, Barry 162
Sanders, Ray 194
San Diego 167
San Francisco 7, 14, 28, 59, 64, 78, 80, 81, 82, 97, 98, 100, 192
San Francisco Armed Forces Induction Center 192
San Francisco Seals 8, 15, 16, 17, 31, 35, 80, 81, 111
Sardi's 157
Schacht, Al 186
Schumacher, Hal 34, 51
Seattle Mariners 168
Seattle Raniers 15
Seidel, Michael 163
Selkirk, George 21, 24, 25, 84, 91, 95, 96, 138, 155, 156, 190, 194
Sewell, Joe 91, 92
Shawkey, Bob 3, 147
Sheen, Charlie 182
Sheldon-Claire Company 186
Shocker, Urban 3
Shor, Toots 157, 158
Silver Spring, Maryland 108
Silvestri, Ken 185
Sisler, Dave (son of George) 169
Sisler, Dick (son of George) 169
Sisler, George 164, 168, 171, 172
Simmons, Al 4
Sinatra, Frank 157
Skowron, Bill 197
Slaughter, Enos 189, 193
Smith, Al 173
Smith, Emmitt 162
Smith, Red 188
Snider, Duke 179, 192
Southern Association 192
Southworth, Billy 115, 189, 193, 195
Soviet Union 170
Spanish American War 10
Sparrow, Harry 11
Speaker, Tris 164
The Sporting News 27, 112
Sports Illustrated 106, 170
Sportsman Park 189, 194
Springfield, Illinois 8
Stainback, Tuck 190
Stanceau, Charley 176, 185

Steinbrenner, George 12, 196, 197, 198
Stengel, Casey 5, 13, 197
Stirnweiss, George 21, 193
Stockton, California 79
Stork Club 157
Sturm, Johnny 165, 186
Sugar Bowl 153
Sundra, Steve 48, 119
Suzuki, Ichiro 168

Tampa 41
Tarzan 35, 36, 147
Terry, Bill 34, 168
This Week in Baseball 152
Time magazine 28, 56
Toots Shor's Restaurant 157, 158
Topping, Dan 197
Toronto (team) 8, 66
Trout, Dizzy 131
Tucson (team) 15
21 Club 157

U.S. Army 130, 132, 191
U.S. Coast Guard 130, 191
U.S. Congress 170
U.S. Navy 130, 132, 140, 183, 186
U.S. Postal Service 151
University of Alabama 153
University of Georgia 117
University of Illinois 24
University of Maryland 113
University of Oregon 65, 87

Valhalla, New York 151
Vance, Joe 120
Veeck, Bill 106
Villanova University 132
Virginia League 120

Walker, Dixie 179
Walker, Harry "The Hat" 189
Walsh, Christy 22, 35
Washburn, George 176
Washington, D.C. 111
Washington Senators 55, 70, 72, 108, 109, 119, 130, 138, 147, 152, 163, 164, 168, 171, 193
Weatherly, Roy 190
Webb, Del 197
Weiss, George M. 105, 106, 107, 123, 159, 175, 183, 197
Weissmuller, Johnny 36
Wensloff, Butch 193
Werber, Bill 21
West Point, New York 191

WGN 109
Wheeling (team) 74, 121
White, Ernie 189
Wicker, Kemp 46, 119
Wilkes Barre (team) 66
Williams, Joe 10
Williams, Ted 100, 113, 166, 167, 176, 186, 192
Winchell, Walter 44
Wolf, Jimmy 164
Wood, Joe 49
World Series 1, 2, 3, 7, 9, 12, 13, 34, 35, 36, 41, 45, 47, 49, 50, 51, 52, 54, 55, 56, 57, 58, 62, 63, 64, 65, 70, 73, 75, 76, 78, 79, 81, 84, 85, 87, 90, 91, 94, 95, 97, 98, 100, 105, 107, 108, 109, 114, 114, 115, 119, 123, 125, 127, 130, 131, 132, 134, 136, 141, 152, 154, 168, 175, 178, 179, 180, 181, 182, 183, 188, 189, 190, 192, 194, 195, 196, 197, 198

World War I 10, 11, 169, 186, 190
World War II 5, 60, 71, 106, 123, 128, 130, 132, 153, 167, 178, 195, 197
Wray, Fay 113
Wrigley, Phil 65
Wrigley, William, Jr. 12
Wrigley Field 85
Wyatt, Whitlow 179, 180, 181, 182

Yale University 41, 43, 85, 105
Yankee Stadium 2, 18, 27, 49, 51, 62, 66, 79, 81, 97, 111, 126, 136, 138, 147, 152, 153, 163, 172, 179, 180, 194, 196
Yankeeland 115
Yawkey, Tom 80, 100
Young, Cy 162

Ziegfeld Follies 33

www.ingramcontent.com/pod-product-compliance
Lightning Source LLC
Chambersburg PA
CBHW030107170426
43198CB00009B/530